THE GRAMMAR OF CONDUCTING

ERRATA

p. 44, line 1.   Delete dot after the half note.

p. 125, Ex. 176.   Metronome indication should be ($\flat$ =88.)

p. 128, Ex. 178.   Add parentheses to the metronome indication $\flat$ -100.

p. 260, Ex. 387a.   The metronome indication should be $\downarrow$ =92.

Ex. 387b.   Add the metronome indication $\downarrow$ =88.

p. 290, Ex. 439.   The first system is Ex. 439a, and the second system, Ex. 439b.

p. 347, 2nd column.   The lines:
Violin Concerto, *14, 33,* 143, *254.*

Berlioz, Hector

should be moved up immediately above:

La Damnation de Faust:

THE GRAMMAR OF CONDUCTING

A Practical Study of Modern Baton Technique

by

MAX RUDOLF

WITH A FOREWORD BY
GEORGE SZELL

G. SCHIRMER, INC.
NEW YORK

ACKNOWLEDGMENTS

The author is deeply indebted to his friends, Mr. George Szell, Dr. Irving Kaplan, and Mr. Leo Kraft. Without Mr. Szell's encouragement, continued interest, and helpful suggestions it is doubtful whether this book would have been completed. Dr. Irving Kaplan contributed invaluable critical and literary assistance in the preparation of the text; Mr. Leo Kraft gave highly competent aid and advice in the preparation of the first draft.

Gratitude is expressed to Mr. Nicolai Malko, who, in 1941, was assisted by the author in his course in conducting. Mr. Malko's lectures confirmed and broadened the author's own views and his friendly cooperation will always be remembered.

The author also wishes to thank Mr. Felix Greissle for many stimulating discussions.

FOREWORD

Modern conducting technique is a comparatively recent musical development. The problems that the contemporary conductor has to face are very different from those of, say, fifty years ago. This is due to the general evolution of conducting from mere time-beating and "keeping things together" to a highly differentiated craft; to the increasing intricacies and complexities of symphonic and operatic scores of the late nineteenth and twentieth centuries; and finally to the general demand for a degree of clarity, precision, and smoothness of orchestral performance undreamed-of even as recently as Richard Wagner's time.

It might be interesting to remember that this general demand for highly polished performances is largely due to the influence of radio and records. While in former days exceptionally flawless performances could be heard only occasionally in a few cities of Europe and America and only by those who were fortunate enough to be present in the hall, such performances have been disseminated during the past few decades through mechanical reproduction to an immense number of listeners all over the world and have thereby created new standards of technical excellence.

It was, of course, at all times important for a conductor to possess good technical equipment so as to be able to communicate his intentions to the players in the most effective manner. But under the new conditions, and especially since the demand for technical perfection of performance has not always been accompanied by a proportionate increase in rehearsal time, a high degree of virtuosity in the handling of the baton is even more imperative than ever.

In most cases this virtuosity has been achieved through practical apprenticeship and the advice and guidance of experienced colleagues, and through the observation and emulation of distinguished conductors. Consequently it is often assumed that baton technique cannot be taught or learned *systematically*. For this reason textbooks on conducting have been regarded as inadequate means of instruction. Such an attitude is just as fallacious as would be a similar attitude toward textbooks on surgery. Obviously, no one would consider allowing a surgeon to operate without adequate practical experience. But it is even less conceivable that a student of surgery could dispense with a thorough study of textbooks dealing with his special craft or art.

In any art some time must elapse before accumulated experience can be summarized in a book. It is only during the last two generations that conducting technique has been developed to the point where it can be systematized. To my knowledge no attempt has been made up to now to write a comprehensive book on this technique. The standard works by Berlioz, Wagner, Weingartner, and others, deal almost exclusively with artistic and interpretational problems, while the many other books either confine themselves to the most elementary instruction, or fail to organize the more intricate and subtle details into a workable system.

In my opinion the present book fills admirably a widely felt need. It seems to me an unprecedented and brilliantly successful attempt to describe and explain the complex technique of conducting in a methodical and yet lively manner. The approach is as novel as it is fascinating, because of the combination of knowledge, experience, and an extraordinary power of observation on the part of the author. This is particularly evident in the diagrams, which at first may seem surprising and unusual in their design, yet demonstrate with provable accuracy the basic patterns of the motions every professional conductor employs. The author also has succeeded in putting down on paper much instructive and valuable material that is typical of "shop talk" among conductors. The student will get an insight into the craftsmanship of recognized masters, while to the practising conductor the book will be an invaluable reference work. I warmly recommend this volume to students, teachers, and musicians in general, and I am inclined to think that it will make most interesting reading even to the average music-lover, who will meet here an aspect of conducting unknown except in professional circles.

GEORGE SZELL

PREFACE

PART MUSICIAN, part actor, the conductor pursues a craft which is not easily defined. Probably very few people have more than a vague notion of what the man with the baton is actually doing. Can his art be taught? Years ago I was assured by a well-known musician that in conducting there is really nothing to learn but the simple rule: the first beat in a bar goes down and the last beat goes up; the rest is experience. This book would not have been written, had I thought he was right. Without underestimating the value of practical experience, I feel certain that there are many things in conducting which can and should be taught. After all, we learn from each other in so many fields, why should we not in conducting?

If a young musician had had the opportunity of observing several accomplished conductors intensively for a number of years in their daily routine, and if he had acquired conducting experience under the eye of an authoritative director, he could become a competent conductor without methodical instruction. Then his position would be comparable to that of a person who had learned a language without any formal study of the grammar, by living for many years in the country where it is spoken. However, few young musicians have such a chance today. The intention of this book is therefore to present, in concentrated form, what a conductor should learn about baton technique during his apprenticeship.

My method of teaching is different from that of most textbooks. Here is a brief outline of the plan of the book.

(1) One of the first things that the student is usually told is that his beat must express the music, with its great variety of feelings. But the advice is of little value unless he has the variety in his beat with which to project this variety of feelings. This cannot be achieved if the conductor has only one way of indicating the rhythm—for instance, only one pattern for beating 4 beats in a measure. It would be impossible to teach all the different gestures and their combina-

tions as used by a master conductor. However, certain fundamental patterns which cover widely different musical situations can be taught methodically.

Six patterns of beating each of the basic rhythms are demonstrated in this book: *non-espressivo, light-staccato, full-staccato, espressivo-legato, marcato,* and *tenuto.* These patterns are based not only upon my own experience but upon the common practice of the foremost conductors of our day. While each conductor has his own highly individual manner of directing, there are certain principles of "good usage" in conducting. This book trains the student in the application of these principles and at the same time gives him opportunity to develop an individual technique. Thus he will be equipped to be a musical leader and not merely a time-beater.

(2) It seems to me that the diagrams found in many textbooks are impractical because they are too small and inaccurate. The present work includes diagrams which are designed so that the student can easily copy them in large size on the blackboard or on a large sheet. The enlarged diagrams can then be used in practising the actual beat, by following the lines with the point of the baton. This method is useful for self-instruction and in the class room, and helps the student to learn a clear and incisive beat.

(3) Perhaps more so in music than in any other art, the student must learn by doing. In order to put the techniques discussed into immediate practice, the book is provided with abundant examples to be played while the student conducts. It has been found that he will learn more readily from short exercises than from a premature attempt to master an entire piece in full score. For this reason I have written short instructive examples which will enable the student to concentrate entirely upon the mechanical problems. These should be practised at many different speeds, in order to train the student to indicate the tempo unmistakably and distinctly.

Other examples have been chosen carefully from musical literature and have been arranged so as to offer the greatest aid to the conducting student, not for their pianistic effect. They include all the important orchestral parts and the pianist may have to simplify them slightly, always bringing out the main themes and preserving the rhythmic structure. They should be played by the teacher or by an experienced student who is able to react to the conducting gestures as an orchestra would. In the interest of economy the examples contain the fewest number of bars which will illustrate effectively the point under discussion. The full orchestral scores should be consulted and used often. It is also recommended that the teacher arrange some of the examples for a small ensemble, so that the students may have the advantage of conducting an orchestra.

(4) The material is presented in a manner which will enable the student to learn quickly and thoroughly. I have not written a treatise on conducting but rather a handbook to train conductors. For this reason all theoretical discussions have been immediately applied to practical musical problems. Furthermore, these have been so arranged that the student naturally proceeds from one to the next, accumulating techniques as he goes on. I am quite conscious of the seemingly improvised nature of certain chapters and of various repetitions, and I realize that some of the most pertinent and useful advice is found in the brief remarks on the musical examples. I consider this sacrifice of academic order well worth while, because such an organization of the material comes closest to personal teaching.

The book includes discussion of full scores and shows how to prepare them from the point of view of baton technique. It can be used by individuals without the aid of an instructor, and it is also planned as a textbook for colleges where conducting is part of the curriculum. Hints are given for the use of the book in classes in conducting.

If my book will contribute to the education of genuine conductors and diminish the number of time-beaters, I shall feel amply rewarded.

MAX RUDOLF

CONTENTS

[xiii]

INTRODUCTION

DIRECTING AN ORCHESTRA IS A COMPLEX JOB

THE CONDUCTOR must be a trained musician, must know how to work with people in a group, and must be able to convey his intentions to his players by means of gestures.

It is very important that the conductor have a thorough knowledge of composition, and he should be familiar with various musical styles. He should also be aware of the problems of musical interpretation. A good working knowledge of instruments, both individually and in combination, is indispensable. The ability to read an orchestral score, and, if necessary, play it on the piano is a vital part of the conductor's equipment. While absolute pitch is not a prerequisite, the conductor's ear should be keen enough to recognize inaccuracy in pitch and to maintain the proper balance. The mastery of all these elements will give him the authority to be a genuine leader.

But all his musicianship and thorough study of scores will help him little unless he knows how to talk to people, work with them, and get results in a quick and direct manner. Knowledge of a few simple principles of group psychology is of great assistance in rehearsing efficiently and in stimulating the players to a good performance.

Musicianship and knowledge of psychology, however, still do not make a conductor. There is a technique of conducting just as there is a technique of playing the piano.

THE TECHNIQUE OF CONDUCTING

This book deals with the technique of conducting, which involves the use of the right arm in wielding the baton, of the left arm to lend support, and the functions of the eyes. The most elementary things indicated by gestures are when to start and stop, the tempo of the music, and the holds and interruptions. These are indispensable, but in themselves are merely sufficient to keep the orchestra together. To obtain an artistic result the conductor must be able to communicate nuances in dynamics, details of phrasing, articulation (legato and staccato), and general expression. For this, mere *time-beating* is not enough; the appropriate gesture for each musical expression must be mastered, before we can speak of *conducting*.

If you watch an accomplished conductor, you will be impressed by the natural unity and coherence of his gestures. His motions seem to be such a simple and direct means of evoking musical expression that you may not realize their thoroughly planned and purposeful nature. These motions constitute a technique for conveying to the orchestra a large number of musical details. In order to teach this technique, the various gestures that the conductor uses will be analyzed and discussed in this book. You may wonder why an activity that appears so easy and natural must be dissected. You may also doubt whether all conductors have worked out their techniques as methodically as this book proposes to do. Actually, if they have not done so, they have attained the same end only by a long process of trial and error.

Whether a conductor studies in the manner proposed by this book, or whether his technique evolves in the course of his experience alone, he will have to pass through a stage of development in which he becomes acutely conscious of technical problems. Most musicians rely at first on their natural feelings and may work for some time with little to guide them but their instinct. But presently they realize that technical control is indispensable to artistic mastery. Once attained, such control gives the artist that expressive simplicity which is the goal of all artistic performance. For the conductor this means that his gestures become second nature and he can give himself entirely to the music.

THE USE OF THE BATON

A conductor who fractured his left arm would still be able to exercise complete control of his group, provided that he had a good baton technique. This is the most efficient tool at his disposal. Therefore, much of the emphasis of this course will be laid upon the use of the baton.

The handiest kind of baton is about twenty inches long and fairly light in weight. It should not be so thin that the point is shaky, making it hard to beat distinctly. The choice of a baton with or without a handle depends upon the individual. You must also decide for yourself what grip is the most convenient. The conductor must be able to control the baton completely and feel perfectly at ease; this is the test of a good grip. The most advisable way to hold the baton is with the thumb, first, and second fingers, and with the butt against the palm of the hand. You will feel more secure in the energetic beats, if you use an even fuller grip.

CONDUCTING WITHOUT BATON

No one can say that conducting without baton is "right" or "wrong". This method has one obvious advantage in that there are two expressive hands instead of one. But even though the baton takes some of the expressiveness from the right hand, there are advantages in using it. Remember that the player's attention is always divided between his music stand and the conductor. It is much easier for the player to follow the baton, especially if the music is unfamiliar or the part is technically difficult, or in accompaniments. The baton is even more important when there is a large ensemble, for then many of the players are quite a distance from the conductor's stand. In the interest of clarity, therefore, the student should learn to conduct with a baton. Nevertheless, the diagrams of this course can be studied without one.

GENERAL EXPLANATION OF THE DIAGRAMS

In order to get the full benefit out of the course, the student should enlarge the diagrams of at least the first ten chapters. Each square of the diagram represents one square inch. The enlarged diagrams, drawn either on a sheet of paper or on a blackboard, will make it possible for the student to practise with a life-size beat.

Because of the two-dimensional nature of the diagrams, different beats along the same line can be indicated only by slight separation of the beat-lines. Straight lines which run close together on the diagram coincide in actual practice.

All counts are marked so that the played· beat coincides with the written count: the baton is at ①when the 1st beat sounds, and moves so as to arrive at ② at the start of the 2nd beat

O   The baton passes through without stopping.

☐   The baton stops at this point.

ATT   Position of attention.

There are four kinds of lines in the diagrams:

indicates the field of beating.

indicates deliberate controlled movement.

indicates very quick movement.

indicates bouncing.

Chapter 1

THE NON-ESPRESSIVO PATTERN (4-Beat)

GENERAL TRAINING OF THE RIGHT ARM

IN DIRECTING MUSIC the right arm describes certain patterns which represent the rhythm. There is a different pattern for each rhythm, and the patterns are modified according to the musical expression. The movements of the baton are: up, down, left, right, and their various combinations.

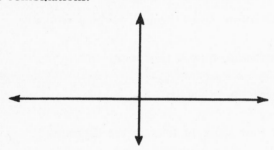

This diagram shows the up-down line and the left-right line used in beating. The general area covered by these lines is called the field of beating, and the lines are the axes of the field. The size of the field of beating may vary widely from one situation to another.

Practise the up-down and left-right motions with the wrist alone, first slowly, then rapidly. To be sure that the forearm does not move, hold it firmly with the left hand. Avoid tension in the wrist and make as large a gesture as possible.

There are two positions of the wrist: palm downward and palm sidewise. Practise with both positions. In practising the left-right movement you may find the palm-downward position stiff. If so, do not try to force it on the wrist; just practise the palm-sidewise position. In actual conducting it is most convenient to use a position half-way between the two, or to change smoothly from one to the other.

In adding the forearm motion to the wrist motion, you must take cognizance of a general rule: the motion increases with the distance of the moving part from the body. Thus, the point of the baton travels farther than the hand, which in turn moves more than the forearm. Use the left hand to hold the arm above the elbow while practising with the forearm. In slow tempo a special precaution should be taken in order to achieve smooth co-ordination of all parts: the hand motion should always be a little behind that of the forearm. This necessitates a turn of the wrist each time the forearm changes direction. For example, suppose the forearm is moving upward and the wrist reaches its highest position; the hand will be pointing half way down, and will complete its upward motion while the arm is already moving downward. Similar relationships apply to both up-down and left-right movements.

The third preliminary exercise uses the whole arm. Work for a smooth motion in which all parts of the arm blend their movements, so that no one part sticks out awkwardly. Think of the baton as an extension of the arm; its motion should be smooth and steady.

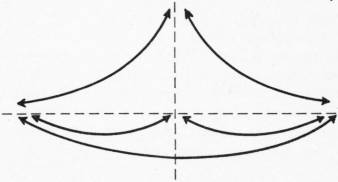

This diagram shows five swinging movements. Practise each with wrist alone, then with wrist and forearm. Vary the size and the speed of your beat, from a snap of the wrist to a slow turn.

These four preliminary exercises should be practised before the work of each of the first ten chapters. In addition, the student should use a few warming-up exercises familiar to violinists and pianists:

shaking the hands freely, lifting the arms and letting them drop suddenly, and so on.

THE NON-ESPRESSIVO PATTERN (4-BEAT)

The first four chapters deal only with music that requires 4 beats in a measure. Several patterns of beating this rhythm will be shown, beginning with the non-espressivo pattern.

The non-espressivo beat is a plain, continuous motion. It is neutral in character and therefore uses mostly straight lines. It is not large in size and is done with no intensity in the forearm motion.

Put the enlarged Diagram 1 on the music stand or tack it onto the wall. Each student can find the height best suited to him by standing before the diagram with elbow relaxed, forearm slightly elevated, and baton extended forward. The point of the baton should then be at the level of the left-right line. (Use the same level for all diagrams!) Stand directly in front of the diagram and let the baton point to the intersection of the up-down and left-right lines, approximately three inches from the surface of the diagram, as demonstrated in the photograph on page 9.

First count aloud without beating: *One-Two-Three-Four* in moderate tempo ($\quad$ =66). When you feel that the tempo is established, continue to count aloud and start moving the baton, following the lines exactly so that the point of the baton passes through the number corresponding to each count. Always keep the baton a few inches from the diagram, but close enough to follow the lines exactly. Try to achieve a smooth motion and avoid stopping on the counts.

A wrist motion is sufficient for this pattern. However, many students will find that they cannot use the wrist alone without feeling some strain. Since it is of utmost importance to feel at ease while beating time, a slight forearm motion may be used in addition to the wrist motion. In this case it should always be remembered that the point of the baton moves more than the hand, the hand more than the forearm.

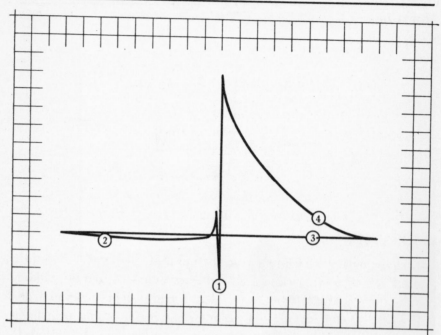

Diagram 1. 4-beat; non-espressivo

The elbow should be held still but relaxed. With practice you will gradually develop the ability to use the wrist alone.

You will observe that on the 1st count the baton is carried upward before it is turned to the left. This upward movement on the 1st count is called the rebound. You will also notice that the distance between the counts is not uniform. The distance between ③ and ④ especially is smaller than the others, while the distance between ④ and ① is much larger. Nevertheless, you will soon learn to adjust your beat automatically so as to keep it even and smooth.

When you are sure that you can follow this pattern without the help of the diagram, check yourself by using a large mirror. Now start beating, watching yourself to see that no part of your body is moving except wrist and forearm. Your whole body should be relaxed and calm. Be sure to keep the elbow quiet but do not press it against your side. Watch your beat, keeping it clear and steady!

THE PREPARATORY BEAT AT THE START

It is a general rule that the conductor gives one extra beat, strictly in tempo, before the music actually begins.

In other words, to start playing on the 1st count you must start beating one count earlier, that is to say on *Four*. However, this beat of preparation which is shown in Diagram 2 is not merely the regular 4th beat, for it starts from the position of "attention" and has the quality of an invitation. It is equivalent to lifting the bow in the string instruments and to taking a breath in the winds. It enables the conductor to get a clean and unified attack.

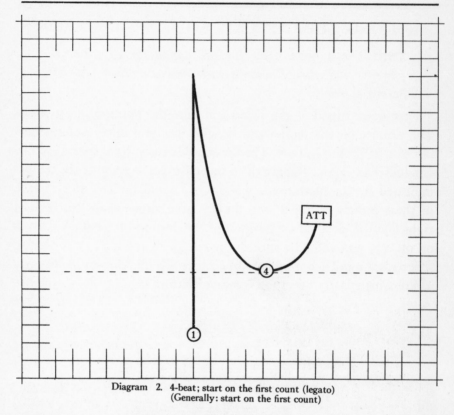

Diagram 2. 4-beat; start on the first count (legato)
(Generally: start on the first count)

Practise the preparatory beat in the following manner. Point the baton to the attention space **ATT** on Diagram 2 and count aloud the previous *One-Two-Three-Four*. Just before *Four*, let the baton move so that it passes through ④ as you count *Four*. Keeping strict tempo, follow the line until you reach ① , where the music presumably begins. Having mastered this, return to the mirror with both arms down and relaxed. Lift the baton and assume the position of attention. Try to feel that by doing this you would really gain the attention of your group. This will be still more effective if you lift elbow and forearm slightly. Count—this time to yourself—and give the preparatory beat. When you reach ① , continue beating as you did with Diagram 1 and beat for several bars. Do this over again several times, starting each time from a completely relaxed position with the arm at the side.

APPLYING THE GESTURES TO MUSICAL EXERCISES

Since it is a good habit for the conductor to watch his players, you should always memorize the first few bars before starting.

Face your friend at the piano and take the position of attention. Concentrate on the tempo and be sure that you know exactly how fast you are going to beat. Then, using what you have learned so far, conduct Exx. 1 a-c. Repeat them several times in each of the tempos indicated by the metronome markings. To end the last note in each of these exercises, simply stop the 4th beat emphatically on the left-right line. (A detailed explanation of the cutting-off gestures is given on pp. 135 and 140.) Be sure that your friend at the piano is playing strictly in time. Do not hesitate to correct him; develop the habit early of knowing exactly what you want and getting it.

In class work, Ex. 1 should be not only played on the piano, but also sung by the group while you conduct. Here you will have to co-ordinate the actions of several people, exactly as you will have to do when you conduct an orchestra. Your preparatory beat will work much better if you take a slight breath simultaneously. There are many exercises in this book that lend themselves to singing, with or without piano accompaniment. Whenever possible the class should sing the melody in those exercises.

Exx. 2 and 3 are to be played on the piano, or can be arranged for a small instrumental ensemble. Ex. 3 is marked 2/4, but use 4 beats in a measure because of the slow tempo.

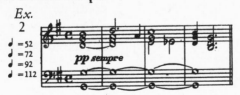

So far you have conducted these exercises *p*. Now repeat them *mf*. To do this, you will have to enlarge the size of your beat. Make your gestures about a third larger than those used for *p*, but do not change their proportions. Keep checking the smoothness and clarity of your beat with the mirror. For the larger beat, use the forearm in addition to the wrist motion.

EMPHASIZING THE BEATS BY "CLICKING"

In Exx. 4 a-c you will find that you want to make your beat very precise, because of the dotted rhythms and syncopations. Especially in slow tempo the beats will have to be emphasized; this is done by "clicking". This is a sharp, quick wrist motion which speeds up the movement of the baton just before reaching a count. Immediately after the count the motion continues at normal speed. Naturally this technique can be applied only when the forearm participates in moving the baton. Remember that clicking always serves the purpose of emphasizing the beat, and that it need not be used where a smooth beat is sufficiently clear.

Use Diagram 3 for practice (♩ = 66). The 1st count is now located on the left-right line, to give space to continue the motion in the same direction after the click. While practising clicking on all 4 counts, you will feel that each beat is emphasized. Learn to do it with ease and certainty, but do not get into the habit of clicking continually!

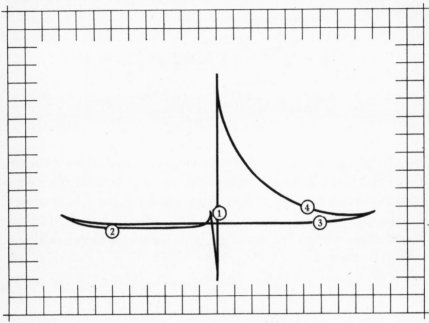

Diagram 3. 4-beat; non-espressivo with clicking on the counts

APPLYING THE NON-ESPRESSIVO PATTERN TO MUSICAL EXAMPLES

By learning the non-espressivo beat first, you start your conducting without any emotional bias and you concentrate upon a clear presentation of the rhythm. But aside from its educational value, you will need it very often in actual conducting.

In practising Exx. 5-9, it is a good habit to hum a few bars of the melody before starting to beat. This will fix the tempo firmly in your mind and enable you to give the preparatory beat strictly in time. Otherwise the preparation might not be in the same tempo as the succeeding beats; the players will be confused and the rhythm will be rather shaky.

Do not use the left hand in directing these examples; its use will be discussed in later chapters.

The metronome markings are those of the original scores—except for those in parentheses, which are the ones traditionally used.

Ex. 5: The harp needs only a clear indication of the rhythm; the quiet flute solo certainly requires no dramatic gestures.

Ex. 6: Indicate the accent in the 3rd measure with a slightly larger *Three*, and click on *Four* but without slowing down. You will feel that the enlarged 3rd beat is a preparation for the accented 4th.

Ex. 7: Since the orchestra has nothing but *pp* accompaniment, the non-expressivo beat is quite adequate.

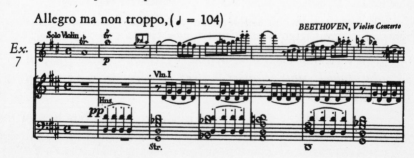

Ex. 8: A minimum of gesture will be sufficient to indicate the tempo for the English horn accompanied by the string section. Here is a good chance to practise keeping the baton in continuous motion in very slow tempo.

Largo, ♩ = 52   DVOŘÁK, Symphony No. 5

Ex. 9: These first bars of *Fingal's Cave* set an atmosphere for the entire piece—more color than expression. For this you need the unemotional non-espressivo beat.

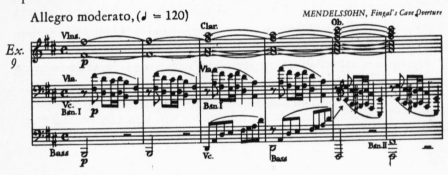

Allegro moderato, (♩ = 120)   MENDELSSOHN, Fingal's Cave Overture

Additional examples for the study of the non-espressivo pattern (4-beat):

Beethoven: Piano Concerto No. 5, 2nd movement—bars 16-24.
Haydn: *The Creation*, No. 12 (Recitative)—bars 1-3.
Nicolai: Overture to *The Merry Wives of Windsor*, bars 1-3, 6, 7.
Shostakovitch: *The Golden Age*, 2nd movement (*Adagio*)—from No. 43.
Tchaikovsky: *Romeo and Juliet* (Overture-Fantasia), beginning.
Verdi: Prelude to *Aïda*, bars 18-23.
Wagner: *Liebestod* from *Tristan und Isolde*, bars 1-5.

Chapter 2

STACCATO PATTERNS (4-Beat)

LIGHT-STACCATO

The light-staccato beat is a quick, straight motion with a stop on each count. The gestures are small.

Diagram 4. The light-staccato beat is done by the wrist alone. In this pattern there is no rebound on the 1st count. Point the baton to 4 and set the tempo at ♩ = 126 in your mind. Then start beating: stop at each count and move very quickly between the counts. Avoid any tension, especially in the forearm. A review of the wrist exercises on pp. 5 and 6 will limber you up so that your wrist will be flexible and your forearm loose. Check your appearance in the mirror

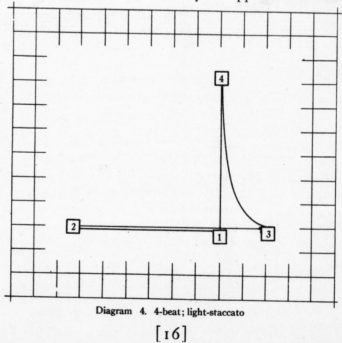

Diagram 4. 4-beat; light-staccato

[16]

to be sure that shoulder and elbow are not moving. Practise light-staccato also at ♩ = 108 and ♩ = 160.

Use Diagram 5 for the start. The motion with which you reach [4] must be very quick and decisive: a snap of the wrist. The preliminary beat is little larger than the other beats. Since this preparation indicates not only the tempo but the staccato quality, you must be sure to make a definite stop at [4] and not to leave it until just before the down-beat.

Exx. 10-16 will give you practice in using this beat. Light-staccato is generally used with tempos of ♩ =100 or faster. However, it can be very effective at slower tempos in *pp* passages (Ex. 13). In the latter case you must be very careful to give a precise preparation and to maintain a steady rhythm.

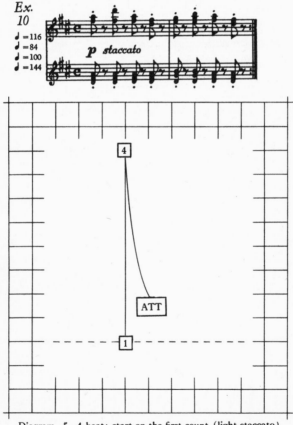

Diagram 5. 4-beat; start on the first count (light-staccato)

Ex. 11

♩ =108
♩ =96
♩ =126

Ex. 12

♩ =138
♩ =120
♩ =168
♩ =104

Ex. 13

♩ =60
♩ =80
♩ =100

Allegro, (♩ = 160)

ROSSINI, Semiramide—Overture

Ex. 14

Vln.I

sotto voce

Str.

Moderato, (♩ = 116)

SULLIVAN, H.M.S. Pinafore

Care-ful-ly on tip-toe steal - ing.

Ex. 15

Ex. 16

Additional examples for the study of the light-staccato pattern (4-beat):

Beethoven: Symphony No. 8, 2nd movement—beginning.
Grieg: *Peer Gynt Suite No. 1*, 4th movement—beginning.
Haydn: Symphony No. 99, 1st movement, *Vivace assai*—beginning.
Shostakovitch: Symphony No. 1, 1st movement, No. 8 (*Allegro non troppo*)—beginning.
Tchaikovsky: Symphony No. 6, 3rd movement—beginning.
Wagner: Prelude to *Die Meistersinger*, passage in E-flat (*Im mässigen Hauptzeitmass*)—3 bars.

FULL-STACCATO

The full-staccato beat is a quick, slightly curved motion with a stop on each count. It is snappy and energetic, with a characteristic "bouncing" on the down-beat. The size may vary from small to large.

Bouncing, a special form of the rebound, is done by a wrist motion. First, practise bouncing without the baton. Lift your forearm and jerk it downward, stopping abruptly at about the left-right line. The wrist must be completely relaxed so that when the forearm stops, the

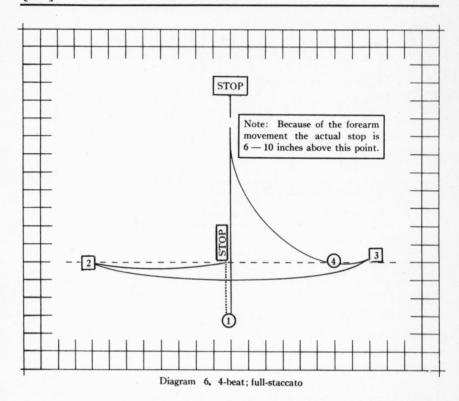

STOP

Note: Because of the forearm movement the actual stop is 6 — 10 inches above this point.

STOP

2

STOP

4   3

1

Diagram 6. 4-beat; full-staccato

hand continues downward and snaps up again immediately. This bouncing of the hand is a natural muscular reaction and must not be hindered by any tension in the wrist.

Diagram 6. Practise at ♩ = 80 and ♩ = 100.

EXECUTION IN *p:* The size of the beat corresponds to the usual enlargement of the diagram. The 1st count is at the bottom of the bounce, and the stop immediately after is on the left-right line. Use very little forearm for the 2nd and 3rd beats; a slight twist will make them snappier. On the 4th beat whip up the arm immediately after the count.

EXECUTION IN *f:* Since the pattern is now about one and one-half times as large as in *p,* use an energetic motion of the forearm for the 2nd and 3rd beats.

As indicated on Diagram 6, the 4th count does not coincide with STOP at the top, though ④ is only a split second from STOP. By

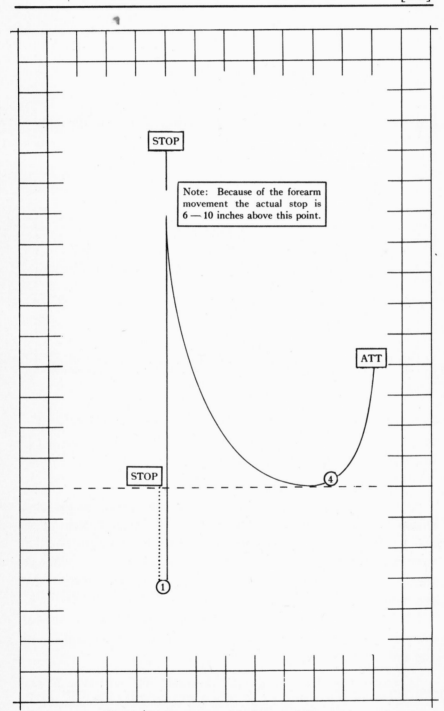

Diagram 7. 4-beat; start on the first count (full-staccato)

making the experiment of beating *Four* at the very top, you will see that it involves a special effort and thus indicates an accent on the 4th count (*accented up-beat*). However, this is an exceptional case (*cf.* Diagram 21) and must be avoided in the regular pattern. But remember that, in the light-staccato, the 4th count actually comes on the highest stop because of the limited size of that beat.

Diagram 7 shows the preliminary beat in full-staccato. In applying it to the exercises, always prepare the tempo in your own mind by counting before you start beating.

Exx. 17 and 18 (each of them to be repeated at least once), practised in the different speeds and dynamics, will train you in the full-staccato. You will help the players by beating very sharply on the rests, so that they can enter precisely on the small-value notes.

Full-staccato is applied in Exx. 19-21.

Additional examples for the study of the full-staccato pattern (4-beat):

Bach: *Brandenburg Concerto No. 3*, 2nd movement.
Bizet: *L'Arlésienne Suite No. 1*, 1st movement—beginning.
Brahms: *Academic Festival Overture, L'istesso tempo, un poco maestoso.*
Haydn: *The Creation*, No. 3 (Recitative)—*Allegro assai.*
Mendelssohn: *Fingal's Cave Overture*, passage starting with bar 76 (one measure before B).
Tchaikovsky: Violin Concerto, 1st movement, *Moderato assai* (after E).

Chapter 3

THE ESPRESSIVO-LEGATO PATTERN
(4-Beat)

The espressivo-legato beat is a curved, continuous motion. It is done with a certain tension in the forearm. The intensity and degree of curve vary with the emotional quality of the music. The size may be anywhere from fairly small to very large.

Diagram 8. Start with the preparatory beat of Diagram 2, but a little larger and with more sweep. Practise with metronome $\quad = 72$, using wrist and forearm. Since the purpose of this pattern is to express a more or less emotional melodic line, you should feel the intensity in the forearm—without too much muscular tension!—and the baton should move as if it were encountering some resistance, a motion similar to the intense drawing of the violin bow in a lyric passage.

The usual enlargement of Diagram 8 gives the size of the *p* beat; practise *mf* with a beat half again as large, and *f* with a beat twice as large. For *f* and *ff* use your whole arm.

While you will have to move the elbow, avoid the mistake of letting it become the center of your conducting motion. Only the tip of the baton offers a clear point of orientation to the players, and movements of the wrist, forearm, and elbow are subordinate to those of the baton. The shoulder must remain still but never tense.

There are many degrees of expression between non-espressivo and molto espressivo, and you should have a wide enough variety of beats to indicate all the shades of intensity. It is therefore important to realize that the espressivo beat is a development of the non-espressivo beat. For poco espressivo, for instance, the pattern of the lines will be bent only slightly, as suggested in Diagram 8a; 8 indicates more

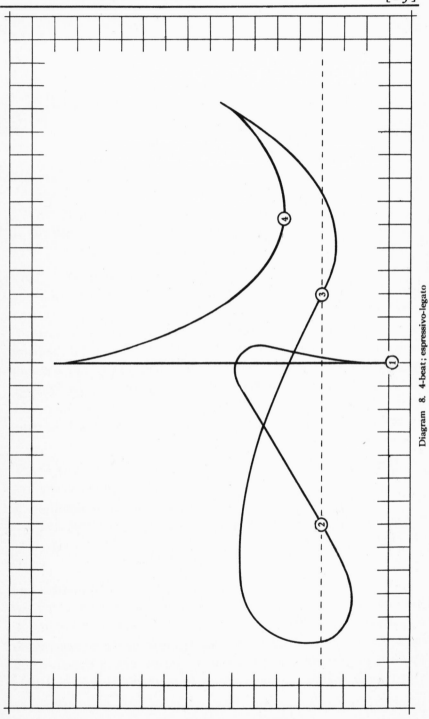

Diagram 8. 4-beat; espressivo-legato

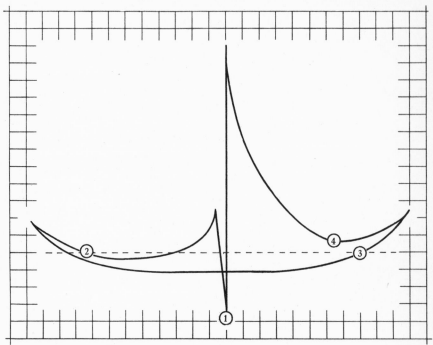

Diagram 8a. 4-beat; espressivo-legato (alternate style)

intensity, and 8b is still more expressive. A highly passionate passage needs an even larger and more curved gesture. Practise before the mirror; start with *p* non-espressivo and, referring to Diagrams 8a and b, work up gradually to *f* molto espressivo.

The relatively neutral patterns of the first two chapters have a quite similar appearance with different conductors. The espressivo beat, however, is more individual; its execution will differ from one conductor to another, but the freedom you gain must not be misused. The orchestra will be confused unless you indicate the counts clearly. There will be occasions when you will need clicking with this beat, especially in slow tempo. The *location* of ①, ②, ③, and ④ remains the same, even though the manner of *connecting* them depends on the musical interpretation. The connecting gestures must be flexible and varied to express the nuances of the melody, which sometimes change from beat to beat in the same bar.

Since the execution of this pattern must be well balanced and graceful, a conductor with very long arms will have to be more careful

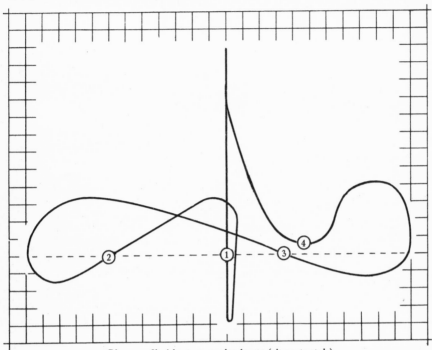

Diagram 8b. 4-beat; espressivo-legato (alternate style)

to control the size of his beat than one with relatively short arms.

The last bar in Ex. 22 needs special attention. The sustained note does not require an espressivo beat; non-espressivo is sufficient. When playing f, however, a gesture of the left hand is needed to prevent the orchestra from playing f⟹. The palm faces upward or inward, and the fingers are somewhat bent. The quality of demand contained in this gesture can be intensified by a slight shaking of the forearm. In other words, while the right hand just beats time (non-espressivo) in this bar, the gesture of the left hand maintains a steady f. The last 2 beats in the 2nd measure of Ex. 23 are treated similarly.

These exercises, like the others written by the author, give you a chance to develop your feeling for a definite and steady tempo.

The skill you gain by practising the same music at different speeds will prove invaluable in your conducting experience.
It is worth while to take great pains with the preliminary beat; students have a tendency to rush it in very slow tempo and to drag it in fast tempo.

Ex. 24: By starting with a somewhat larger beat than the usual *p*, you will be able to build the musical phrases. Then you will express the decreasing intensity of the 2nd bar by the decreasing intensity of your gesture. *Four* in the 2nd and 4th bars is like a preliminary beat, preparing the following phrase. The emphasized 3rd beat in the last measure should also be prepared (without delaying the tempo!); carry the 2nd beat farther to the left, and you will naturally give more expression to the 3rd beat.

Ex. 25: In the 2nd measure, use a very small gesture for *Three*—then on *Four* prepare for the next bar. The intensity in the forearm, usually characteristic of the espressivo beat, would be too heavy for this graceful music. Therefore lead the melody with a light forearm, poco espressivo.

Ex. 26: The conductor must devote as much attention to the counterpoint in the 'cellos as to the melody. All the beats must be espressivo and the intensity of the gesture should express the rise and fall of the melody.

Ex. 27: While the espressivo beat will guide the strings in the melody, the winds need a very accurate indication of the rhythm (clicking may be used, but not necessarily on all the counts). The crescendo in the 4th measure requires an increasing gesture.

Ex. 28: The character of this music indicates a light and graceful gesture. Here again you should not "feel" your forearm.

Additional examples for the study of the espressivo-legato pattern (4-beat):

Brahms: Symphony No. 3, 2nd movement—passage starting at F.
Elgar: *Enigma Variations, Op. 36*, Variation No. 5—beginning.
Franck: Symphony in D minor, 1st movement—*Lento*.
Mascagni: *Cavalleria Rusticana*, Prelude—bars 2-12.
Puccini: *La Bohème*, 1st act, Rodolfo's aria (*Andante lento*).
Verdi: Overture to *La Forza del Destino, Andante mosso* at C.

Chapter 4

STARTING ON OTHER COUNTS

ACCORDING TO THE RULE on page 9, you are supposed to give one extra beat, strictly in tempo, before the first "played" beat. Thus, if the music starts on the 4th count, start beating *Three*; if it starts on the 3rd count, start beating *Two*; if it starts on the 2nd count, start beating *One*. Your preparation must also include the dynamics: a larger gesture prepares *f*, a smaller gesture *p*.

START ON THE 4TH COUNT

Diagram 9. It has been pointed out that the preliminary beat, because of its quality of invitation, is not identical with the regular

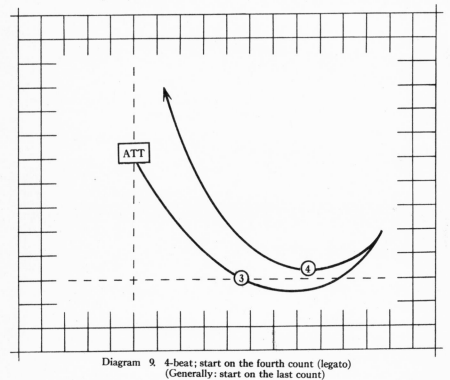

Diagram 9. 4-beat; start on the fourth count (legato)
(Generally: start on the last count)

pattern. Even in non-espressivo it is slightly curved, unlike the usual straight line. The more expressive the music, the more expressive the preparation should be. But do not give too much weight to the preliminary beat, which is always gentler than the first played beat. Be especially careful in espressivo: undue tension of the forearm will give too great an intensity to the preliminary beat and make it difficult for the players to start. Apply these ideas to your practice of Ex. 29.

Diagram 10. As in all staccato beats, use a snappy and decisive motion in the preparation. You can indicate the tempo clearly only

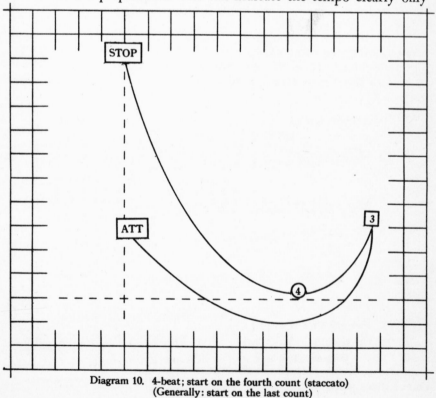

Diagram 10. 4-beat; start on the fourth count (staccato)
(Generally: start on the last count)

by making a definite stop at $\boxed{3}$, otherwise the staccato quality is lost and the players do not get a precise feeling of the tempo. Keep this in mind while practising Ex. 30.

Ex. 31: Use poco espressivo and a small beat.

Ex. 32: For this very energetic start, raise the whole arm on the preparatory beat (the baton pointing downward!), while the elbow may go slightly backwards to increase the impetus of the start. Check in the mirror to be sure that the gesture appears convincing but not too violent. Beat staccato *ff*.

Ex. 247 (1 bar only): Accent the start in a similar but less violent manner.

Ex. 33: Although the first phrase is slurred, the theme does not have legato character, therefore beat staccato. (*Cf.* the remark at the end of this chapter.)

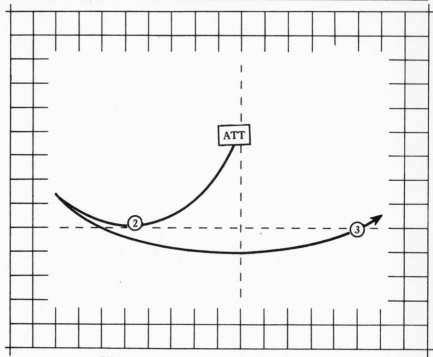

Diagram 11. 4-beat; start on the third count (legato)

START ON THE 3RD COUNT

Diagrams 11 and 12. You will feel that the change of direction from left to right included in the preparation gives the quality of invitation to the beat. Practise Exx. 34 and 35.

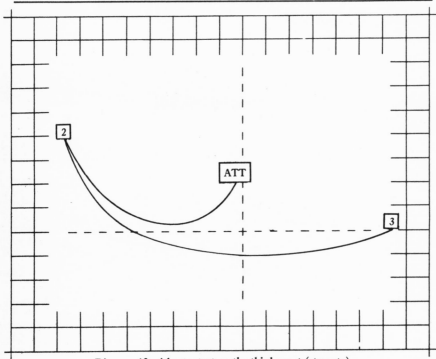

Diagram 12. 4-beat; start on the third count (staccato)

Ex. 36: Beat non-espressivo.

Ex. 37: Beat in 4 in spite of the time-signature ¢ ; 2-beat is not applicable because of the slow tempo. The first two notes are detached, the rest legato; beat accordingly. Your preparatory gesture should be very gentle, to match the graceful music.

Ex. 38: Vigorous staccato.
Ex. 39: *f* legato.

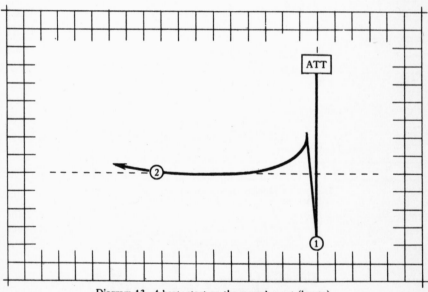

Diagram 13. 4-beat; start on the second count (legato)

START ON THE 2ND COUNT

Diagrams 13 and 14. Again the change of direction leads the players into their attack. The staccato preparation in this case requires a large bounce, but should be very elastic and by no means heavy. Lifting the forearm slightly on the rebound will emphasize the introductory character. In light-staccato, however, use the wrist only. The gesture then is considerably smaller. For training use Exx. 40 and 41.

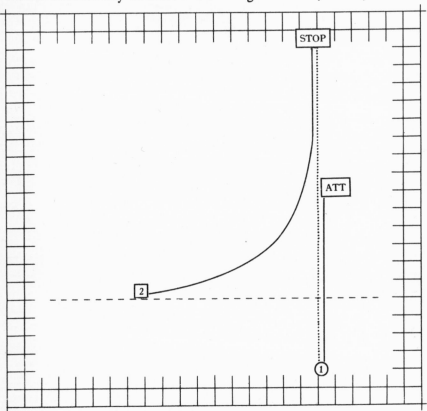

Diagram 14. 4-beat; start on the second count (staccato)

Ex. 42: Start *p* legato, crescendo to *f*. After a large down-beat (*fp*) make the 2nd beat much smaller and crescendo again.

Exx. 43 and 44: *p* legato, poco espressivo. The quarter rest on *One* does not affect the manner of preparation.

Ex. 45: *f* staccato, but not too sharp, since the music is solemn and the bowing should not be too detached.

Keep in mind the various positions of attention! Once you lift the baton do not leave the position of attention until you give the preparatory beat. Before lifting the baton, be sure where to point it. Remember this simple rule: *when the attack is on the 1st count, point the baton to the right. To start on the other counts point it to the center.* There is one exception. For a spectacular attack on the 4th count, point the baton to the left. This position allows a very large preliminary beat (whole arm gesture). Try it, but do not use it too often.

Additional examples:

Start on the 4th count:

Beethoven: Symphony No. 3, 2nd movement.
Brahms: Symphony No. 2, 2nd movement.
Haydn: *The Creation*, No. 24—Aria.
Mozart: *Die Zauberflöte*, No. 21—Finale.
Puccini: *Madama Butterfly*, 2nd act—beginning.
Verdi: *Il Trovatore*, 2nd act (No. 4—Chorus).

Start on the 3rd count:

Haydn: *The Seasons*, No. 34—Cavatina.
Prokofieff: *Classical Symphony*, 3rd movement.

Start on the 2nd count:

Bach: Cantata No. 21 (*Ich hatte viel Bekümmernis*), No. 3—Aria for Soprano.

Chapter 5

THE 3-BEAT

NON-ESPRESSIVO AND ESPRESSIVO-LEGATO

DIAGRAM 15. Apply the same procedure as for Diagram 1. To start on the 1st count, use Diagram 2 (changing the figure ④ to ③) and practise before the mirror at different tempos.

Diagram 16. The explanations of Chapter 3 apply to this pattern. Diagrams 16a and b show poco espressivo and molto espressivo. Enlarge according to dynamics.

Ex. 47: Practise with poco espressivo to molto espressivo.

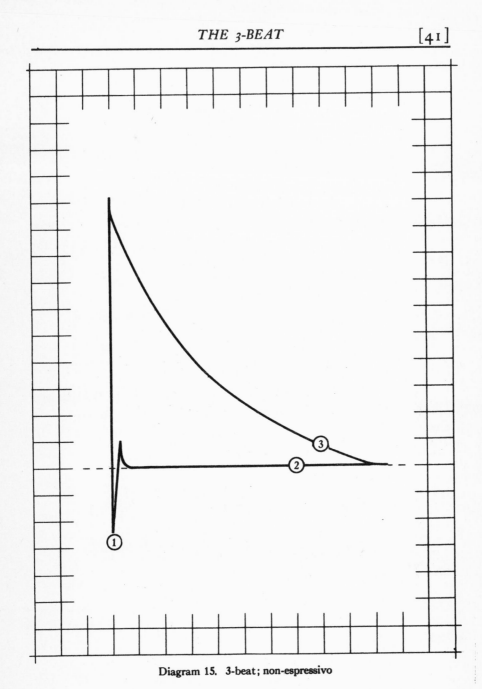

Diagram 15. 3-beat; non-espressivo

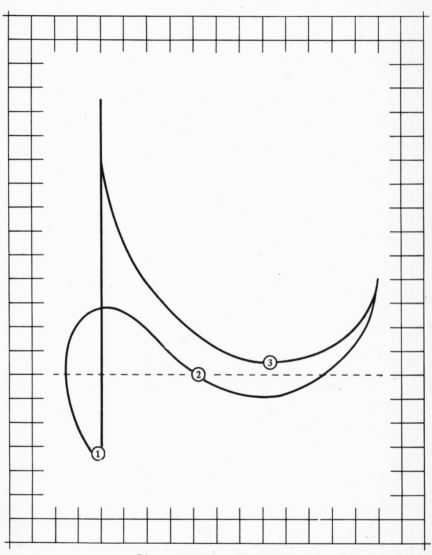

Diagram 16.   3-beat; espressivo-legato

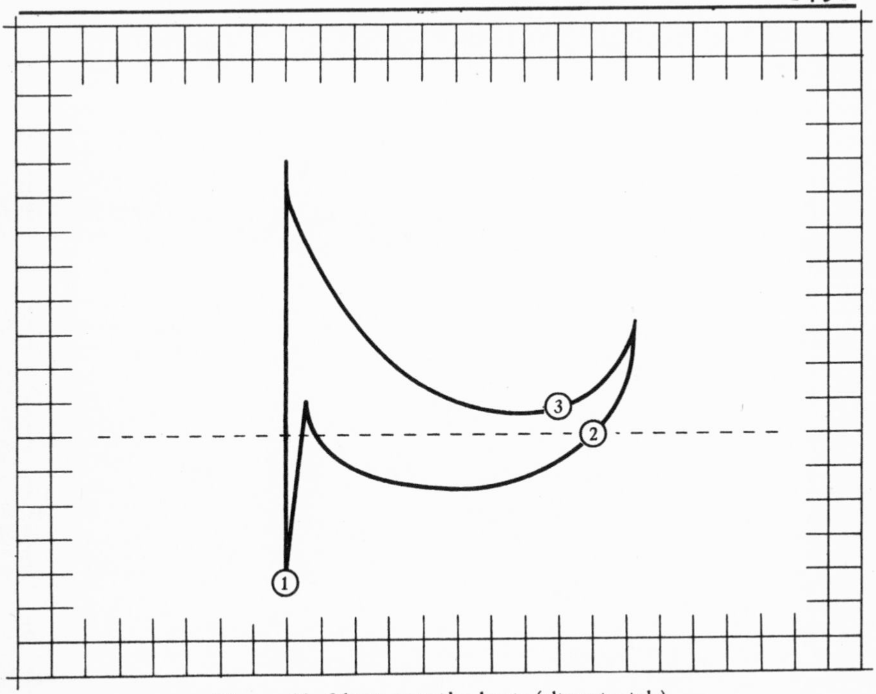

Diagram 16a. 3-beat; espressivo-legato (alternate style)

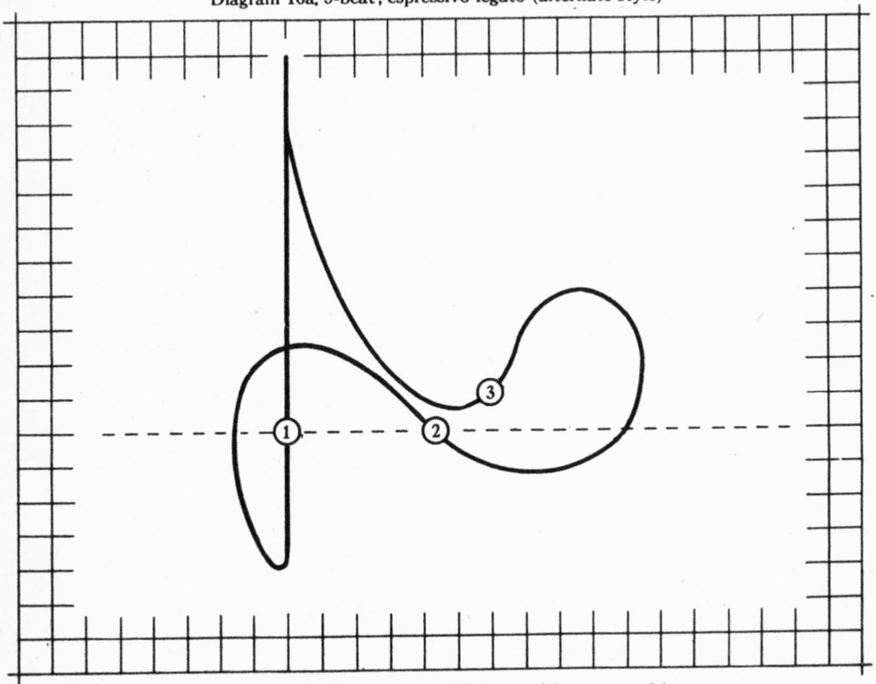

Diagram 16b. 3-beat; espressivo-legato (alternate style)

Ex. 48: Beat in 3, indicating each ♩. with one beat. Use non-espressivo.
Ex. 49: Very small non-espressivo.

Ex. 50: Molto espressivo.

LIGHT-STACCATO AND FULL-STACCATO

Diagrams 17 and 18. Compare the explanations of Chapter 2. For the start apply Diagram 5 (light-staccato) and Diagram 7 (full-staccato), changing the figure 4 to 3 . Practise at different speeds.

For training in 3-beat staccato use Exx. 51 and 52.

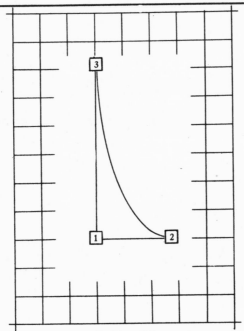

Diagram 17. 3-beat; light-staccato

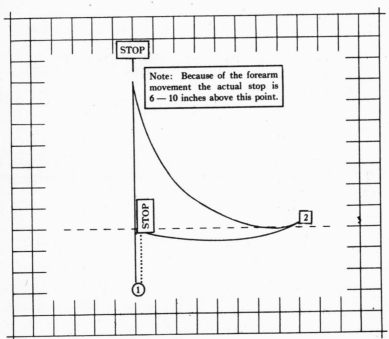

Note: Because of the forearm movement the actual stop is 6 — 10 inches above this point.

Diagram 18. 3-beat; full-staccato

Ex. 53a: Light-staccato. The legato in the flutes (bar 4) does not affect the beat, which remains staccato. This is justified not only by the staccato accompaniment, but because the staccato pattern is often applied to fast legato passages when a strong pointing out of the rhythm is indicated.

Ex. 53b: 2 bars full-staccato (not too large) followed by 2 bars light-staccato.

EXAMPLE 53 a-b

Ex. 54: Full-staccato, large gesture.

Tempo di Bolero, ♩ = 76 — RAVEL, *Bolero*

Ex. 55: Light-staccato. Make your preparation sufficiently fast. **Here,** as in the first 2 bars of Ex. 53a, the strings are playing pizzicato, which often requires staccato beating.

Tempo di Mazurka, ♩ = 160 — GRIEG, *Peer Gynt Suite No. 1*

START ON THE 2ND AND 3RD COUNTS

Use Diagrams 19 and 20 for the start on the 2nd count, Diagrams 9 and 10 for the start on the 3rd count (changing figures as usual). Practise Exx. 56-59.

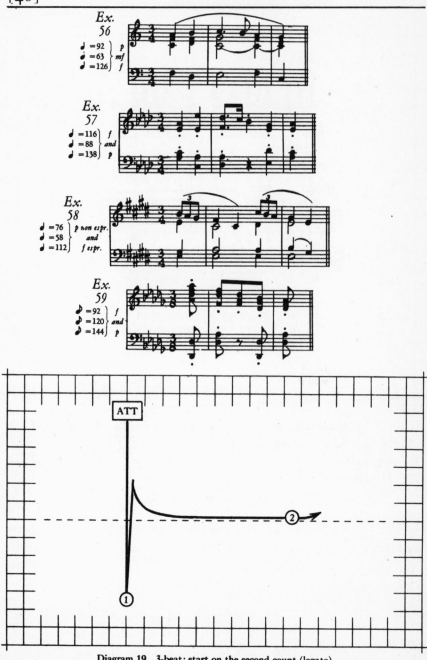

Diagram 19. 3-beat; start on the second count (legato)

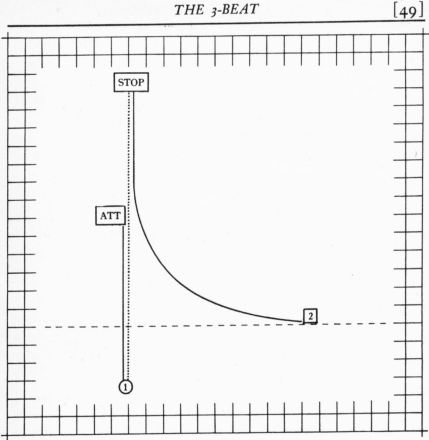

Diagram 20. 3-beat; start on the second count (staccato)

Ex. 60: Full-staccato.
Ex. 61: Non-espressivo.

Ex. 62: Poco espressivo, always legato (a staccato beat would be inadequate for the eighth-note C in bar 1, which is only slightly detached).

Exx. 63 and 64: Full-staccato but not too large. Your preparation must be very precise to indicate the correct tempo: Allegretto in Ex. 63, Allegro in Ex. 64.

Additional examples for the study of 3-beat:

Non-espressivo:

Beethoven: Symphony No. 5, 2nd movement—bars 39-46.
Brahms: *Variations on a Theme by Haydn*, Variation No. 8.
Elgar: *Enigma Variations, Op. 36*, Variation No. 9—beginning.
Rimsky-Korsakov: *Capriccio Espagnol*, 2nd movement—beginning.
Stravinsky: *L'Oiseau de Feu* (Suite), Finale—beginning.

Espressivo-legato:

Grieg: Piano Concerto, 2nd movement.
Leoncavallo: *Pagliacci*, 1st act, *Cantabile* (*Un tal gioco*).

Sibelius: *The Swan of Tuonela*, 3 bars after G.
Tchaikovsky: Serenade for Strings, 3rd movement.
Wagner: Overture to *Tannhäuser*, bars 17-31.

Light-staccato:

Dukas: *L'Apprenti Sorcier*, 3 bars before No. 2—(*Vif*).
Haydn: Symphony No. 97, 3rd movement—Trio.
Rossini: Overture to *La Gazza Ladra*, *Allegro*.
Stravinsky: *Feu d'Artifice*, beginning.
Tchaikovsky: *Nutcracker Suite, Danse Arabe*—beginning.

Full-staccato:

Brahms: Symphony No. 4, 4th movement—passage starting at C.
Moussorgsky: Polonaise from *Boris Godounoff*.
Offenbach: *Les Contes d'Hoffmann*, 2nd act—Minuet in A major.
Shostakovitch: *The Golden Age*, 1st movement—passage starting at No. 2.
Strauss, Richard: *Salome, Dance of the Seven Veils*—beginning.

Start on the 3rd count:

Beethoven: Symphony No. 8, 3rd movement.
Brahms: German Requiem, 2nd movement.
Franck: Symphony in D minor, 2nd movement.
Handel: *Messiah*, Aria—*The trumpet shall sound*.
Purcell: *Dido and Aeneas*, Nos. 4, 11, 17, 23, and 31.
Schumann: Symphony No. 1, 2nd movement.

Chapter 6

SUDDEN CHANGES OF DYNAMICS AND ARTICULATION

SUDDEN CHANGE FROM *p* TO *f* AND VICE VERSA

IT HAS ALREADY been pointed out that the dynamics of the music can be expressed by the size of the gesture. There are two other ways of indicating volume of sound, and all three will be discussed in this chapter.

(1) CHANGING THE SIZE OF THE BEAT

Exx. 65 and 66: The danger here is that you may over-emphasize the last *p* beat, preparing for the *f*. This can be avoided by using a field of beating in the *p* bars that is about 6 inches higher than the normal. You will then have ample room for a large *f* down-beat. The transition from *f* to *p* (in the repeats!) is done simply by a sudden diminution of the down-beat. Use non-espressivo for *p* and espressivo for *f*. The preliminary gesture is small in Ex. 65, large in Ex. 66.

Ex. 67: The last *p* beat must be somewhat larger to prepare for the *f*, but must not appear to indicate a crescendo. On the rest in bar 4, beat *p* to prepare the repeat. For *p* staccato, use the light-staccato or full-staccato. Maintain your tempo, do not speed up in *f*, and do not slow down when changing back to *p*!

Ex. 68: Beat *f* on the rest in the 4th measure to prepare the repeat.

These exercises offer practice in the sudden change of dynamics on the 1st count in a measure. Changes on the other counts, which are less difficult to execute, are directed in a similar manner.

(2) Using the Left Hand

It has already been demonstrated how to indicate *f* with the left hand (page 27). In the gesture which expresses *p*, the palm of the hand, fingers together, faces the orchestra. These two gestures do not take the place of indicating dynamics with the beat, but are rather supporting gestures. (The one exception is in a *f* passage with sustained notes, as in Ex. 22, in which a large and cumbersome baton motion is usually avoided by means of a *f* gesture in the left hand.)

Repeat Exx. 65-68, using the left hand. The *f* gesture of the left hand must come exactly on the first *f* beat; the *p* gesture, however, should come a little ahead of the *p* beat. In other words, the left hand gesture, following the last *f* beat immediately, indicates a sudden warning before the *p* passage begins. Practise turning your left hand quickly on the last eighth-note of the measure.

In staccato, use the left hand to indicate the change to *p* only, and not for the change to *f*. Avoid time-beating movements in the left hand!

(3) Moving the Right Hand Nearer To or Farther Away From the Body

The right hand may beat close to the body, or it may move away a considerable distance. To emphasize a *f* beat, the right hand may move away from the body suddenly. Likewise a sudden retreat of the hand close to the body makes the change to *p* more effective.

Apply this to the examples without using the left hand. Support by the left hand and motion by the right hand as described are rarely used together. Their combination is a very powerful dramatic gesture and should be reserved for great climaxes.

The following examples may be used for applying the various techniques.

Reprinted by permission of the copyright owners,
Boosey & Hawkes, Inc., New York, N. Y.

In some of the Beethoven excerpts there are two sets of metronome markings: the one printed in the score and, in parentheses, the one that indicates the traditional tempo. Discussion of the reliability of Beethoven's metronome markings would lead us too far afield. The fact is that they are not always followed strictly by many of the foremost conductors.

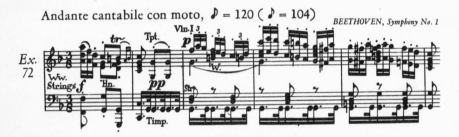

Additional examples for the study of sudden dynamic changes:

4-beat:

Haydn: Symphony No. 101, 2nd movement—bars 11-12.
Mozart: Symphony No. 39, K. 543—2nd movement.
Mozart: Violin Concerto No. 5, K. 219—2nd movement.
Schubert: Symphony No. 9, 1st movement—Introduction.

3-beat:

Beethoven: Symphony No. 5, 2nd movement.
Brahms: Symphony No. 2, 1st movement at B and 20 bars after H.
Franck: Symphony in D minor, 2nd movement—3rd bar from the end.
Haydn: Symphony No. 92 (*Oxford*), 1st movement—*Allegro*.

CHANGE FROM LEGATO TO STACCATO AND
VICE VERSA

Make the experiment of having your friend at the piano play Ex. 73 (♩ = 66) while you are beating the 1st bar staccato and the 2nd legato, contrary to the music. The player will neither feel comfortable in his legato line nor be sure of the rhythm of the staccato chords. This experiment, better than a long explanation, proves the necessity of articulating the beat in agreement with the music—in spite of certain exceptions already mentioned and others to be discussed later on.

As to the execution of the transitions, you will not find it difficult to go from legato to staccato. Just begin to beat staccato on the count at which the detached playing begins; if this is the 1st count, use "bouncing". To change from staccato to legato, beat staccato as usual on the last staccato count, but instead of waiting on the STOP during the count, let the hand *immediately* continue in a legato motion to the next count. Practise this technique in slow tempo until you feel able to apply it to the faster metronome markings.

Exx. 73-79: Practise all the transitions from legato to staccato and vice versa by doing all the repeats.

There are different ways of performing staccato: from very short and sharply attacked notes to moderately detached playing; from a vigorous *f* staccato to a very gentle touch. A conductor can make his players understand what kind of staccato he wants by his beat alone. Furthermore, learn to articulate so distinctly that while your friend at the piano is playing a scale, let us say, he will know when to play legato or staccato just by following your baton. To do this, you will have to think ahead of your beating; if you are not sure of what you want, you will never convince the player.

Chapter 7

CRESCENDO AND DECRESCENDO

IN CHAPTER 6 you practised the *sudden* change from *p* to *f* and vice versa. This discussion deals with the *gradual* change.

CHANGING THE SIZE OF THE BEAT

As the dynamics gradually increase or decrease, your gesture changes its size. If there is a crescendo from *p* to *f* in one measure, the 2nd beat will be markedly larger than the 1st, the 3rd still larger, and the 4th will indicate *f*. But if you have two or more bars at your disposal, the increase of size is sometimes so slow (crescendo poco a poco) that the change from beat to beat is hardly noticeable. The same applies to decrescendo.

Practise first before the mirror, beating in 4 and 3 (♩ = 80) and indicating *p* ———— *f* in one measure, then in two measures, finally in three or more measures. In legato, start non-espressivo or poco espressivo. As a rule, the non-espressivo pattern is not suited for very large gestures because here it looks awkward. Therefore, do not carry this beat too far in crescendo, but change to espressivo. This also applies to light-staccato, which should change gradually to full-staccato. Practise similarly *f* ——— *p*.

Now use Exx. 80-83. Each of these has 4 different dynamic markings. Thorough practice will make your beat flexible and improve your control considerably. Be economical in the use of your arm and avoid exaggerated gestures. To direct *p* ——— ——— *p*, it is often sufficient to add some forearm motion to the wrist movement which is used to lead the *p*.

[58]

USING THE LEFT HAND

Crescendo is indicated by lifting the left hand, palm facing upward, from the level of the hip to eye level. The hand is held up as long as you want to maintain f. For decrescendo, turn the hand *slowly* so that the palm faces the players; then start dropping the hand gradually, the palm still towards the orchestra, until it reaches the starting position. (The reason for turning the left hand slowly is that a sudden turn would indicate sudden p instead of decrescendo!)

Practise these movements by allowing yourself first one measure, then two, then three or more measures for crescendo. Count aloud in 4 and in 3. Practise decrescendo the same way. Take great care not to make any time-beating movements with the left hand. The up-and-down motions must be absolutely smooth and continuous. Students sometimes have trouble in achieving this smoothness in the left hand while the right hand is beating time. Practise the co-ordination of both hands, and check in the mirror.

In applying the left-hand gestures to Exx. 80-83, you should realize that they constitute a very strong support. Therefore you will not need as large beats as you did with the right hand alone. Try to balance the movements of both hands and avoid exaggerations. Crescendo in staccato does not need the expressive left-hand gesture. However, the left hand is considerably more effective than the right in securing a diminuendo or p subito in both legato and staccato.

Another point that must be considered is connected with the psychology of the orchestra. Many players have a tendency to play loudly at once when they see "cresc." and softly when their parts indicate "decresc." or "dimin." On the other hand, the orchestra does not easily give all its strength to the climax of a crescendo unless stimulated by the leader. So you will have to be fairly restrained at the beginning of a crescendo but very energetic at the climax.

The conductor must not yield to the temptation to increase the tempo when directing a crescendo, or to slow down during a diminuendo passage.

Ex. 84: Diagram 8 is recommended. During the 4th bar, lift the *left hand* half-way to indicate f espressivo in bar 5 (*cf*. Ex. 22). Turn the palm during the 1st beat of bar 6 and drop the hand slightly. With the 1st beat in bar 7, the left hand moves back to indicate *f*; it is turned again during the 3rd beat and dropped slowly. The *right hand* uses the 4th beat in bar 4 (quarter-rest) for a fairly large and very expressive preparation for the following *f*. In the 6th measure use small gestures for the 2nd and 3rd beats, but a larger preparatory beat to attack the second *f* entry. The 8th bar requires restrained gestures.

Ex. 85: Beat espressivo. In the 3rd measure, gradually put the left hand into action. After the climax in the 5th bar a strong diminuendo follows, which requires convincing gestures of both hands.

Ex. 86: Increasing intensity of the gestures indicates the increase in the volume and sonority of the string orchestra. A strongly contrasted motion is needed for the *p* subito.

Ex. 87: In a case like this, do not enlarge your beat for the crescendo in the drum; it is much more effective to save the first large gesture for the preparatory beat (full-staccato) needed on *Three* for the *ff* attack on *Four*. Small beats will do to start the drum player and to beat the first 2 counts.

Ex. 88: Full-staccato. It is not advisable to use too large beats in staccato when the tempo is lively, because the gestures would become too hectic. Instead, indicate the crescendo by increasing the intensity and sharpness of your staccato beat. Support the climax with the left hand.

Ex. 89: Poco espressivo. Increase the size of the beat in the 5th bar only slightly and gradually; then use the left hand to indicate the sudden *p* in bar 7. Keep your gestures small and graceful.

Ex. 90: Start beating non-espressivo with restrained gestures, and indicate the 3 small crescendos (bars 2-6) with slightly enlarged beats. For the crescendo starting in the 7th measure, use either of the methods you have learned, but be economical with your gestures! If you have exhausted your resources by bar 13 (*f*), nothing is left to build up the climax in bar 25. This *ff* requires a special preparation, made by beating the last beat in bar 24 full-staccato with *Three* on STOP. This is the *accented up-beat* mentioned in Chapter 2 (p. 22); *cf*. Diagram 21.

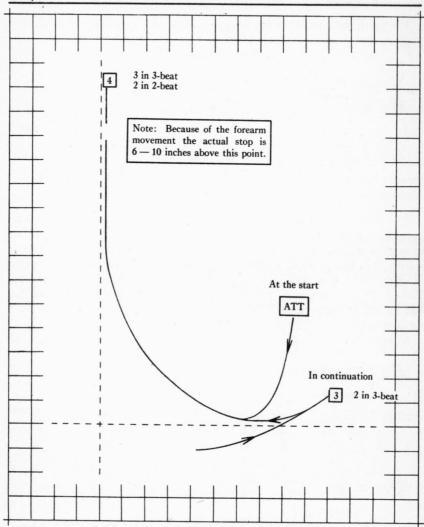

4 3 in 3-beat
2 in 2-beat

Note: Because of the forearm
movement the actual stop is
6 — 10 inches above this point.

At the start

ATT

In continuation

3 2 in 3-beat

Diagram 21. Accented up-beat

A general remark may be added here. The detailed suggestions made
in this and the following chapters are to some extent a matter of individual interpretation. It is not assumed that they constitute the only
right way of execution, for there are often several "right" ways to
conduct a particular piece of music. Nevertheless, it is important that
the student be shown at least one of the right ways, and thus get a
start on the road which leads away from mere time-beating and to-

ward the development of his ability to convey artistic intentions to his players.

Additional examples for the study of crescendo and decrescendo:

4-beat:

Beethoven: Symphony No. 6, 2nd movement.
Bizet: *L'Arlésienne Suite No. 1*, 1st movement—last 10 bars.
Dvořák: Symphony No. 5 (*From the New World*), 2nd movement.
Sibelius: Symphony No. 2, 2nd movement—passage starting at D.
Tchaikovsky: Symphony No. 5, 1st movement—Introduction.

3-beat:

Beethoven: Symphony No. 2, 2nd movement.
Berlioz: *Menuet des Feux-Follets* from *La Damnation de Faust*.
Mendelssohn: *Elijah*, Aria No. 21—*Hear ye, Israel*.
Saint-Saëns: *Samson et Dalila*, 2nd act—Dalila's aria, *Amour, viens aider*.
Wagner: Overture to *Tannhäuser*.

Chapter 8

FACING THE ORCHESTRA

ORCHESTRAL SEATING ARRANGEMENT

THIS CHAPTER REQUIRES a bit of imagination on the part of the student. A young actor not only memorizes his part and acquaints himself with the poetic and spiritual values of the play; he prepares himself by imagining that he is acting his part on the stage. Self-training of this kind is very useful for the young conductor. When you apply your baton technique to the study of scores, you should act as though facing an orchestra. You must therefore have a definite mental picture of the seating plan. It is of minor importance which of the traditional arrangements you choose, whether the 1st violins are on your left and the 2nds on your right, or all the violins on your left, etc. The main requirement is that you have a certain seating arrangement in mind while practising. It will increase your flexibility if you think of one seating plan now, and of another the next time you practise.

CUING

The question of when to cue in the players will be discussed in greater detail in Chapter 24, but whether you give a cue or not, you should be aware of the entries. This means that you must know the score so well that you know what each instrument is doing all the time.

There are three ways of giving a cue: with the eyes, with the baton, and with the left hand.

Some conductors like to show their superior knowledge of the score by throwing the left hand in the direction of the entering instruments as the first note of the entry is played. The players dislike it, and quite justifiably. Cuing is helpful only if done a little in advance of the entry and, while a spectacular gesture may impress the public, it is apt to make the players nervous. Do not get into the habit of giving all cues by pointing. The left hand should be used primarily to indicate a special kind of attack, or the expression with which the particular entry is to be played.

In directing your baton toward a group of entering instruments, you can address the players effectively by turning and facing them. This technique should be used, however, only when a very dramatic entrance is required. If used too often the repeated change of the field of beating upsets the clarity of the beat, as any strong gesture used too frequently loses its effectiveness. Moreover, indication of entries by stretching the whole arm, as though you wanted to stab the players, is not a good habit.

The best way of cuing in your players is usually to look at them. Turn your eyes toward the players one count in advance in moderate tempo, and about 2 counts in fast tempo. Using your eyes is best for two reasons: first, you should not use more motion than you need in conducting; second, the expression of your eyes and your general facial expression can tell the players more about your intentions than fancy hand-waving.

A review of some of the exercises will give you an opportunity to combine the picture of the orchestral set-up with your conducting technique and to use your eyes for cuing in the players.

Ex. 5: Shortly after assuming the position of attention, look at the harp, then start. Not too soon, but not later than the 4th beat in bar 2, turn your eyes toward the flute.

Ex. 7: Since the orchestra pauses in the 1st bar, your beats are small but distinct in order to keep the rhythm clear. In the 4th beat, include an unobtrusive preparation for the horns by turning your eyes toward them. The G-minor chord in the next bar is played by the strings without 1st violins; turn the head slightly toward the right section. At the same time think about the grace-notes (G, B♭, A) in the solo violin, while beating the last count in bar 2, so as to start bar 3 exactly with the soloist.

Ex. 9: To start, address the string section in a general way without pointing out any special group. You may have to prevent the double-basses from starting too loudly, as they sometimes do: put your left hand unobtrusively in p position. Watch the entries of clarinets, oboes, and 2nd bassoon.

Ex. 14: After attention, turn the body and baton half-way to the left. This establishes closer contact with the 1st violins, which is desirable when they have a passage of solo-like quality. Be sure that the rest of the orchestra can see the beat.

Ex. 16: Do not turn your baton to the left, since it would be awkward to move the field of beating a few seconds later to the right for the 2nd violins. Address the different string groups by turning the head only.

Exx. 53a and 55: In this fast tempo, turn your eye toward the flutes in Ex. 53a and to the 1st violins in Ex. 55 at least two beats before the entries.

Ex. 90: Address the violins and then the violas (+ bassoons) for the small crescendos. In the 13th bar there are simultaneous entries of the oboes, horns, and trombones. During the preceding bar, look at the oboes and horns, then concentrate on the accented trombone entry. Your beats on the accented counts played alternately by trombones and clarinets should be especially sharp. Cue in the flutes, 4 bars later the kettle-drum, and on the ff the trumpets.

CONDUCTING A COMPLETE WORK

At this point the student will have sufficient command of the elements of conducting to apply his training to an entire composition. To conduct a piece of music one must know it intimately. This knowledge must include not only notes but also dynamics, orchestration, and the harmonic and formal structure. The importance of the rhythm, also, cannot be emphasized too much.

> *Only if the conductor approaches his task with a definite idea of the rhythmic requirements for each instrument, can he control a rehearsal efficiently and direct a good performance.*

Those who memorize easily should learn the score by heart; others should know it so well that they need refer to it only every few bars. If you know the sequence of the phrases, memorizing is much easier.

The use of a good phonograph recording is quite stimulating, because it supplements the musical imagination. It is helpful in memorizing the score and in giving a vivid picture of the orchestration. But using a record for practice gives you only a passive experience, for you tend to follow rather than to lead. The best active practice is to hum or sing while you conduct, or to be assisted by a skilful pianist who can follow your beat intelligently. This develops the feeling for leading, while following the record does not. Reserve the phonograph for checking your thorough knowledge of the score.

At the beginning of your practice, put yourself into the mood of the music. Fix the rhythm firmly in your mind, by humming the first few bars or thinking them to yourself. Then call your imaginary orchestra to attention. The authority of this gesture must be in keeping with the particular character of the opening, which may vary from quiet and contemplative to vivacious and energetic.

Study and practise scores Nos. 1 and 2 discussed in the Appendix.

Chapter 9

THE 2-BEAT

NON-ESPRESSIVO AND ESPRESSIVO-LEGATO

DIAGRAM 22. In 2-beat it is absolutely essential to follow the diagram exactly. Otherwise it is easy to slip into a habit that is confusing to the players—namely, to use almost identical gestures for the 1st

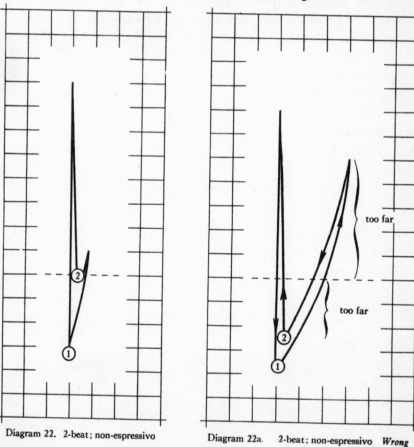

Diagram 22. 2-beat; non-espressivo   Diagram 22a.   2-beat: non-espressivo *Wrong*

[70]

and 2nd beats. Avoid carrying the rebound of the 1st beat too far up (*cf.* Diagram 22a). ②) must be *on* the left-right line, not below! It will help you in practising to imagine that you are lifting something off the left-right line with the point of the baton at ② .

For the start on the 1st count, use the preliminary beat of Diagram 2. Practise Ex. 91.

Diagram 23. Use this pattern in slow and very expressive music. The double curve looks almost like a subdivided 2nd beat (*Two-and*), but there is no rhythmic subdivision here; the double curve gives more space to execute the 2nd beat smoothly and fluently. Diagram 23a is used often, especially in a tempo faster than ♩ = 60. Diagram 23b is recommended for molto espressivo.

All of these diagrams, both non-espressivo and espressivo-legato, can be applied only in slow and moderate tempos. The legato gestures for 2-beat in rapid tempo are discussed in the chapters on the tenuto pattern and on free style.

Practise Exx. 92 and 93. For the latter you need the start on the 2nd count shown in Diagram 24.

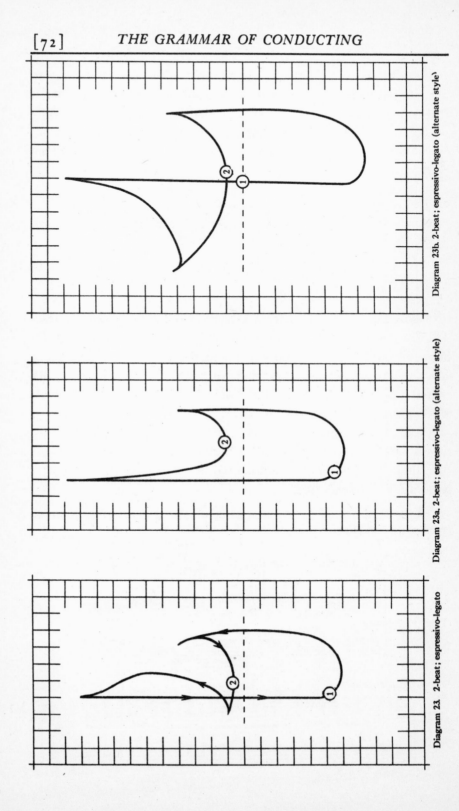

Diagram 23b. 2-beat; espressivo-legato (alternate style)

Diagram 23a. 2-beat; espressivo-legato (alternate style)

Diagram 23. 2-beat; espressivo-legato

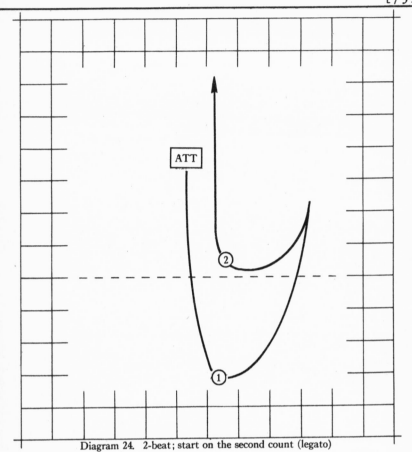

Diagram 24. 2-beat; start on the second count (legato)

Exx. 94 and 95: A calm and well-controlled beat is required. Ex. 94 is non-espressivo and Ex. 95 poco espressivo.

Ex. 96: Espressivo-legato. Click on the counts to maintain a definite rhythm for the triplets played by the winds.

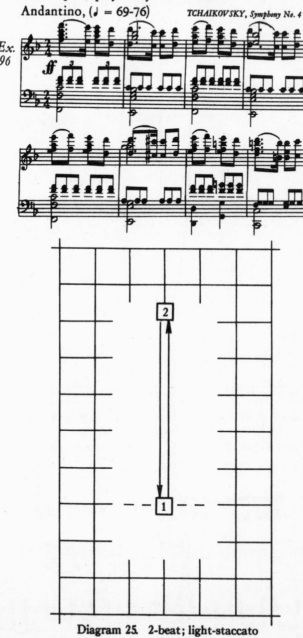

Diagram 25. 2-beat; light-staccato

Ex. 97 (first three bars only): Start on the 2nd count; use a very intense espressivo gesture.

LIGHT-STACCATO AND FULL-STACCATO

Diagrams 25 and 26 show the patterns for staccato. Use Ex. 98 for practising light-staccato and full-staccato. Ex. 99 starts on the 2nd count. On the preliminary beat (Diagram 27), lift the forearm swiftly with the hand turned downward at the lower STOP. Thus the baton points down and gives more impetus to the *f* attack. For light-staccato the size is smaller.

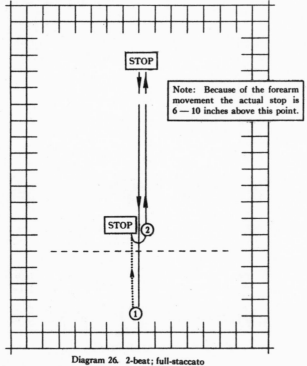

Diagram 26. 2-beat; full-staccato

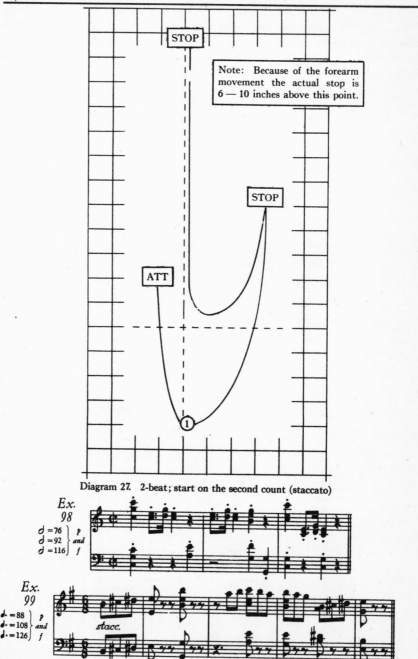

Note: Because of the forearm movement the actual stop is 6 — 10 inches above this point.

Diagram 27. 2-beat; start on the second count (staccato)

Ex. 100: Full-staccato, energetic gestures. A sharp 2nd beat in bar 2 will get a good trombone entrance strictly in time. Beat *One* in the 4th bar similarly, and emphasize the 2nd beat in the 5th bar after which the horns and violas come in.

Ex. 101: Light-staccato; beat in the center. Your small but distinct movements should be seen equally well by the 1st violins playing the theme, and the 2nd violins playing the staccato counterpoint.

Exx. 102 and 103: Use full-staccato in Ex. 102, light-staccato in Ex. 103, in spite of the legato marking.

Ex. 104a: Full-staccato.
Ex. 104b: Light-staccato.

Exx. 105 and 106: Both start on the 2nd count, Ex. 105 in full-staccato,
Ex. 106 in light-staccato. Beat the preparation in the correct tempo!

DYNAMIC CHANGES

For dynamic changes review the explanations of Chapters 6 and 7. Practise Ex. 107; in order to indicate the dynamics exactly as they occur in the music, your mind must always be ahead of your hand.

Ex. 108: An excellent opportunity to practise the well-balanced co-operation of both hands. In bars 5 and 6, use the right hand alone. In bar 7, use the left hand again. Apply the pattern of Diagram 23a with clicking on the accented beats.

Allegretto pastorale, ♩. = 60

GRIEG, *Peer Gynt Suite No. 1*

Ex. 109: In the 3rd and 7th measures, the 1st beat is large, the 2nd small.

Ex. 110: For the sudden *p* in the 3rd bar, put up the left hand just in time to announce the change without affecting the last *f* eighth-note. After the legato beat in the first 3 measures, change to a gentle staccato, becoming somewhat sharper with the gradual crescendo. Reverse this procedure for the diminuendo.

Ex. 111: For the articulation *cf*. Ex. 110. In cases like this it helps to think of the structure of the music (periods of 4 bars each) in building up a gradual crescendo. Do not forget the cues!

CHANGE FROM LEGATO TO STACCATO

The explanations of Chapter 6 apply to the following exercises:

Additional examples for the study of 2-beat:

Non-espressivo:

Bruckner: Symphony No. 4, 1st movement—beginning.

Mendelssohn: Violin Concerto, 1st movement—beginning.

Stravinsky: *L'Oiseau de Feu* (Suite), *Ronde des princesses*—beginning and last 19 bars.

Tchaikovsky: Serenade for Strings, 4th movement—beginning.

Espressivo-legato:

Borodin: Symphony No. 2, 2nd movement—passage starting at F.

Brahms: Symphony No. 4, 1st movement.

Mascagni: *Cavalleria Rusticana*, Santuzza's aria, *Voi lo sapete*—Introduction.

Rachmaninoff: Piano Concerto No. 2, 3rd movement—*Maestoso* (second theme).

Smetana: *The Moldau*, passage starting at bar 40.

Verdi: Overture to *Les Vêpres Siciliennes*, passage starting at I (bars 185-199).

Light-staccato:

Beethoven: Symphony No. 6, 4th movement—beginning.
Mendelssohn: Overture to *A Midsummer Night's Dream.*
Mozart: Overture to *Le Nozze di Figaro*, beginning.
Rimsky-Korsakov: *The Flight of the Bumble-Bee.*
Rossini: *Il Barbiere di Siviglia*, 2nd act—Tempest Music.
Tchaikovsky: *Nutcracker Suite: Ouverture miniature*, and *Danse des Mirlitons.*

Full-staccato:

Bach: *Brandenburg Concerto No. 1*, 3rd movement.
Berlioz: *Marche Hongroise (Rakóczy March)* from *La Damnation de Faust.*
Brahms: Symphony No. 2, 4th movement—passage starting at A.
Dvořák: *Carneval Overture.*
Franck: Symphony in D minor, 1st movement, *Allegro non troppo.*
Rimsky-Korsakov: *Capriccio Espagnol*, passage starting at M.

Start on the 2nd count:

Bach: Suite No. 2 in B minor, Badinerie.
Beethoven: Symphony No. 8, 4th movement.
Gluck: *Orphée et Euridice*, 2nd act, 2nd scene—*Cet asile* (*Grazioso* 6/8).
Gounod: *Faust*, 1st act, 2nd scene—No. 3 (Chorus).
Haydn: Symphony No. 103, 1st movement—*Allegro.*
Mozart: *Don Giovanni*, 1st act—No. 1, Introduction.

Dynamic changes:

Beethoven: Symphony No. 4, 1st and 4th movements.
Berlioz: Overture *Le Carnaval Romain*, *Allegro vivace.*
Bizet: *Carmen*, Prelude to the 1st act.
Haydn: Symphony No. 88, 4th movement.
Mozart: Overture to *Le Nozze di Figaro.*
Rossini: Overture to *Guillaume Tell*, *Allegro vivace* 2/4.

Chapter 10

THE 1-BEAT

WHEN THE TEMPO of a piece of music is very fast, the conductor will be unable to give all the beats without confusing the players. In many classic scherzos, the written tempo of 3/4 is so fast that it is much more convenient to give only 1 beat in a measure. The same is true for most waltzes. Many classic pieces with the time-signature 2/4 are also done in this way, as are a number of modern pieces written in 4-time and even 6-time (Sibelius, Symphony No. 2, 3rd movement in 6/8, *cf.* Ex. 332; Stravinsky, *L'Oiseau de Feu* (Suite), *Danse infernale* in 6/4).

NON-ESPRESSIVO

Diagram 28. The diagram shows that the downward movement is quicker than the upward movement. Avoid any stop at the top of the beat. For the start use Diagram 29 or Diagram 2; the choice between the two is a matter of personal preference.

Ex. 114

♩. =80
♩. =60
♩. =100

p

ESPRESSIVO-LEGATO

Diagram 30. This pattern implies a subdivision into 3-time; when that is not desired, use Diagram 30a. In any case, do not stress any part of the beat except ①. Since the execution of the beat depends upon the individual gesture and the character of the music, feel free to vary the pattern, which is only one of several possibilities.

[83]

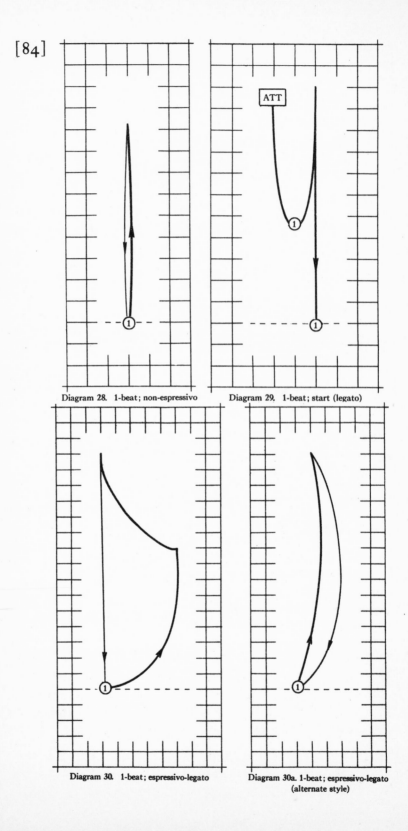

[84]

ATT

Diagram 28. 1-beat; non-espressivo

Diagram 29. 1-beat; start (legato)

Diagram 30. 1-beat; espressivo-legato

Diagram 30a. 1-beat; espressivo-legato
(alternate style)

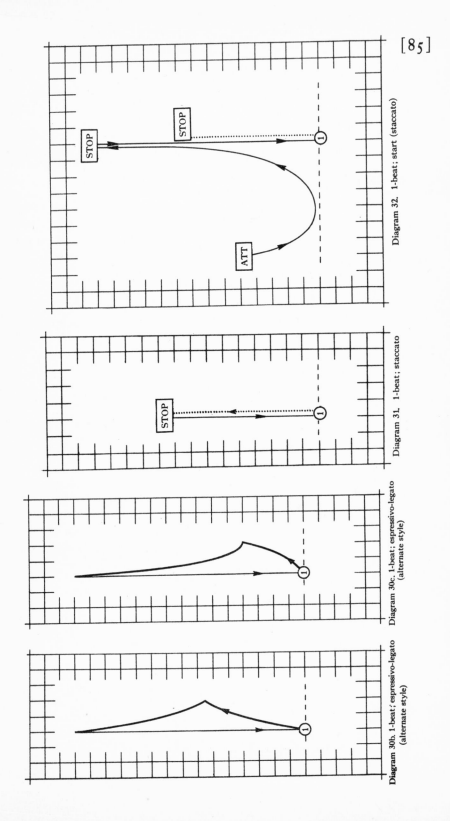

[85]

Diagram 32. 1-beat; start (staccato)

Diagram 31. 1-beat; staccato

Diagram 30c. 1-beat; espressivo-legato (alternate style)

Diagram 30b. 1-beat; espressivo-legato (alternate style)

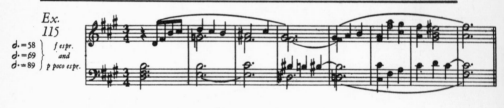

STACCATO

Diagram 31. This pattern covers both light-staccato and full-staccato. For full-staccato the size is larger and the bounce sharper, with more arm movement. The intensity of the beat depends upon the speed with which you snap the baton up. If this movement is moderately slow, the staccato is rather gentle; if you make a special effort to whip the baton up, the orchestra will play very sharply. In practising the start (Diagram 32, also 5 or 7), remember that the preliminary beat must express the type of staccato that you want from the players. Exx. 116 and 117 give you varied practice.

DYNAMIC CHANGES AND CHANGE FROM LEGATO TO STACCATO

Ex. 118: Practise first with the right hand alone, then support with the left hand.

Ex. 119: The technique explained in Chapter 6 is used here.

MUSICAL EXAMPLES

Ex. 120: Beating this in 3 would disturb the smooth flow of the melody, therefore 1-beat is always used here. Beat the first 8 bars legato non-espressivo, the following accompaniment figure staccato, very gently.

Ex. 121: A graceful espressivo beat is recommended. The non-espressivo 1-beat pattern would be too dull, while beating 3 beats in a measure would be too agitated.

Ex. 122: A flexible espressivo beat is needed to build up the melodic line.

Reprinted by permission of the Oxford University Press, London
(U. S. A. Agents: Carl Fischer, Inc.)

Exx. 123 and 124: Very small but precise light-staccato.

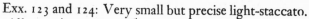

Copyright, 1941, by G. Schirmer, Inc.

Ex. 125: Full-staccato. Do not be too quick with the diminuendo, since the orchestra is apt to quiet down too suddenly.

Ex. 126: Because of the strong rhythmic element, beat staccato, first gently, but with full-staccato at *ff*.

Ex. 127: 4 bars legato, 2 bars full-staccato, then sudden change to light-staccato.

Ex. 128: 1st bar full-staccato, 2nd bar light-staccato with the character of a preparation for the 3rd; light-staccato in bars 4-7, and full-staccato in the 8th measure.

Additional examples for the study of 1-beat:

Non-espressivo:

Beethoven: Symphony No. 5, 3rd movement—passage starting at bar 324.
Dvořák: *Scherzo Capriccioso*, bars 7-16.

Espressivo-legato:

Gounod: *Faust*, Ballet No. 1 (A major)—starting at the double bar.
Strauss, Johann: *Emperor Waltz*—No. 1.
Verdi: Overture to *La Forza del Destino, Allegro agitato* 3/8.
Weber-Berlioz: *Invitation to the Dance*, passage starting at No. 7.

Staccato:

Beethoven: Symphony No. 9, 2nd movement.
Dukas: *L'Apprenti Sorcier*, starting at No. 6.
Elgar: *Enigma Variations, Op. 36*, Variation No. 4.
Handel: Concerto Grosso No. 5, 3rd movement (*Presto* 3/8).
Rossini: *Il Barbiere di Siviglia*, 1st act—Finale I, *Allegro* 3/4 in E-flat major.

Dynamic changes:

Beethoven: Symphony No. 5, 3rd movement.
Berlioz: *Symphonie Fantastique*, 2nd movement (*Un Bal*).
Dvořák: *Slavonic Dance in C major, Op. 46, No. 1.*
Schubert: Symphony No. 9, 4th movement.
Tchaikovsky: *Nutcracker Suite, No. 3—Valse des Fleurs.*

Chapter 11

THE MARCATO PATTERN

The marcato beat is a heavy motion with a stop on each count. It is forceful, sometimes aggressive in character and medium to large in size. The gestures connecting the counts are slower than in staccato; they are either straight or curved (espressivo) depending on the music.

There are two types of marcato, both done with a strong and vigorous gesture. For the first type, which uses straight lines to connect the counts, apply Diagram 4. Since marcato is used only in loud dynamics (*mf* to *ff*), the size will have to be at least three times that of the light-staccato pattern. Also remember that you must not move too quickly. ⟨4⟩ at the top of the field of beating is characteristic of this type of marcato. To gain the impetus needed for a start on the 1st count, use the accented up-beat of Diagram 21. Start on the other counts with a full-staccato preliminary beat.

Diagrams 17 and 25 are applied in a similar manner for marcato in 3-beat and in 2-beat. Diagram 33 shows the execution of 1-beat marcato. It is characterized by an intense holding on to ⟨1⟩ and a quick but energetic up-down motion which gives the impetus for the next marcato attack.

[91]

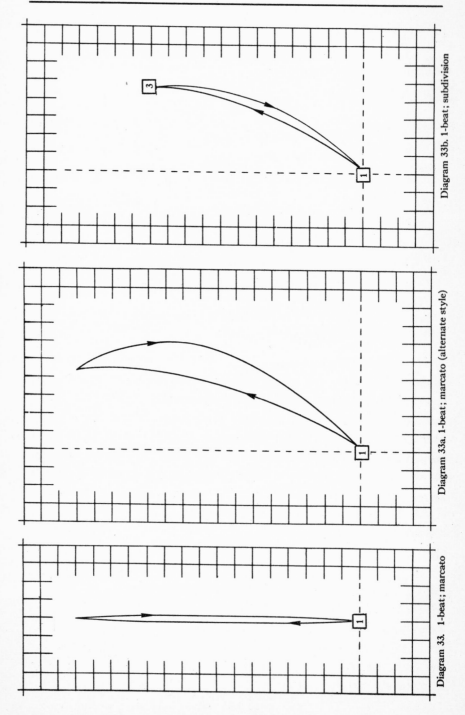

Diagram 33b. 1-beat; subdivision

Diagram 33a. 1-beat; marcato (alternate style)

Diagram 33.   1-beat; marcato

Ex. 129: An excellent example for practising marcato with straight lines. If a score is available, conduct the entire *Hallelujah*. Try to find a few instrumentalists to assist the class, which sings the chorus. Conduct legato beginning with the words "The kingdom of this world", 7½ bars in all.

Allegro, (♩ = 108)

HANDEL, *The Messiah*

Since *The Star-Spangled Banner* is in every conductor's repertoire, learn it now and practise beating marcato in the first and last parts.

The marcato with curved lines is used for rather slow music of passionate intensity and strong rhythm. It combines the lyric expressiveness of the legato beat with the rhythmical decisiveness of the staccato. In 4-beat, apply Diagram 8 or 8b, making a full stop on each count. The slowness of the tempo permits you to do this and still have time for an espressivo movement to the next count. Remember that while the connection between counts depends somewhat upon individual interpretation, the location of the counts remains fixed. Apply Diagrams 16, 23, and 30 for this type of marcato in 3-beat, 2-beat, and 1-beat, respectively.

Ex. 130: The curved-line marcato beat at once expresses the lyric quality of the melody and gives a heavy definite rhythm for the accompaniment.

Ex. 131: Gradual intensification from non-espressivo (*pp*) to marcato (*ff*). Start with a fairly small gesture; gradually increase both the size and the accentuation of each beat till bar 5. Use the straight-line marcato.

Ex. 132: Similar to Ex. 130 but in 3-beat. The advantage of marcato in such cases over espressivo (even with clicking) is that it keeps the heavy brasses from dragging, as they are otherwise likely to do.

Ex. 133: The heavy brass chords and syncopated strings demand the marcato.

Ex. 134: Though the time-signature is 4/4, this music is beaten alla breve (2-beat). Make the experiment of beating legato; try it again staccato. You will not be very comfortable either way, and only the marcato beat will give you the feeling that you are in control of this music. Think of the different orchestral groups as you conduct, and cue them in.

Ex. 135: The heavy chords starting with the 2nd bar require a strong marcato beat. Decrease not only the size but the heaviness of the beat until you reach *p* non-espressivo.

Ex. 136: 1-beat marcato with a very lively connecting motion.

Additional examples for the study of the marcato pattern:

4-beat:

Bach: *Brandenburg Concerto No. 1*, 1st movement.
Liszt: *Les Préludes, Andante maestoso* 12/8.
Shostakovitch: Symphony No. 5, 3rd movement—passage starting at No. 89.
Wagner: Funeral March from *Die Götterdämmerung*, *ff* passages.

3-beat:

Brahms: German Requiem, 2nd movement—13 bars after B.
Handel: Concerto Grosso No. 6, 3rd movement (Musette)—passage starting at bar 81.
Puccini: *Tosca*, 1st act—beginning.
Sibelius: Symphony No. 2, 4th movement—3 bars before B (*Pesante*).

2-beat:

Beethoven: Symphony No. 5, 4th movement—beginning.
Liszt: *Hungarian Rhapsody No. 2*, 4th bar from the end (*Andante*).
Rachmaninoff: Piano Concerto No. 2, 1st movement—beginning.
Rimsky-Korsakov: *Scheherazade*, 1st movement—beginning.

1-beat:

Brahms: Piano Concerto No. 2, 2nd movement—passage starting 38 bars after C.
Schumann: Symphony No. 4, 3rd movement—bars 9-14.

Chapter 12

START AFTER THE COUNT

IF THE MUSIC DOES NOT START on the count but on a fractional value, ignore the fraction in your beating and give the same rhythmic preparation that you would if the music began on the next full count. Do not try to beat the fractions, but rather feel them within the regular preparatory beat.

In class work Ex. 137 should be sung. There is a danger that the singers may not enter correctly, although the beat is right. However, the valuable experience gained by the student as a result of direct contact with the group is easily worth the time spent in interrupting and repeating.

In Exx. 137 a-g, give the preparation as though the music began on the 1st count, in h-j as though it began on the 2nd count; in k and l prepare the 3rd count, and in m the 4th. If you have a definite idea of the rhythm you can give a convincing preparation, and then the fractional values will come out correctly and automatically. Each of these short exercises should be repeated immediately in different tempos.

Exx. 138 and 139: Eighth-note before the 1st count. The preliminary beat is *pp* legato in Ex. 138 and *f* staccato in Ex. 139.

Exx. 140 and 141 (1 bar only): The two openings are similar. But while the attack works easily in fast tempo, it is more difficult in slow tempo. In the slow start as shown in Ex. 141 it is difficult even for experienced conductors to get a unified attack from the orchestra. There are at least three ways of executing Ex. 141: (1) Strictly according to rule: the staccato preparation has the value of a quarter-note (do not wait for the ♪, but keep going without hesitation!). (2) The preliminary beat has the value of an eighth-note. (3) Free style: make the preparation as though the ♪ were on *One* and give 2 down-beats, one for each of the two chords. (Another way of conducting this opening is explained in the last paragraph of Chapter 24.)

Ex. 142: Although the 2nd measure is not the actual start, the allegro part of the overture starts here after a pause (⌒) and the technique of preparing to resume the music is the same as that used at the start. Point the baton to the left side of the beating field to get a large, clear preliminary beat.

ROSSINI, *L'Italiana in Algeri—Overture*

Exx. 143-145: The down-beat should express the solemn dignity of the music in Ex. 143, while the preparation for Exx. 144 and 145 is a very snappy full-staccato.

Used by permission of the copyright owners, Editions Salabert, Paris

Used by permission of Leeds Music Corporation, Am-Rus Edition, New York, N. Y.

Ex. 146: Poco espressivo, legato.

MENDELSSOHN, *Symphony No. 4*

Exx. 147 and 148: Same rhythmic pattern in different tempo.

SULLIVAN, *The Mikado*

HAYDN, *Symphony No. 94*

Ex. 149: *f* marcato.

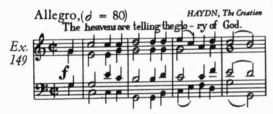

Ex. 363 (bar 1): A sharp up-beat secures a precise ♪ at the attack.

Exx. 150 and 151: Similar rhythms, contrasting tempos.

RIMSKY-KORSAKOV, *Scheherazade*

Ex. 152: Very energetic staccato.

Exx. 153 and 154: Same rhythm, different tempos and dynamics. The preparation has the character of an up-beat.

Exx. 155 and 156: 1-beat in 2/4 time. Ex. 155 requires light-staccato, Ex. 156 full-staccato. The preparatory gesture again has the character of an up-beat.

Exx. 157, 158, and 257a: In these examples the entrance occurs immediately after the down-beat. Proceed in strict tempo and without hesitation from the first down-beat to the next. Do not wait unnecessarily for the notes in the 1st bar to be played, or the tempo will drag. The preparation here does not feel like an up-beat, but has the solidity of an actual strong beat.

By permission of Novello & Company, Ltd., London

USE OF AN EXTRA BEAT

Because of the difficulty of executing certain starts after the count, especially in fast tempo, conductors sometimes give an extra beat to secure precision.

Thus in Ex. 159 you may beat *One-Two* to establish the tempo with certainty.

MOZART, *Eine kleine Nachtmusik*

Ex. 160: You may beat *Two-One*, but a very small *Two* at the top of the field of beating, with a quick turn of the hand followed by a large staccato down-beat (*One*).

Copyright by C. F. Peters
Reprinted by permission of the copyright owner, Mr. Walter Hinrichsen

In a similar way extra beats are sometimes used for Exx. 148, 151, 152, and 257a. Remember: use the extra beat only if you cannot get a satisfactory result without it. If you want to use the extra beat, you have to inform the players.

Additional examples for the study of the start after the count:

4-beat

After the 1st count:
Beethoven: *Fidelio*, No. 5—Terzett.
Schumann: Overture to *Manfred.*
Verdi: *Aïda*, 4th act—2nd scene.

After the 3rd count:
Brahms: German Requiem, 5th movement.
Stravinsky: *Ragtime.*

After the 4th count:
Enesco: *Roumanian Rhapsody No. 1.*
Handel: Concerto Grosso No. 6, 4th movement (*Allegro* 4/4).
Rossini: *Il Barbiere di Siviglia*, 1st act—Finale I.

3-beat

After the 1st count:
Bach: *St. Matthew Passion*, No. 49—Chorus.

After the 2nd count:
Bach: Suite No. 4 in D major, Réjouissance.
Haydn: *The Seasons*, No. 21—Introduction (*Autumn*).
Rossini: *Il Barbiere di Siviglia*, 1st act—Rosina's Cavatina.

After the 3rd count:
Barber: Overture to *The School for Scandal.*
Handel: *Messiah*, Part II, Aria—*Thou art gone up on high.*
Wagner: *Die Walküre*, 3rd act—*Ride of the Valkyries.*

2-beat

After the 1st count:
Mendelssohn: Overture to *Ruy Blas, Allegro molto.*
Tchaikovsky: Symphony No. 4, 2nd movement.
Wagner: Overture to *Der Fliegende Holländer*, 6 bars before L (after the General Pause).

After the 2nd count:
Beethoven: Symphony No. 2, 4th movement.
Brahms: Symphony No. 4, 1st movement.
Puccini: *La Bohème*, 3rd act.

1-beat

Beethoven: Symphony No. 5, 3rd movement.
Dvořák: *Scherzo Capriccioso.*
Elgar: *Enigma Variations, Op. 36*, Variation No. 2.
Puccini: *La Bohème*, 1st act.
Tchaikovsky: Serenade for Strings, 2nd movement.

Using an extra beat:

Berlioz: *Marche Hongroise (Rakóczy March)* from *La Damnation de Faust.*
Mozart: Symphony No. 39, K. 543—4th movement.

Chapter 13

THE 6-BEAT

THERE ARE TWO STYLES used in beating 6-time: the so-called German style, taught in most textbooks and used by the majority of conductors until recently; and the Italian style, now becoming more popular. The choice between them is a matter of personal preference; in general you will find the German style is very useful for slow and expressive music, while the Italian is handier in quick tempo. Especially in operatic conducting, the economy of gesture gives the Italian style the advantage. The student should study both styles to find out from personal experience which is better suited to him or whether he will desire to make use of both.

GERMAN STYLE

Diagram 34. Think of ②and ⑤as being interpolated into the 4-beat pattern. Use the wrist alone for these 2 "added" beats except in very expressive passages. For the espressivo patterns see Diagram 35. Practise before the mirror in a fairly slow tempo, then use Ex. 161.

Diagrams 36 and 37 show the staccato beat (whether to use 36 or 36a is a matter of choice). Practise with Ex. 162.

[107]

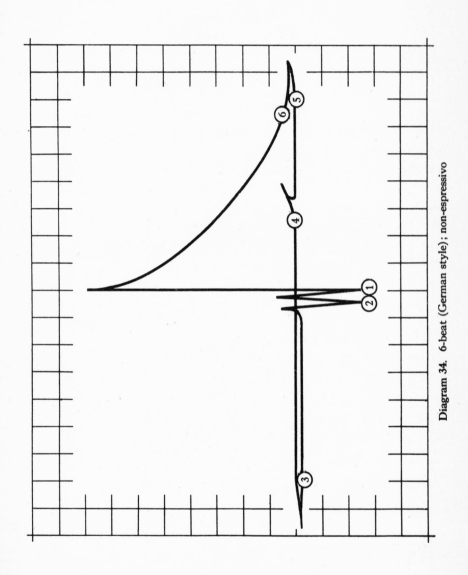

Diagram 34. 6-beat (German style); non-espressivo

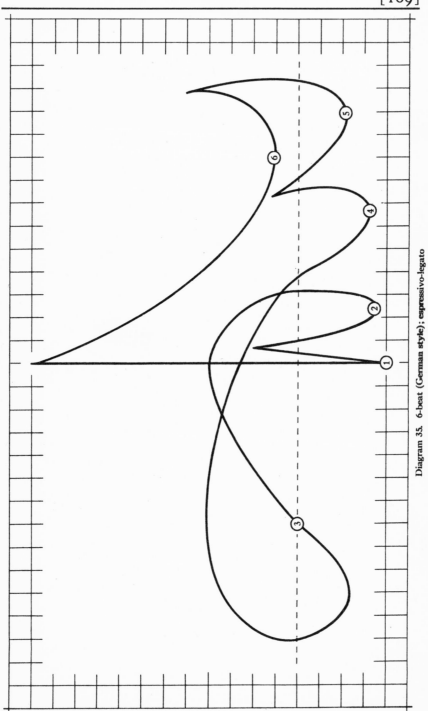

Diagram 35. 6-beat (German style); espressivo-legato

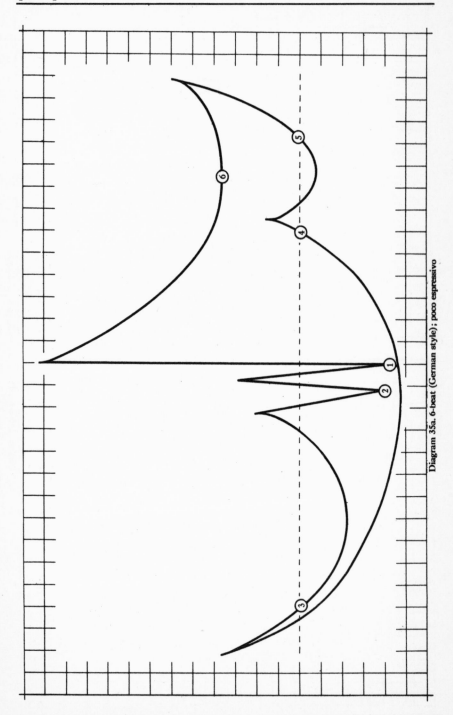

Diagram 35a. 6-beat (German style); poco espressivo

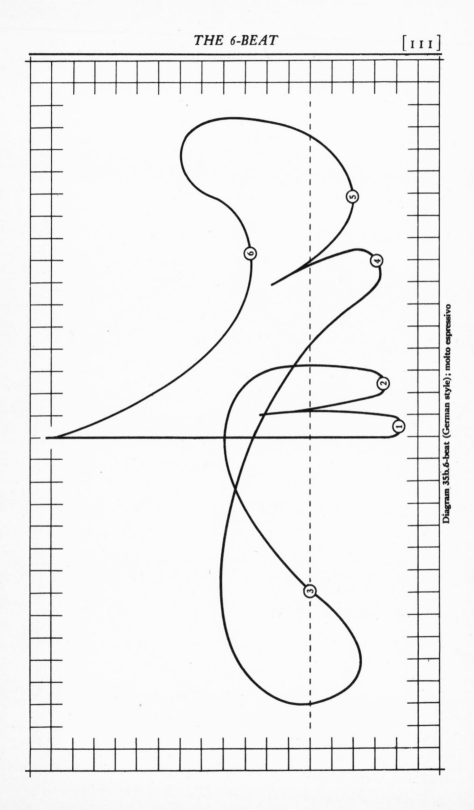

Diagram 35b.6-beat (German style); molto espressivo

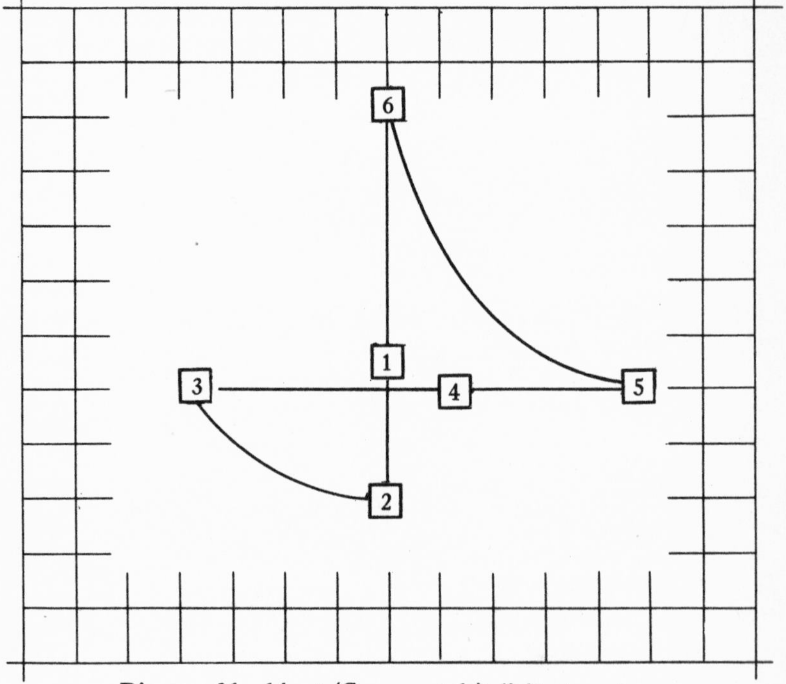

Diagram 36.   6-beat (German style); light-staccato

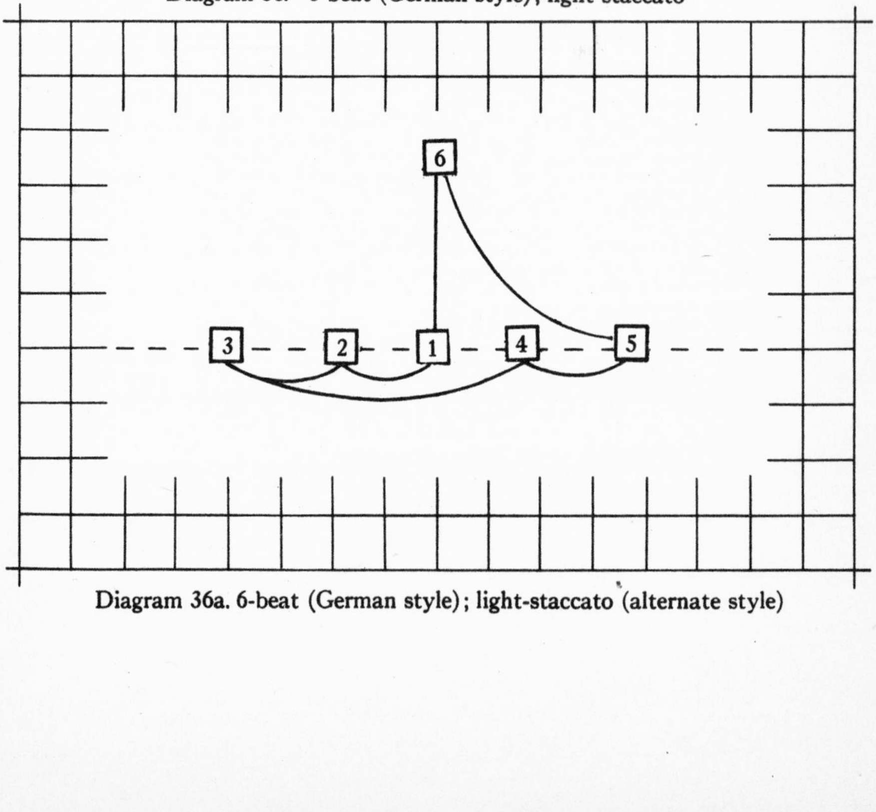

Diagram 36a. 6-beat (German style); light-staccato (alternate style)

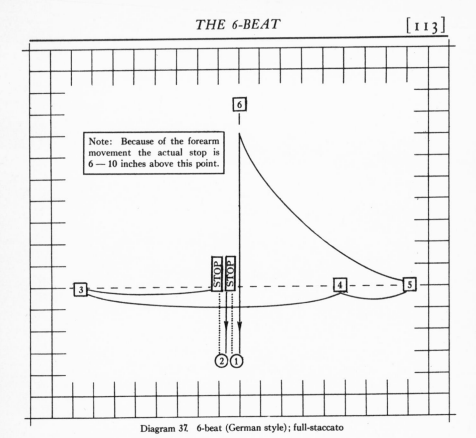

Note: Because of the forearm movement the actual stop is 6 — 10 inches above this point.

Diagram 37. 6-beat (German style); full-staccato

To start on the	apply diagrams
1st count	2, 5, and 7
2nd count	28 and 32
3rd count	13 and 14
4th count	11 and 12
5th count	11 and 12 (slightly farther to the right)
6th count	9 and 10

ITALIAN STYLE

Diagram 38. This pattern is fairly close to a subdivided 2, which means that the 1st and 4th counts are considerably more marked than the others. By enlarging the pattern and adding to the curves of the lines you can easily work out the espressivo.

Diagrams 39 (39a) and 40 demonstrate the staccato.

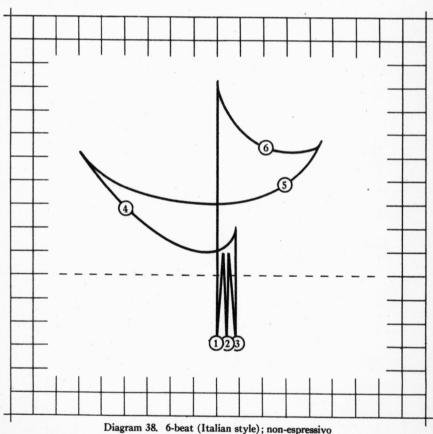

Diagram 38. 6-beat (Italian style); non-espressivo

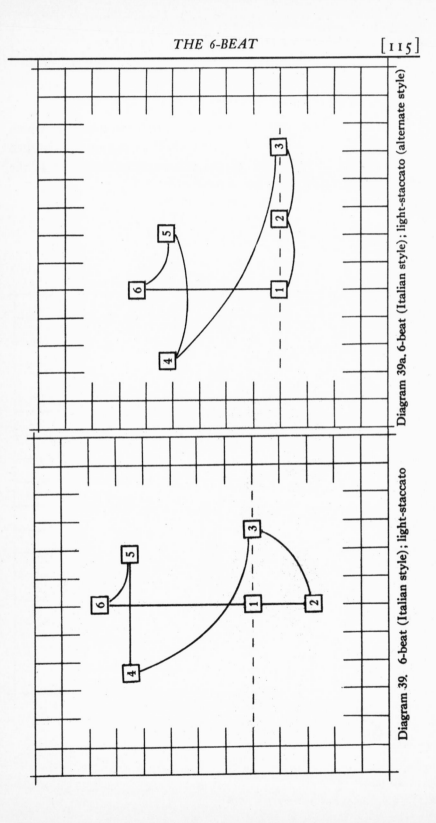

Diagram 39. 6-beat (Italian style); light-staccato

Diagram 39a. 6-beat (Italian style); light-staccato (alternate style)

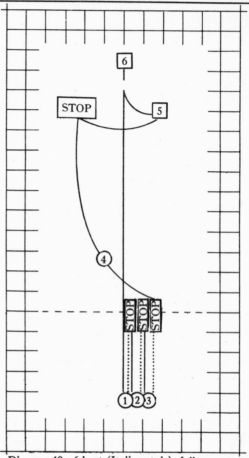

Diagram 40. 6-beat (Italian style); full-staccato

To start on the	apply diagrams
1st count	2, 5, and 7
2nd count	28 and 32
3rd count	28 and 32
4th count	9 and 10
5th count	11 and 12
6th count	9 and 10

Ex. 163a: Marcato, not too heavy and fairly small; with the diminuendo change to non-espressivo. Ex. 163b: Full-staccato, accented up-beat on 6 in bar 1. Ex. 163c: Molto espressivo, legato.

Ex. 164: The wood-wind entry requires a certain emphasis on *One* in bar 2, then beat very quietly non-espressivo. The 5th beat in bar 3 is used for a cut-off (discussed in Chapter 15).

Ex. 165: Legato poco espressivo; the gesture must be very graceful.

Ex. 166: Gentle staccato for the strings; use the 3rd beat to prepare the entrance of the winds (non-espressivo).

Ex. 167: Start after the count. Give the preparation as though the music would start on the 6th count.

Additional examples for the study of 6-beat:

Non-espressivo:

Brahms: Symphony No. 1, 1st movement, 1st and 2nd bars after A.
Mozart: Symphony No. 40, K. 550—2nd movement (also espressivo).
Verdi: *Aïda*, 3rd act, Aïda's aria starting at D.
Wagner: Overture to *Der Fliegende Holländer*, *Andante 6/4.*

Espressivo-legato:

Debussy: *Nuages.*
Massenet: *Manon,* 1st act, Prelude, *Andante sostenuto* 6/8.
Mendelssohn: *Elijah,* No. 37—Arioso.
Schubert: Symphony No. 5, 2nd movement (also non-espressivo).

Staccato:

Berlioz: *Symphonie Fantastique,* 3rd movement (also legato).
Kodály: *Psalmus Hungaricus,* passage starting at No. 25.
Mozart: *Die Zauberflöte,* No. 16—Terzett.
Rossini: Overture to *Semiramide,* passage starting at the 20th bar of *Andantino* 6/8.

Marcato:

Bach: Cantata No. 11 (*Lobet Gott in seinen Reichen*), No. 11—Chorale.
Wagner: Prelude to *Parsifal,* passage for brass instruments, 6/4.

Dynamic changes:

Brahms: Symphony No. 1, 1st movement—passage starting at bar 9.
Haydn: Symphony No. 96, 2nd movement.
Mozart: Symphony No. 38, K. 504 ("Prague")—2nd movement.
Verdi: *Aïda,* 1st act, 1st scene—Radames' aria, starting at B.

Chapter 14

SUBDIVISION

WHEN THE MUSIC is so slow that the regular beat would not give the conductor enough control or intensity, the beat is divided into fractional parts. This chapter deals mainly with the execution of the subdivided patterns; their application will be discussed in greater detail in Chapters 25 and 26.

The general principle is that unless the musical expression demands otherwise, the main beats are larger and more emphatic than the subdivisions. To start in subdivided time, always give the preliminary beat in terms of the smallest unit that you are actually beating.

8 BEATS IN A MEASURE

Diagram 41. The weaker beats ②, ④, and ⑥ are usually done with wrist motion only. Conductors differ in their manner of beating ⑦ and ⑧. Some always beat ⑦ at the top of the field. The main reason for not doing so is that it emphasizes the 7th beat and destroys the smooth flow. Use this technique only when you want to accent the 7th beat.

The various patterns (staccato, espressivo, etc.) can be deduced easily from the diagram. In many cases it will add to the distinctness to click on the main counts: ①③⑤⑦.

Ex. 168: Non-espressivo; the preliminary beat has the value of an eighth-note. Conduct the strings as accompaniment, but know exactly what is going on in the oboe solo. The conductor must be able to deal with fractional values very easily in order to correct his players. The study of Bach will train the conductor's mind to recognize these small values quickly even in the most complicated passages. (Bach's violin sonatas afford especially good practice.)

Adagio assai, (♪ = 76)   BACH, *Cantata No. 21*

Ex. 168

Ex. 169: The tympani player needs your very distinct beat, but without too large a gesture. Study the whole introduction to the symphony. There should be sufficient flexibility in your beat to keep the subdivision from becoming stiff.

Adagio, (♪ = 108)   MOZART, *Symphony No. 39*

Ex. 169

Ex. 170: For the start *cf.* Ex. 141. Insist that after your eighth-note up-beat the ♪ be played strictly in tempo.

Andante maestoso, (♪ = 100)   ROSSINI, *Il Barbiere di Siviglia*

Ex. 170

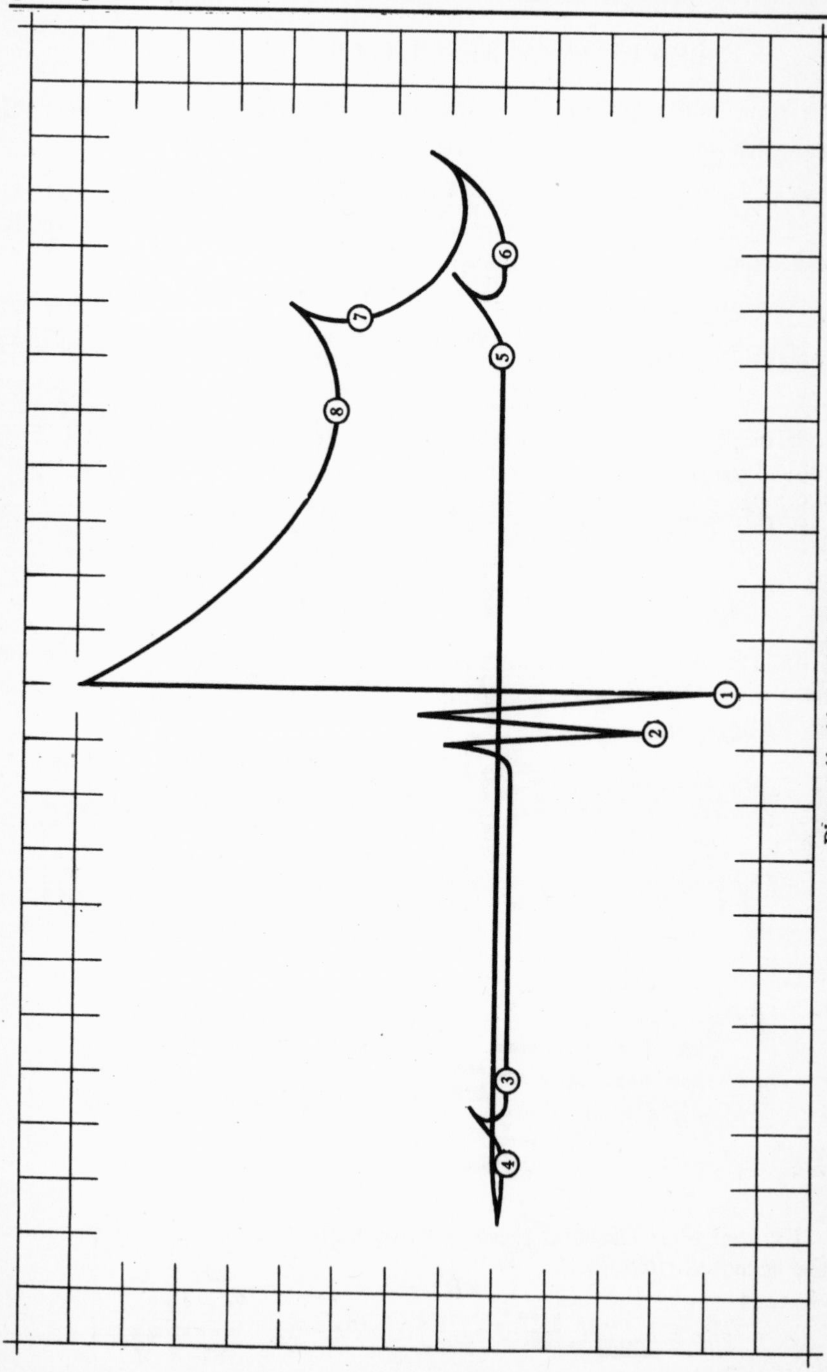

Diagram 41. 4-beat subdivided in 8

4 BEATS AS A RESULT OF SUBDIVISION

2-time with subdivision is shown in Diagram 42. The following examples give practice in different applications of this pattern.

Ex. 171: The 1st bar requires regular 4-beat; then use a subdivided 2/4 (= 4/8) to lead the melody. In bars 3-5 the subdivision should be hardly noticeable; use it in bars 6 and 7.

Ex. 172: Only the 2 last bars need subdivision because of the *sf* and the 32nd-groups.

Ex. 173: Here the subdivision, starting with *ff*, is the best way to control the accented ritenuto.

Ex. 133: The most effective way of directing the allargando is to subdivide the beat.

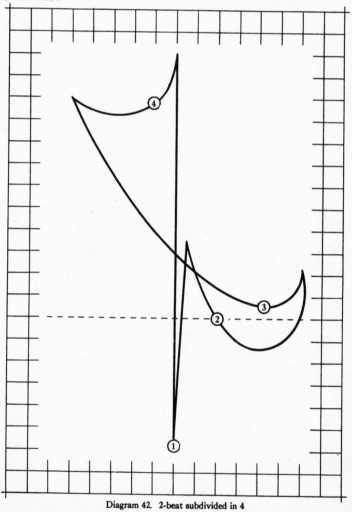

Diagram 42. 2-beat subdivided in 4

12 BEATS IN A MEASURE

4-time with each beat subdivided triply is shown in Diagram 43. Now it is even more important to keep the main beats—①④⑦⑩ —clear and distinct, to avoid any misunderstanding on the part of the players. For this reason a number of conductors prefer the slightly different pattern of Diagram 43a.

Exx. 174 and 175: Use slightly curved motions for the graceful music of Ex. 174. The restrained mood of Ex. 175 requires small neutral beats.

Ex. 176: This should be sung, and the various entries indicated precisely by the conductor.

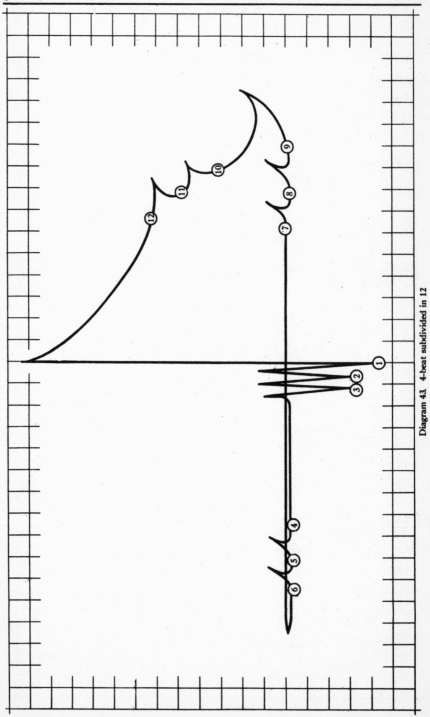

Diagram 43. 4-beat subdivided in 12

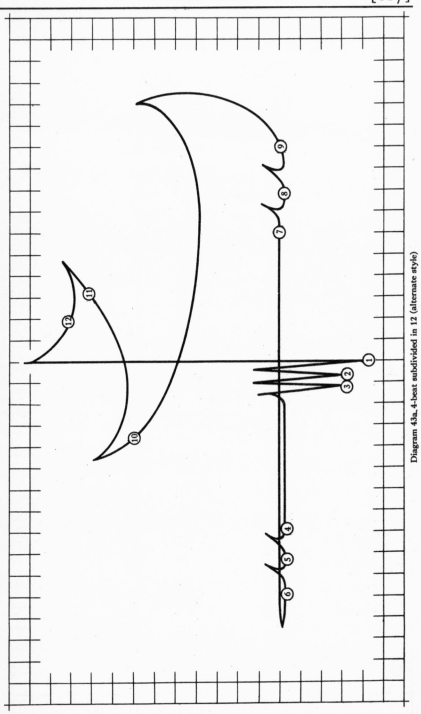

Diagram 43a. 4-beat subdivided in 12 (alternate style)

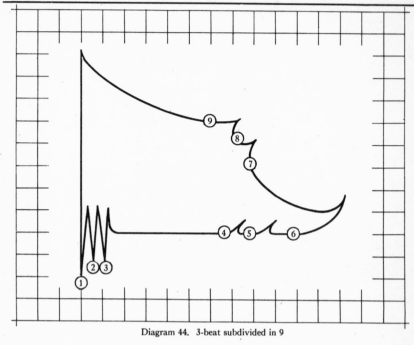

Diagram 44. 3-beat subdivided in 9

9 BEATS IN A MEASURE

Diagram 44. This pattern is 3-time with each beat subdivided triply.

Ex. 177 (bar 1): Non-espressivo.
Ex. 178: The 2nd measure requires 9 beats, legato.

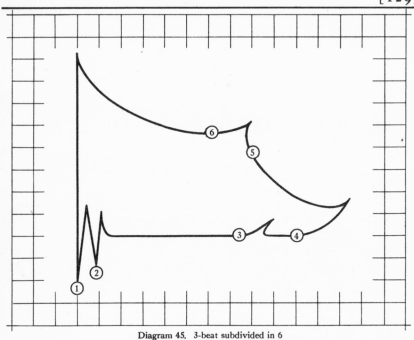

Diagram 45. 3-beat subdivided in 6

6 BEATS AS A RESULT OF SUBDIVISION

6-beat resulting from subdivision is different from regular 6-beat; it is 3-time or 2-time subdivided.

(1) The pattern for 3-time subdivided is shown in Diagram 45.

Ex. 179: Poco espressivo. In bar 2 use the 2nd eighth-beat to prepare the *f* chord by carrying the baton over to the left side of the field of beating.

Ex. 180: Start with non-espressivo; on the 2nd eighth-beat in bar 2, suddenly enlarge the gesture, which then becomes smaller while you direct the diminuendo.

Adagio, ♪ = 76

Ex. 180

BERLIOZ, *Harold en Italie*

Ex. 181a: In bar 1, use strong marcato gestures for the main counts while the subdivided beats serve as preparation.

Ex. 181b: The character of the music requires emphatic motions on each of the 6 beats, but keep the pattern unmistakably clear.

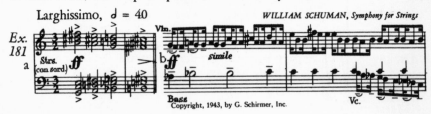

Larghissimo, ♩ = 40

Ex. 181 a

WILLIAM SCHUMAN, *Symphony for Strings*

Copyright, 1943, by G. Schirmer, Inc.

(2) 2-time with each beat subdivided triply is shown in Diagram 46 (*cf.* the Italian pattern for 6-beat).

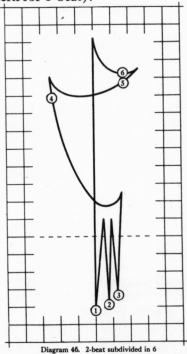

Diagram 46. 2-beat subdivided in 6

Ex. 182: Regular 6-beat, especially in the German style, would be too academic and would not conform to the pulsation of the music. Start with relatively small gestures and bring out the crescendo.

Ex. 183: Start beating in 2; with the rallentando, subdivide, and at "rall. molto" use the regular 6-beat pattern (Italian style). Return to beating 2 beats in a measure for the last bar.

1-BEAT WITH SUBDIVISION

1-beat with subdivision occurs only in fairly fast 3-time; it is used when the regular 3-beat would be awkward and the regular 1-beat would lack distinctness or intensity. It can be done in 3 different ways.

Although the student will be referred to the espressivo patterns of Diagram 30, there is a marked distinction between 1-beat espressivo and 1-beat with subdivision. The object of the former is to add expression to the simple 1-beat, but without rhythmic accentuation. Consequently a very smooth and relatively large gesture is used. In the subdivided 1-beat, the fractions of the rhythm are clearly indicated with a more or less staccato quality of the gesture. Thus, even though the motions may be small, there is no doubt as to the fractional parts of each measure.

(1) As a special case of 3-beat, the gesture is very small, and the 2nd beat, instead of going to the right, goes upward at a very small angle (Diagram 30b). This pattern is useful when an occasional indication of the 3 beats is needed, although the rhythm is felt primarily in 1-beat.

Ex. 184: 1-beat in bars 1 and 2. You may start subdividing in the 3rd measure, using flexible wrist motions; the syncopations in bars 5-7 require a very clear subdivision. Return to 1-beat in bar 9.

(2) When the pulsation felt is *One-Two*(-*three*), apply Diagram 30. The gesture indicating the 3rd count is not only very small, but weak. The outline of each bar is practically a 2-beat in 3-time, in which each bar can be considered as |♩ ♩ |.

(3) When the pulsation felt is *One*-(*two*)-*Three*, use Diagram 30c, or apply a regular 2-beat. The outline of each bar can be considered as |♩ ♩ | .

Ex. 185: Neither a regular 3-beat nor a regular 1-beat would do justice to this music, both being too academic. *One- (two)-Three* is felt in bars 1-8, *One-Two(-three)* in bars 9-12; beat accordingly.

Additional examples for the study of the subdivided patterns:

12 beats in a measure:

Bach: *St. Matthew Passion*, No. 47—Aria.
Debussy: *Prélude à l'Après-midi d'un faune*, at No. 3.
Verdi: *Rigoletto*, No. 14—Duetto finale, passage starting at the 25th bar of *Andante* in D-flat major.

9 beats in a measure:

Brahms: Symphony No. 1, 1st movement—bar 8.
Wagner: Prelude to *Parsifal*, passage starting at *sehr gehalten*.

8 beats in a measure:

Handel: Concerto Grosso No. 12, 1st movement.
Haydn: Violoncello Concerto, 1st movement.
Rossini: *Il Barbiere di Siviglia*, 2nd act—Quintet.
Schubert: Symphony No. 2, 1st movement—Largo.

6 beats in a measure (3-time):

Beethoven: Symphony No. 4, 2nd movement.
Copland: *A Lincoln Portrait*, beginning.
Haydn: *The Creation*, No. 29 (Recitative)—Prelude to Part III.
Rachmaninoff: Piano Concerto No. 2, 2nd movement—bars 13, 16, etc.
Sibelius: Symphony No. 3, 1st movement—7th bar after No. 4, 2nd bar after No. 12, etc.

6 beats in a measure (2-time):

Brahms: Piano Concerto No. 1, 1st movement.
Enesco: *Roumanian Rhapsody No. 1*, passage starting at No. 7, *Posato*.
Mascagni: *Cavalleria Rusticana*, Prelude—bars 20-27.
Wagner: Overture to *Der Fliegende Holländer*, passage of 3 bars at *Un poco ritenuto* (four times).

4 beats in a measure (2-time):

Haydn: *The Creation*, No. 18—Terzett.
Schubert: Symphony No. 2, 2nd movement.
Tchaikovsky: Serenade for Strings, 1st movement—bar 8.
Verdi: Overture to *Les Vêpres Siciliennes, Allegro agitato*. (Start beating 2 but subdivide whenever necessary to lead the sixteenth-passages and the syncopations; the subdivision ends 7 bars before D but is resumed at E.)

1-beat with subdivision:

Bizet: *L'Arlésienne Suite No. 1*, 2nd movement, middle section.
Dvořák: Symphony No. 5 (*From the New World*), 3rd movement—after the double bar.
Strauss, Johann: *Tales from the Vienna Woods*, Waltz No. 1, at *poco ritenuto*.
Tchaikovsky: *Nutcracker Suite*, No. 3—*Valse des Fleurs*. (The question when to subdivide depends on the interpretation.)

Study and practise scores Nos. 3 and 4 discussed in the Appendix.

Chapter 15

RESTS

PROPER HANDLING of the rests is one of the important requirements for smooth conducting. There are 3 different uses to which
the conductor puts those beats where the music is not actually sound-
ing: (1) to cut off the tones preceding the rest when necessary,
(2) to indicate the counts during the pause, (3) to prepare the next
attack.

(1) The cut-off is used only after a sustained tone, not after a detached one. However, not every sustained tone followed by a rest
need be cut; use it only when a unified release is difficult to achieve
automatically. This is the case more often in slow tempo than in fast,
and more often in loud passages than in soft.

You may cut off with the right hand alone, either by clicking or
by making a definite stop on the rest. The left hand may also be used,
and in several different ways. The effect of the gesture is that of a
command: be quiet! Some conductors move the arm in toward the
body, palm inward, closing the hand simultaneously. Another effective way is to snap the hand downward, palm facing down.

(2) A small non-espressivo beat is usually sufficient to indicate the
rests when neither cut-off nor preparation is needed.

(3) When a rest is followed by an attack, use the rest for preparation, especially if it is the last of several in succession. In most
cases the preparatory gesture will not have to be as emphatic as at
the start, since the rhythm is already established.

Ex. 186: The first rest is for cut-off (in slow tempo), the second for a
slight preparation. In the 3rd measure cut off on *Two*, mark the time on
Three, and prepare on *Four*. Follow this procedure throughout the example and do not forget that the half-note in bar 5 ends exactly on *Four*.

Ex.
186

Ex. 187a: No cut-off because of staccato. Do not yield to the temptation of beating staccato during the rests, except of course for preparation.

Ex.
187

Ex. 84: Click on the 4th counts in bars 3 and 4 to get a clean release.

Ex. 170: Use the left hand which supported the *ff* for an incisive cut-off, allowing the right hand to find the most convenient position for the light-staccato that follows. Use the rests in the 2nd bar for preparation. In bar 3, beat the first 2 eighth-rests small, non-espressivo; beat the following (preparatory) eighth sharply and further to the left, to make room for a large gesture to attack the *ff* chord.

Ex. 179: Review this, applying what you have just learned.

Ex. 188: The beat on the first rest may be quite small, even skipped if you are very sure of the rhythm. Here are two different types of preparation on rests; *Three* in bar 1 is an accented up-beat for *f* staccato, *Three* in bar 2 prepares *p* legato.

Allegro con brio, ♩.= 60 (♩ = 160)

Ex.
188

Ex. 189: Subdivided 3-beat. The preparation at the end of bar 3 should also include the *sf* at the beginning of bar 4.

Ex. 190: Beat alla breve. Use the 2nd count in bar 2 to prepare the staccato.

Ex. 191: The drum-roll requires no special leading from the baton while the other instruments rest. Beat full-staccato to prepare the chords.

Ex. 192: Be sure that the time-marking beats in bar 3 are neutral and do not lead the 1st violins into a false entry—as has happened in prominent orchestras! Beat light-staccato in the 4th measure.

Ex. 193: 1-beat. The first and second G.P.'s (General Pauses) are used for preparation. Mark time in the 7th bar and prepare in the 8th. A time-beater, not a conductor, would use the same large down-beats throughout this example.

Ex. 194: The 2nd and 3rd beats must be hardly noticeable. This increases the tension of the music and the attention of the orchestra.

Ex. 195: A new section with change of tempo begins here. To establish the rhythm and character of the Allegretto vivace, beat the rests light-staccato. In such cases the neutral beat would not give the conductor the needed control.

LISZT, *Piano Concerto No. 1*

RESTS AT THE BEGINNING OF A PIECE

Although there is no rule telling how to beat when the piece starts with several rests, you must always establish the tempo definitely. Since the rests appear in the parts and are counted by all the players, including those who do not come in at the very start, skipping could cause confusion. Whether to beat the rests in a neutral manner or with some kind of expression depends upon the character of the opening. In any event, do not beat the rests in a way that could lead the players into a premature attack.

Exx. 196 and 197: While no special treatment is needed in 196, a non-espressivo start in 197 would lack tension; start light-staccato, and beat full-staccato on the 4th count (preparation).

Ex. 198: To get a good pizzicato entry, beat both quarter-rests staccato.

Ex. 199: A completely neutral 1st beat would lose the drama of the opening; directly from ATT at the top of the field of beating, give a fairly

large but not too emphatic down-beat, and continue with a preparatory staccato on *Two*. (If *One* is too emphatic, the horn players may mistake it for the preparation!)

Allegro non troppo, (♩ = 84)

TCHAIKOVSKY, *Piano Concerto No. 1*

RESTS AT THE END OF A PIECE

Rests often occur after the last played note of a piece, either to fill up the last bar or, where the last bar is part of a group, to fill out the metrical balance. Naturally rests of this kind do not require any beat at all. The last beat is for the last played note, with cut-off if needed.

The concluding cut-off is done by moving the baton downward or sidewise with a very quick gesture. In *f* it is sharper and more forceful than in *p*. The *p* ending may be done with a quick turn of the wrist or by drawing the baton swiftly toward the body. In both *p* and *f* the cut-off gesture must not suggest any accent. The left hand may support the right-hand movements in *f* with an energetic gesture (in *ff* even using the fist), in *p* in the way described on p. 135.

Ex. 200: The concluding chord is usually played tenuto and therefore requires a cut-off gesture.

Adagio, ♪ = 84

BEETHOVEN, *Symphony No. 4*

RESTS IN ACCOMPANIMENT

The following two examples show the special care with which rests must be treated in accompaniments.

Ex. 201: Neutral beats in the 1st bar. Be sure you are in time, or even a little ahead, on the 2nd beat in bar 2, and synchronize your preparatory 3rd beat with the triplet in the solo violin, to be in position for the 4th beat. Give a sharp beat before each of the syncopated chords with neutral beats between. Prepare the last measure (*fp*) by picking up the beat from the violin.

Allegro moderato, ♩ = 126   *TCHAIKOVSKY, Violin Concerto*

Ex. 202: Here it is very important to know the words as well as the music, and to be sure which syllable falls on which beat. The preparatory beats must be flexible, because the singer is allowed a certain liberty in recitative. Your down-beat in the 3rd bar coincides with "cin-", followed by 2 secco chords in strict tempo. If necessary, wait on *Four* so as to be sure that the next down-beat comes exactly on "dir-". Do not drag the neutral beats, and be ready for the next down-beat! The singer tradition-ally holds the high A♭; wait for him on *Two* and time your preparatory beat to be with "-to" precisely on *Three*. Use the accented up-beat on *Four* to prepare the fanfare in the brass.

VERDI, *Aïda*

By permission of G. Ricordi & Co., Milan

A very handy general rule to remember is this:

> *When there are several rests in the accompaniment, keep with or a trifle ahead of the tempo, but always allow your-self one beat at the end for a good preparation. If necessary, wait just before giving this preparatory beat.*

Additional examples for the study of beating rests:

Barber: Overture to *The School for Scandal*, bars 6 and 7.
Beethoven: Symphony No. 8, 1st movement—15 bars from the end.
Dukas: *L'Apprenti Sorcier*, beginning of *Vif* 3/8.
Haydn: Symphony No. 102, 4th movement (Coda).
Kodály: *Háry János* (Suite), 1st movement, bars 73-76.

Rossini: Overture to *Semiramide*, last bars of *Andantino* 6/8; bars 63-65 of *Allegro*.
Shostakovitch: Symphony No. 1, 1st movement—bars 8 and 9.
Sibelius: Symphony No. 2, 2nd movement—3rd bar after D; also at P.
Wagner: Prelude to *Parsifal*, passage in 6/4.

Rests at the beginning of a piece:

Bach: Mass in B minor, *Et resurrexit.*
Bizet: *L'Arlésienne Suite No. 1*, 1st and 2nd movements.
Haydn: Symphony No. 86, 4th movement.
Sibelius: Symphony No. 2, 1st movement.
Verdi: *Aïda*, Prelude to the 1st act.

Rests in accompaniment:

Beethoven: Violin Concerto, 1st movement.
Bizet: *Carmen*, all recitatives.
Grieg: Piano Concerto, 1st and 3rd movements.
Haydn: *The Creation*, No. 12—Recitative.
Mozart: *Die Zauberflöte*, 1st act, No. 8 (Finale)—Recitative.
Rachmaninoff: Piano Concerto No. 2, 3rd movement.

Chapter 16

RITARDANDO AND ACCELERANDO

JUST AS THERE ARE more or less gradual changes in dynamics, so there are gradations in the speed of music. Often the student will find that he does not get the results he wants in speeding up and slowing down. The following general advice will be helpful. The conductor's mind must be ahead of his hand. The way you *lead into* the count on which the change starts should prepare the players. If you do not think of the change until you are *on* the count, it will be sudden and awkward instead of gradual and smooth. However, this preparation must not start the change prematurely; it only warns the players that one is coming. *It is helpful to use a slightly larger beat before a ritardando and a slightly smaller beat before an accelerando.*

A quick change in the size of the beat is also very effective in indicating "a tempo". For "a tempo" after ritardando, use a smaller beat; after accelerando, use a larger beat.

Once a tempo change has been started it gains a certain momentum of its own, and the conductor must be careful that he does not cause exaggeration by indicating too much on the subsequent beats. A tempo change must be planned, just as a dynamic change must be. Know exactly how fast or how slow you want to be when the change is completed, and you will achieve a smooth and continuous gradation.

Practise ritardando and accelerando with return to tempo, on all counts and in different rhythms. Have your friend at the piano improvise simple chords while following your beat. Practise the changes in varying degrees from poco ritard. to molto ritard. and similarly with accelerando. The following should be remembered:

[144]

For more ritard. on the		wait longer before moving
1st beat		to the left
2nd "	in 4-beat	" " right
3rd "		" " left
4th "		up
1st "		to the right
2nd "	in 3-beat	" " left
3rd "		up
1st "	in 2-beat	up (rebound)
2nd "		up
"	in 1-beat	up

By practising ritardando and accelerando according to these suggestions, you avoid the spasmodic gestures that mar the conducting of inexperienced leaders and disturb the security of the players.

Ex. 203: (1) No preparation is required for poco rit. within an entire bar. (2) Since you have only 2 beats for the ritard., prepare it. (3) Prepare; subdivide for the eighth-notes. (4) Very gradual. (5) Small exact beat on *Three* in bar 2 (a tempo).

Ex. 204: (5) Be sure to return to the exact tempo—no faster!
Ex. 205: (5) The 2 last chords are "a tempo"; wait on *One* in bar 4, then beat the eighth-rest and the 2 chords strictly in time.

Ex. 204

1)   poco rit.
2)   rit.   molto rit:
3)   rit.   accel.
4)   accel.   rit.
5)   poco rit.   a tempo

Ex. 205

1)   poco rit.
2)   molto rit.
3)   accel.   rit.
4)   rit.   a tempo
5)   molto rit.   a tempo

Exx. 206 and 207: Only by following the markings painstakingly can you get the full benefit of these exercises.

Ex. 206

1)   accelerando   rit.   a tempo   rit.
2)   molto rit.   animando   poco rit.   molto rit.   a tempo
3)   rit.   a tempo
4)   molto rit   animando

                                                          poco rit.

1)		animando	rallent.
2)		molto rit.	a tempo
3)	rit. poco a poco		
4)	rit.		accel.
5)	accel.		a tempo

Ex. 208: Subdivide in the 4th measure; "lento" is twice as slow as the 1st tempo. In bar 5 a beat on *Two* is superfluous; cut off with a small gesture to the right. *Cf.* p. 140.

Andantino, ($\d = 100$)   NICOLAI, *The Merry Wives of Windsor—Overture*

Ex. 209: Gradual ritard. in bars 2-5; "a tempo" immediately in the 6th bar; "meno" in the 8th, with no transition.

Allegro, ♩ = 152 — DVOŘÁK, Symphony No. 5

Ex. 210: In the 4th measure, wait on *Two* and use *Three* to prepare the "a tempo". For this type of preparation *cf.* Ex. 32 (p. 33).

GERSHWIN, *Rhapsody in Blue*

Copyright, Harms, Inc., New York, N. Y.
Reprinted in this book by permission of the copyright owners

Ex. 211: 2 bars strictly in tempo (many conductors use subdivision in these 2 bars); well-planned stringendo with complete stop on the *ff*; subdivide *One* (bar 7), using the rest for an eighth-note preparation in the original tempo.

Adagio, (♩ = 56) — BRAHMS, Symphony No. 1

Ex. 130: Despite the large orchestration, a heavy and large beat is not required. On the contrary, a small energetic beat for accelerando keeps the brass instruments well under control. Do not do much for the rit. or the orchestra will overdo it.

Ex. 212: Subdivide in bar 6 and the 1st quarter in bar 7, using the rest for preparation as in Ex. 211.

Ex. 213: You get the full advantage of this example by following a singer in his individual rendering of Pagliaccio's lament. Subdivide in bars 9-13. In this case subdivision is used to control the sustained chords of the accompaniment, but the subdivisions should be unobtrusive.

Ex. 214: You may subdivide in the 3rd measure, but give a sharp up-beat on *Two* in bar 4 to return to "a tempo".

Ex. 215: Subdivide for the first ritenuto. After the stringendo use a larger beat to start "ritenuto" (the composer undoubtedly meant rallentando) and slow down, first by subdividing, then changing to 3-beat.

Ex. 216: The accelerando in bar 3 is rather marked. Click on *Two* in the 6th measure to bring the basses in with the harp, which plays very slowly. The notes marked "rubando" are quite fast; wait on *Six*, then give an eighth-note preparation, as though the sixth count were subdivided.

Additional examples for the study of ritardando and accelerando:

4-beat:

Barber: Overture to *The School for Scandal*, 9th bar after F.
Brahms: *Variations on a Theme by Haydn*, 9 bars from the end.
Prokofieff: *Peter and the Wolf*, passage starting at No. 54.
Tchaikovsky: *Overture 1812, poco a poco rallentando* (bar 340).

3-beat:

Bizet: *Carmen*, 2nd act, No. 12—Gipsy song.
Brahms: Symphony No. 2, 1st movement, passage starting 15 bars after M.
Harris: *When Johnny Comes Marching Home*, starting at bar 231.
Tchaikovsky: Symphony No. 4, 1st movement—*Ritardando*, 4th bar after E.

2-beat:

Dvořák: *Slavonic Dance in A-flat major, Op. 46, No. 3.*
Liszt: *Les Préludes*, passage starting at E.
Mendelssohn: Overture to *A Midsummer Night's Dream*, end of the development section.
Schuman, William: Symphony No. 3—passage starting at bar 288.

1-beat:

Beethoven: Symphony No. 9, 2nd movement—8 bars before *Presto*.
Dukas: *L'Apprenti Sorcier, Vif* 3/8, several passages.

TEMPO TRANSITIONS BY CHANGING THE NUMBER OF BEATS IN A MEASURE

When a ritardando or accelerando is not temporary—that is to say, when it leads to a slower or faster section—it is often necessary to change the number of beats in a bar. If you are using 2-beat, a slower section may require 4-beat or 6-beat, while a faster section may find 1-beat useful. Subdivision is very helpful as an intermediate step. The conductor, however, must be sure that a change of the number of beats in a measure is clearly understood by the players—even when it is marked in the parts, and especially when it is not.

First indicate the change of tempo by slowing down or speeding up for a few counts, without changing the number of beats; then switch to the new rhythmic pattern.

Ex. 217 (1): A smooth transition can be achieved by emphasizing *One* and *Three*, and weakening *Two* and *Four* in the 3rd bar, changing to subdivision (Diagram 42) in the 4th or 5th bar, and using the regular 2-beat in bar 6. (A number of conductors of the German school prefer to make the transition on the third beat by gradually shifting upward the left-right motion until it coincides with the up-down line. Here also the emphasis on *One* and *Three* increases, while *Two* and *Four* become weaker and disappear.)

(2): Start subdividing in bar 5 to lead easily into 4/4. Both of the methods discussed above will work.

(3): The changes are more sudden and require a more concentrated beat.

Ex. 218: (1) For the accelerando first weaken *Two*, then *Three*, until they disappear. (2) *Three* reappears first in the ritardando, then *Two*.

Ex. 219: Subdivide in the 3rd measure and change to 2-beat.

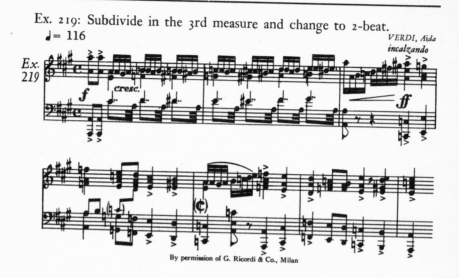

By permission of G. Ricordi & Co., Milan

Ex. 220: You have 9 bars for accelerando with change from 2-beat to 1-beat. Beat *Two* with less and less emphasis until it disappears altogether, but without losing control over the rhythm, and arrive at Presto without any last-second readjustment.

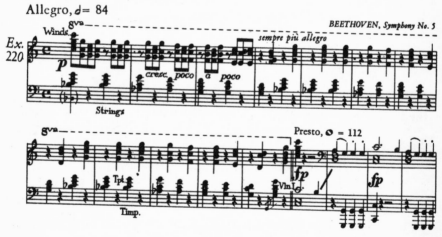

Ex. 221: Do not subdivide until bar 4; subdivision in the 3rd bar would exaggerate the ritardando.

OFFENBACH, Orphée aux Enfers—Overture

Additional examples for the study of tempo transitions which involve a change of the number of beats in a measure:

Changing from 4-beat to 2-beat:

Grieg: *Peer Gynt Suite No. 1*, 4th movement.
Liszt: Piano Concerto No. 1, 1st movement, use 2-beat at *animato* after B.
Strauss, Richard: *Tod und Verklärung, alla breve* at the 30th bar of the *Allegro molto agitato.*

Changing from 1-beat to 3-beat:

Barber: *Essay for Orchestra*, 6th bar after No. 21.
Strauss, Johann: *Emperor Waltz*—Coda, several bars before *Tempo di Valse.*

Changing from 3-beat to 1-beat:

Stravinsky: *L'Oiseau de Feu* (Suite), *Danse infernale*, at No. 29 or earlier.

RITENUTO

A special technique is used for a sudden marked slowing down of the tempo. In ritenuto there is no gradual change; one beat is in tempo and the very next is much slower. The beat used for this is in effect a wait on the count without stopping the motion.

This technique is especially useful in accompaniment, where the more or less unpredictable changes on the part of the soloist force the conductor to wait on a certain count. A sudden complete stop would confuse the players, but the flexible ritenuto beat keeps the orchestra under control.

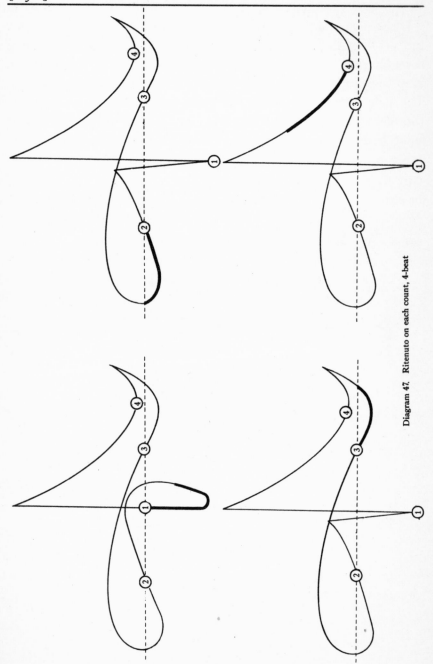

Diagram 47. Ritenuto on each count, 4-beat

Diagram 47. The heavy black line indicates an extremely slow and very intense movement, as though the baton were being drawn through a strongly resisting substance. The length of time you can keep moving the baton while still on the count will surprise you. The point where the heavy line changes back to the medium line (normal speed) must be distinct in the beat, for the release at this point leads to the next count. Practise first on all counts without music.

Ex. 222: The solo part may be either sung or played. Practise first with the conductor indicating the ritenuto and "a tempo". Then have the soloist take his own liberty in the rhythm and lead the accompaniment only.

Chapter 17

THE TENUTO PATTERN

The tenuto beat is a smooth motion with a stop on each count. It resembles the marcato, but lacks the aggressive impetus of that beat. Each beat is sustained with or without intensity, depending on the music. The size varies from small to large.

Diagram 48. The connecting gesture between two counts serves as release and preparation. It should not be hurried (as in staccato) or leisurely (as in legato). Diagram 48a allows a more expressive connection. This expressive form of tenuto is characterized by a "holding on" to the count, as though you were loath to let go of it. This is still more evident in the pattern of 48b, which gives strong emphasis to single counts, especially when marked——◁ or ——◁ ▷—— . The technique is similar to the ritenuto (p. 155), but with great intensity—coming from the forearm—on the very slow part of the pattern (heavy line).

The tenuto beat is used for chords that are detached but held, and for melodic passages of portamento character. The preliminary beat for tenuto is legato. The piano is not the ideal instrument for music of tenuto character. The exercises should therefore be played by a small ensemble.

Diagram 49 is useful for those not too frequent occasions when you want to limit yourself to a very academic time-beating. This "dry" tenuto lacks the strong holding quality of the expressive form.

Since there are no new problems in 3-beat tenuto, apply the principles of Diagram 48. The 2-beat tenuto is shown on Diagrams 50 and 50a; the "dry" pattern (Diagram 51) is recommended for legato passages in very fast tempo, the stops on *One* and *Two* being very short. For 1-beat apply Diagram 33.

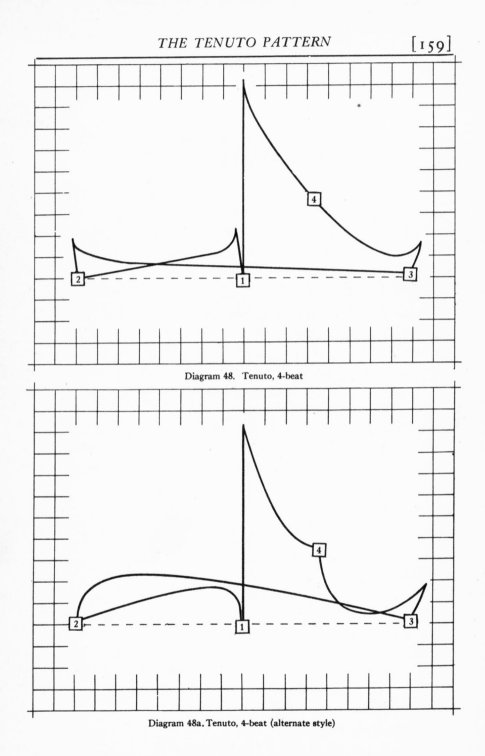

Diagram 48. Tenuto, 4-beat

Diagram 48a. Tenuto, 4-beat (alternate style)

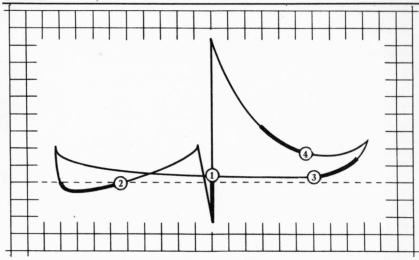

Diagram 48b. Tenuto, 4-beat (alternate style)

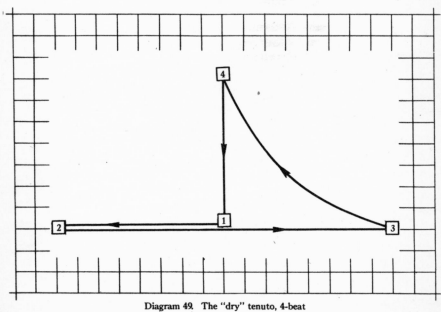

Diagram 49. The "dry" tenuto, 4-beat

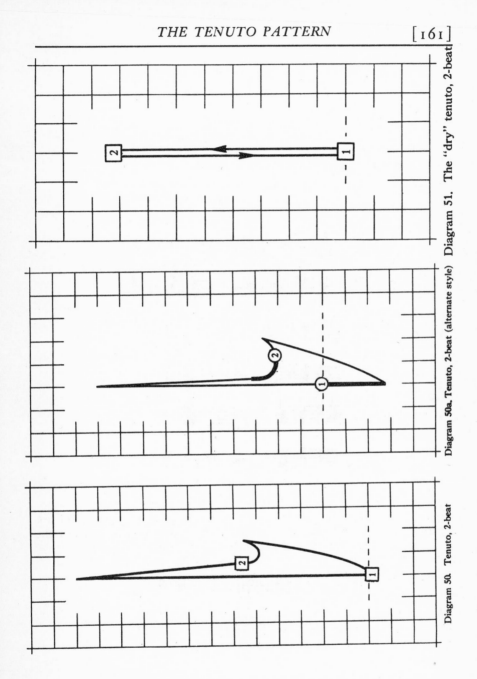

Diagram 51. The "dry" tenuto, 2-beat

Diagram 50a. Tenuto, 2-beat (alternate style)

Diagram 50. Tenuto, 2-beat

Ex. 223: Use Diagram 48 or 48a.
Ex. 224: Use Diagram 48b.
Ex. 225: Same procedure as in Diagram 48 applied to 3-beat.
Ex. 226: Diagram 50.

Ex. 227: Since each half-note is to be held until shortly before the succeeding chord, beat tenuto only on *One* and *Three*. *Two* and *Four* are legato gestures and are easily reduced to connecting links between the tenuto beats. They may even be slightly out of tempo—a little late.

Ex. 228: The sustained chords require the tenuto beat.

Ex. 229: Use the tenuto beat for the *pp* accents in the first bars; for the *ff* chords use the more emotional pattern of Diagram 50a.

Ex. 230: The brass chords in bars 5 and 6 need the tenuto for the intense sustained quality. Support with left hand.

Ex. 231: At the "rit." the accompaniment should be carefully synchronized with the solo. Subdivide the triplet if necessary. If 2 pianos are available, the practice will be more realistic. The ending in the 3rd and 4th bars is of a type found in many pieces: repetition of the same chord detached. This is best controlled with the tenuto beat.

Ex. 232: Subdivision throughout; tenuto for the solo-passage (1st violins).

Ex. 233: Indicate the crescendo in the 2nd measure by increasing the expressiveness in the tenuto beat.

Ex. 234: Same technique as in Ex. 227.

Ex. 200: Tenuto beat will insure the full value of the closing *ff* eighth-note chords.

Chapter 18

HOLDS (I)

THE PROPER HANDLING of holds and interruptions is one of the hardest problems confronting the student conductor. Although it is hardly possible to establish simple general rules, some degree of systematization can be achieved. This is done by dividing holds into those that occur at the end of a piece; those during a piece, and either followed or not followed by rests; and holds followed or not followed by breaks.

CONCLUDING HOLDS

Many pieces have a fermata on the last played note. Regardless of the note value, beat only one count and sustain it as long as you feel the music requires. The manner of execution depends upon the orchestration and the dynamics.

The effectiveness of a *f* is greatly increased by raising the baton for the fermata. Merely stopping the motion of the baton is not sufficient to sustain a *f* or *ff*; only a diminuendo would result. Maintain the volume by indicating intensity with either the right or left hand. The left-hand gesture was explained on p. 27. The right hand may make a similar gesture by shaking the baton, but do not exaggerate. Some conductors indicate a continued *f* by moving the baton very slowly, the same way as in the ritenuto beat (Diagram 47). In *p*, simply stopping the baton on the fermata is sufficient. In *pp*, the left hand keeps the orchestra subdued.

The end of the hold is indicated by a cut-off. The gestures are similar to those for a general cut-off, described on p. 140. Because of the indefinite length of the hold, however, the cut-off must be especially decisive in order to insure the simultaneous stopping of all the players. Although the gesture must be sudden and quick, it must still avoid any suggestion of an accent at the very end unless an accent is marked by the composer.

Ex. 235: Do not beat *Four* in the last bar; sustain a moderate *f* with the left hand.

Ex. 230: The hold actually starts on the 2nd beat of bar 7; do not beat for the last bar.

Exx. 236 and 237: While in 236 the last pizzicato chord will take care of itself, the 1st violins in 237 need an extra gesture of the left hand for a cut-off. This gesture should be unobtrusive and clearly directed toward the violins, so that none of the wind players will mistake it for the concluding cut-off.

Exx. 238 and 239: Both examples illustrate diminuendo on the fermata. The first starts *fff* and is played by the winds (the last string chord again takes care of itself), while the second starts softly and dies away in the strings. Indicate the diminuendo in 238 by gradually lowering both hands, if the right hand was in a raised position; if not, use the left hand alone. A wind chord, no matter how soft, always requires a cut-off. The "morendo" in 239 may be expressed by a "dying-away" gesture which is very effective for strings: both arms slowly fall to the side with no definite cut-off.

Exx. 229 and 231: Two endings with ⎯⎯⎯⎯ ⎯⎯⎯⎯ , expressed by raising and lowering both hands together, or the left hand alone. The size and intensity of the gesture depend upon the orchestra's response.

BEETHOVEN, *Die Weihe des Hauses—Overture*

Ex. 240: The uplifted left hand sustains the *ff* tutti while the right hand directs the kettle-drum. The baton waits on *One* and cuts the drum-roll on *Three*, then joins the left hand for the tutti cut-off.

Ex. 241: Beat the first 3 counts in the last bar. The 4th beat is super-fluous since the pizzicato needs no cut-off. Sustain the violins throughout with the left hand.

SHOSTAKOVITCH, *The Golden Age*

Ex. 242: Since only part of the orchestra has a fermata on the last chord, and the other part holds the 4th and 5th counts, you must beat all 6 counts. The 6th beat is small, so that it cuts off part of the orchestra and does not look like the concluding cut-off.

REGER, *Mozart Variations*

HOLDS DURING A PIECE, NOT FOLLOWED BY A REST

Such holds may or may not require a cut-off. If they do, there may be only a short break for "breathing", or there may be a longer pause. The length of the pause often depends upon the individual interpretation. Consider how differently the fermata in *The Star-Spangled Banner* is treated by conductors! Only the techniques are discussed here. Their application to the following examples may vary, depending on the personal taste of the conductor.

(1) *If there is only a slight interruption after the hold, the cut-off gesture is also the preparation for the next count.*

Diagram 52 shows the technique of making a hold and cut-off on any count in 4-beat. On each count *the beat is repeated:* ⊡ is for the hold, ① is for the cut-off and also serves as preliminary to ②. In most cases, click on the repeated count for a clear release.

The principle of repeating the beat after the hold is applied to 3-beat, 2-beat, and 1-beat in Diagrams 53-55. It can easily be applied to all other patterns.

When the note under the fermata is of greater value than one count, it is not necessary to repeat any beats, as will be seen in the following examples.

Ex. 243: The hold in bar 2 is treated according to Diagram 52. The fermata in the 4th measure, however, includes several counts; stop on ⊡ for the hold, then (skipping *Two*) beat ③, which serves the double purpose of cutting off the hold and preparing ④. Thus only 3 gestures are used in this measure.

Chorale Setting by J. S. Bach

Ex. 244: For the hold in the 2nd bar, stop on ⊡ and use ② for cut-off and preparation.

Chorale Setting by J. S. Bach

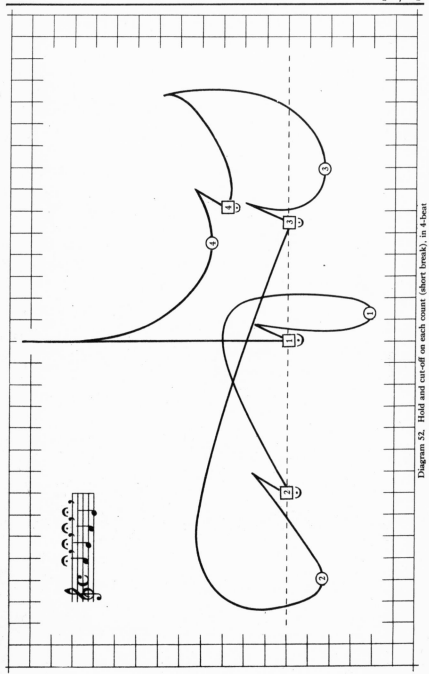

Diagram 52. Hold and cut-off on each count (short break), in 4-beat

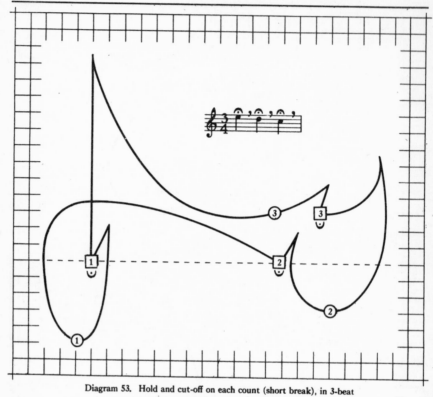

Diagram 53. Hold and cut-off on each count (short break), in 3-beat

Ex. 245: In bar 4 stop on $\boxed{3}$ cut off and prepare with $\textcircled{4}$

Chorale Setting by J. S. Bach

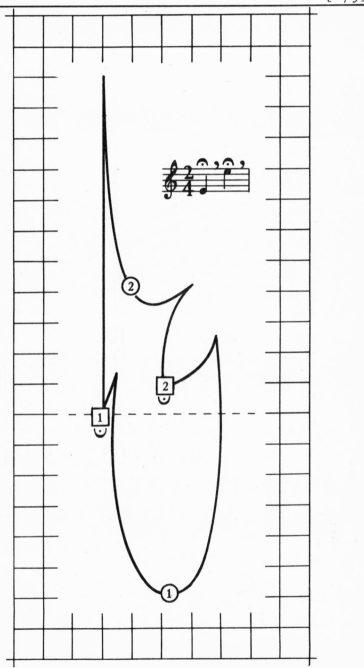

Diagram 54. Hold and cut-off on each count (short break), in 2-beat

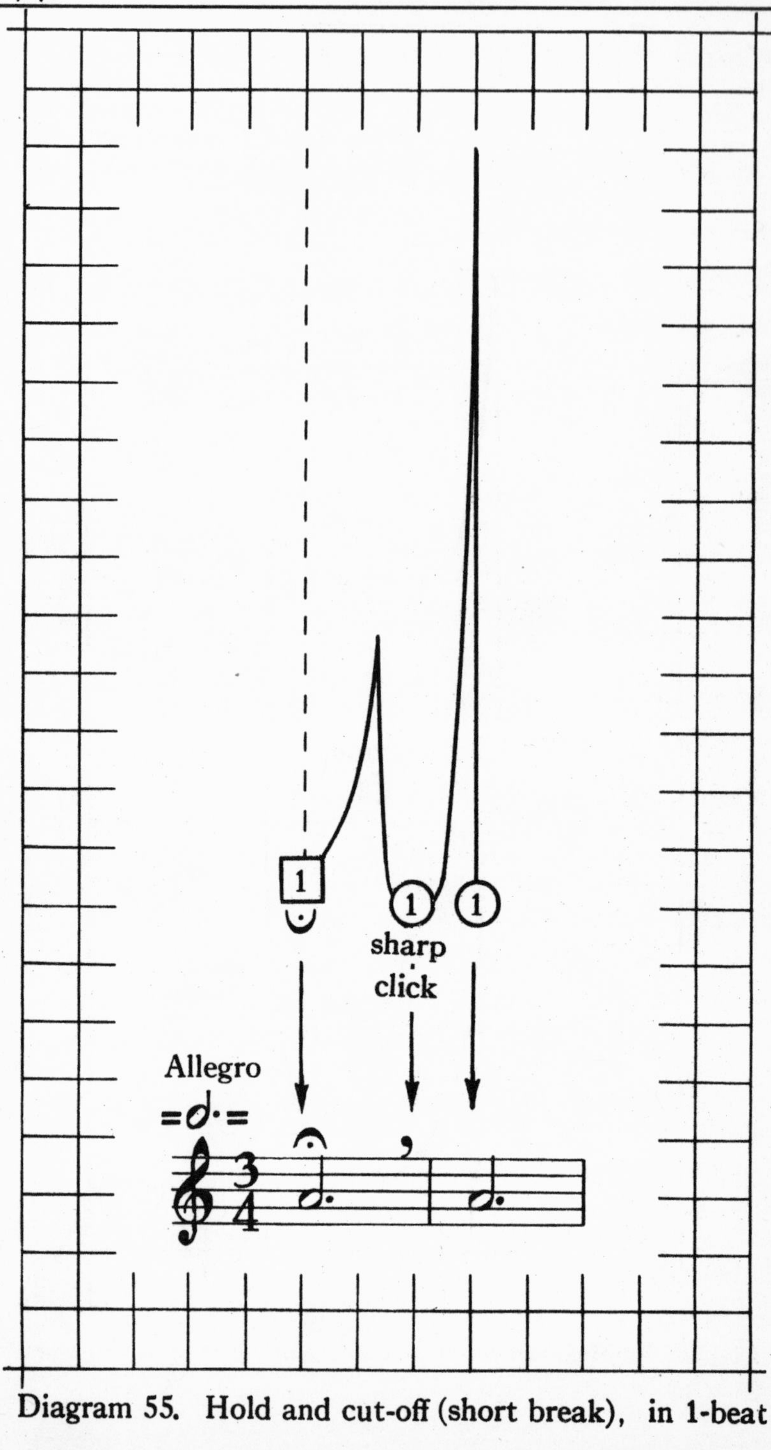

Diagram 55. Hold and cut-off (short break), in 1-beat

Ex. 246: Since the cut-off also serves as preparation, it must have all the different expressions of the preliminary beat. In bar 2 it is full-staccato. In the last measure the orchestra has a half-bar rest. After a sharp cut-off of the second fermata, use a neutral down-beat (synchronized with the first chord of the piano) and prepare the staccato chord with *Two*.

Ex. 247: In bar 2 use a full-staccato cut-off, which prepares the tutti attack.

Ex. 248: Stop on **[1]** in the 4th bar. Following the usual procedure by beating the cut-off **③** strictly in tempo results in a whole-beat pause. Considering the very slow tempo, the conductor may prefer to shorten the pause, perhaps by as much as half, using an eighth-note beat.

Exx. 249-251: Use Diagram 54. Change from *f* to *p* in 251 with a definite but small cut-off.

Ex. 252: Apply Diagram 55. Though the held note comes after the beat, just stop on *One* and wait for the orchestra to finish the bar.

BEETHOVEN, *Symphony No. 9*

Ex. 253: When a fractional value occurs after a fermata, do not change the regular procedure (*cf.* Chapter 12, Start After the Count). Thus the 3rd fermata is treated just as the first two are.

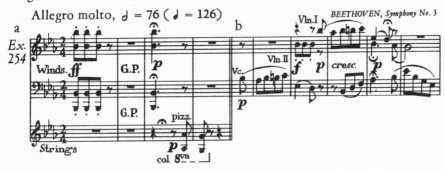

Ex. 254: The two types of combined cut-off and preparation, one with and one without repeated beat, are illustrated in 254a and b. In the 3rd measure of 254a only two gestures are used: the hold is on **1**, while **2** cuts off the winds and also prepares the string entrance (staccato gesture!). This way of beating does not follow the notation, for the dotted quarter should be held until after *Two*. However, *it is not unusual for the beat to contradict the notation under a fermata, provided the beat is convenient and will not confuse the players.* In Ex. 254b the hold for the 1st violins is on D, and not E♭ as in many editions. The cut-off gesture (2nd beat repeated!) should be rather gentle and smooth, so as to have a very slight break.

Ex. 255: All counts are subdivided except the very first. The 1st eighth-beat on *Two* has two functions: it cuts off the fermata and prepares the entrance of oboes and bassoons. For the start *cf.* Ex. 141.

The following two examples have rests after the holds. They are discussed here because the technique involved is the same as in the previous examples, owing to the fact that the rest actually includes only part of the count.

Ex. 256a: Beat 1 in bar 2 and wait for the lower instruments with their fermata, then beat ②for cut-off and preparation.

Ex. 256b: Wait on 2 ; a sharp down-beat on *One* in the following bar cuts off the fermata and prepares the next attack.

Ex. 247 (bar 4): While the second fermata may be executed without repeating the 3rd beat, most conductors desire a longer break and therefore repeat *Three*. But if this is done, beat the repeated *Three* downward so that the players will not confuse it with *Four*.

Additional examples for the study of fermatas followed by a short break:

Beethoven: Symphony No. 6, 1st movement—bar 4.
Carpenter: *Sea Drift*, 3 bars before No. 5.
Copland: *A Lincoln Portrait*, bar 211.
Franck: Symphony in D minor, 2nd movement—bar 100.
Haydn: *The Creation*, No. 32 (Duet)—*Allegro* section.
Rimsky-Korsakov: *Scheherazade*, 4th movement—11 bars from the end.

> (2) *If the interruption after the hold is longer than one count, a different technique is used. There are two separate gestures, one for the cut-off and one for the preparation.*

The nature of this cut-off is similar to that at the end of a piece. The execution, however, is now determined by the fact that the music continues after the pause. Consequently, the cut-off gesture carries the baton from one complete stop (⌒) to another (ATT) in the most simple and direct manner. To prepare the attack after the pause, use the position of attention and the regular preparatory beat just as at the start.

There can be no hard and fast rule for the application of these gestures. The procedure depends on the position of the baton at the fermata and on where you want the baton to be at attention. Diagram 56 shows some of the more useful of the many possibilities. Whenever an upward or sidewise cut-off could be mistaken for a direction to continue, use a downward cut-off.

Ex. 257a: The two fermatas can be done in three different ways: cut-off and preparation done with the same down-beat (difficult for the players); separate gestures for cut-off and preparation, strictly in time; separate gestures with a pause between. Most conductors treat the first 5 bars as an introduction, taking the cut-off and the down-beat after the first fermata in tempo, but making a pause after the second fermata, as shown in Ex. 257b. For the cut-off gesture after the first hold, consult Diagram 55. The cut-off after the second hold must carry the baton to where it can start the 2nd violins in the clearest and most comfortable way.

Ex. 257 a / b — Allegro con brio, ♩ = 108. BEETHOVEN, Symphony No. 5. Vln. II / Vla. Strings *ff* Cl. *p* — Cut-off gesture of the value of one bar.

Exx. 258 and 259: In these examples a definite break is made after the slow introduction before starting the fast movement. The conductor must feel for himself how long to wait on the pause. For the 1st bar of Ex. 258 *cf.* what was said about Ex. 170. After the fermata in Ex. 259, the music continues with a start after the count, since the "vivace" goes alla breve.

ROSSINI, *Il Barbiere di Siviglia—Overture*

HAYDN, *The Seasons*

Ex. 260: The first *ff* is a kind of introduction in itself and is followed by a short silence. Raise the baton for the fermata and use a strong down-beat for the cut-off. The *p* subito in bar 5 needs the sudden appearance of the left hand. Be careful not to have the baton too high in cutting off the second hold, so as to be in a convenient position for the allegro attack.

BEETHOVEN, *Symphony No. 1*

Exx. 261 and 262: Pauses indicated by the composers: in Ex. 261 by using the sign ∥ , in Ex. 262 by inserting a fractional rest with a fermata.

MENDELSSOHN, *Midsummer Night's Dream—Nocturne*

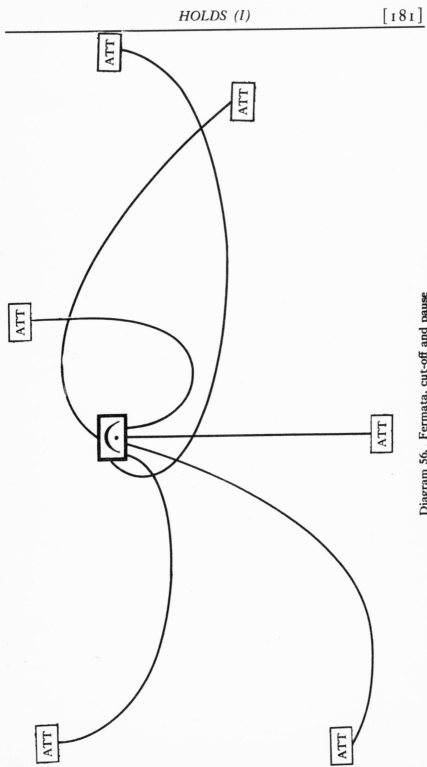

Diagram 56. Fermata, cut-off and pause

Additional examples for the study of fermatas followed by a longer pause:

Beethoven: Symphony No. 3, 4th movement—bar 348 (before *Poco Andante*).

Brahms: Symphony No. 1, 4th movement—before the beginning of the *Allegro* section.

Haydn: Symphony No. 103, 1st movement—before the beginning of the *Allegro* section.

Rossini: Overture to *Tancredi*, bar 121 (beginning of the recapitulation).

Sibelius: Symphony No. 3, 1st movement—3 bars from the end.

Smetana: *Dance of the Comedians* from *The Bartered Bride*, 2nd bar.

> (3) *Even if there is no interruption after the hold and no cut-off is required, a gesture is needed to resume the progress of the music.*

The type of gesture to be used depends on the notation, and the different possibilities are illustrated in the examples.

Exx. 215, 263, and 264: Since the note under the fermata has a greater value than one count, wait on the first beat of the held note and use the second, or in general the last, for preparation with no cut-off. While this gesture leads unequivocally into the next count in strict tempo, it must be smooth rather than sharp, so that players cannot mistake it for a cut-off.

MENDELSSOHN, *Midsummer Night's Dream*

Ex. 265: Sometimes the method of skipping beats on a fermata can lead to misunderstanding about the release and the continuation of the music. Whenever this may occur, it is necessary to beat all the counts. In the present example, the bass instruments may enter prematurely unless the 4 counts in bar 3 are clearly indicated. Wait on *Two* for the hold; the preparatory 3rd beat should not be too large, while *Four* is done with an incisive motion. In the 1st measure, do not neglect the correct indication of the rests; *Two* and *Three* are neutral but distinct beats, *Four* is preparatory.

Copyright, 1943, by G. Schirmer, Inc.

Ex. 266: When the same notes are tied over to the next count, with no new instruments entering, no additional gesture is required; just continue beating after the hold according to the notation. In the 4th bar, release the winds with the left hand.

In the following nine examples the beat used for the hold is repeated. However, this is done differently from the cut-off and preparation discussed under (1) and (2). As you see in Diagram 57, the baton leaves the hold without any special gesture and merely resumes the motion with which it entered the hold. The smoothness of this motion precludes the possibility of clicking.

A number of conductors use the pattern of Diagram 57 even to direct fermatas which are followed by a short break, making the motion after the hold more emphatic to indicate the release. But this gesture lacks the incisiveness of Diagram 52, and the student conductor will do well to adhere to the method taught in section (1).

Ex. 267: Stop on the 3rd beat in bar 2; the repeated *Three* will tell the clarinetist to continue with the triplet.

Copyright, Harms, Inc., New York, N. Y.
Reprinted in this book by permission of the copyright owners

Ex. 268: In 268a the beat after the hold can have the value of either a quarter or an eighth. By beating a quarter you will make the sixteenth-note a little calmer. In slow passages like 268b, subdivision of the last beat gives more control at the fermata. Lead into the next bar with either an eighth- or a quarter-beat.

OFFENBACH, *Orphée aux Enfers—Overture*

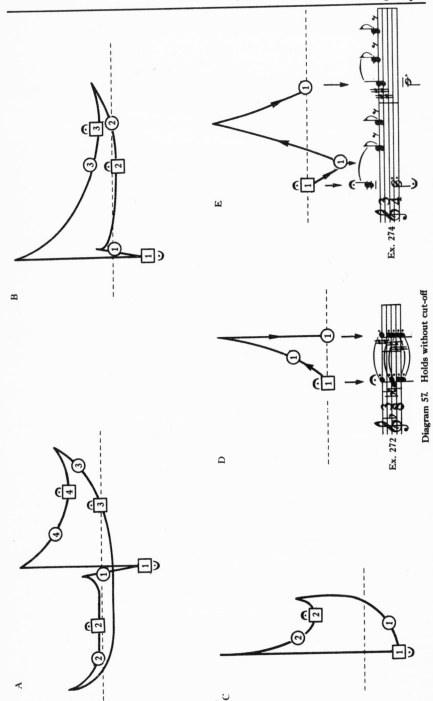

Ex. 272   Diagram 57.   Holds without cut-off

Ex. 269: The repeated *Two* is a small gesture to indicate the change to *p*.

MOZART, *Die Entführung aus dem Serail—Overture*

Ex. 270: The first two fermatas need an especially smooth continuation so that the various entries blend into one another. After the third, however, use a sharp staccato gesture to cut off, and to prepare the sudden *ff*.

Ex. 271: Hold on *Two* and continue with a preliminary eighth-beat.

MASCAGNI, *Cavalleria Rusticana*

Ex. 272: Use Diagram 57d, noting the difference between this technique and that used for Ex. 252 (Diagram 55).

BERLIOZ, *Roméo et Juliette*

Ex. 273: Allow sufficient time for the G after the hold, without rushing the repeated 5th beat.

RIMSKY-KORSAKOV, *Scheherazade*

Ex. 274: The beat after the hold (up-beat quality) must express the change of tempo and dynamics. Use Diagram 57e.

J. STRAUSS, *Vienna Blood*

Ex. 275: While the 'cellos and basses hold the B, give a small but well-timed preliminary beat for the Allegro, with no break.

BEETHOVEN, *Leonore Overture No. 3*

Sometimes, especially in accompaniment, there is no time for a regular preparatory beat. A short smooth gesture is needed which, without being in tempo, leads convincingly into the next count. The pattern for this is identical with the tenuto of Diagrams 48 and 48a.

Ex. 276: Use this technique for connecting the two fermatas in bar 2; a small 3rd beat serves as cut-off.

Ex. 277: Stop on the 3rd beat and, using the short connecting motion, pick up *Four* with the singer.

Copyright, 1935, by Gershwin Publishing Corporation, New York, N. Y.

Ex. 213: The 13th measure calls for the same procedure in 2-beat.

Ex. 261: An application of this smooth connecting gesture (from *One* to *Two*) to purely instrumental music.

Additional examples for the study of fermatas without cut-off:

Without using an extra beat:

Beethoven: Symphony No. 6, 3rd movement—bar 203 (end of the section in 2/4).

Borodin: Symphony No. 2, 3rd movement—last bar.

Gershwin: *Rhapsody in Blue*, 1st and 15th bars.

Haydn: Symphony No. 97, 4th movement—27 bars from the end (a similar passage occurs earlier in this movement).

Rimsky-Korsakov: *Scheherazade*, 2nd movement, bars 415 and 417 (in bar 419, an extra gesture is required: *Two* is repeated!).

Schuman, William: Symphony No. 3—Part 2, bars 139-141.

Using an extra beat:

Berlioz: *Symphonie Fantastique,* 1st movement, 46th bar of the *Allegro* section (*Two* must be repeated to lead the violas and 'cellos which play different notes on the downbeat after the fermata!).

Borodin: Symphony No. 2, 3rd movement—2nd and 3rd bars after B. (*Three* must be prepared because of the change of harmony.)

Franck: Symphony in D minor, 1st movement—bar 186 (in bars 188 and 190, no extra beat is required!).

Sibelius: Symphony No. 2, 1st movement—4 bars before P.

Strauss, Johann: *Voices of Spring*—82nd bar of the Coda.

Chapter 19

HOLDS (II)

HOLDS FOLLOWED BY RESTS

Ex. 278: The beat on the rest serves to cut off the hold and prepare the following count.

Chorale Setting by J. S. Bach

Ex. 279: For the 1st measure use Diagram 57c. In bar 2, an incisive down-beat secures a clear release and prepares *Two*.

Ex. 280: In the 2nd bar, wait on *One*, skip *Two*, and cut off on *Three*. Then wait for the singer, who traditionally starts after the cut-off. Synchronize your 4th beat (*p* staccato!) with "waste-".

Additional examples for the study of fermatas followed by rests:

Borodin: Symphony No. 2, 3rd movement—1 bar before A.
Franck: Symphony in D minor, 2nd movement—bar 96.
Kodály: *Háry János* (Suite), 4th movement—3rd bar after No. 2.
Rimsky-Korsakov: *Scheherazade*, 2nd movement—bars 111 and 121.
Rossini: Overture to *Semiramide*, 62nd bar of the *Allegro* 4/4.

HOLDS ON RESTS

Exx. 191, 208, and 350: In cases like these, neglect the rests. Just keep the baton up during the interruption in readiness for the next attack.

Ex. 281: The fermata is on a whole-rest. Beat a neutral *One* for cut-off, and wait; *Two* serves as preparation.

FRANCK, *Symphony in D minor*

Ex. 141: The fermatas are directed in a similar manner.

Exx. 282 and 283: The notation is not followed literally. In Ex. 282 the stop is on *One*, for the orchestra needs no further beat to play the three chords. After the pause, prepare on *Two*. Execute the 2nd bar of Ex. 283 as though the fermata were on the 5th eighth, using the last eighth for preparation.

Allegro marcato
con molto fuoco, ♩ = 92   WEBER, Euryanthe—Overture

Ex. 282

(♪ = 76)   WAGNER, Tristan und Isolde

Ex. 283

Ex. 284: There are two ways to conduct this passage. You may cut the first chord with *One* in the 2nd bar and then wait; a sharp up-beat on *Two* starts the violins. Alternatively, the chord may be cut with the baton in high position (no down-beat!); after the pause, beat *One-Two*, but remember that *One* must not be too emphatic or it may be mistaken for the attack.

Molto vivace, (♩ = 104)

Ex. 284

WEBER, Der Freischütz—Overture

Ex. 285: The players start counting the Presto from the 1st beat after the fermata; therefore beat *One-Two* at the beginning of the new tempo. You will be in a position for this if you beat the *sf* in bar 2 with a vigorous rebound and keep the baton high during the pause. (*Cf.* the first movement of Tchaikovsky's Sixth Symphony, in which a similar transition occurs at the end of the introduction. After the pause, beat the rests to establish the new tempo.)

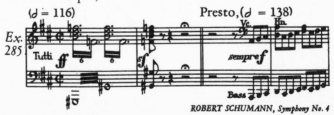

(♩ = 116)   Presto, (♩ = 138)

Ex. 285

ROBERT SCHUMANN, Symphony No. 4

Ex. 286: In the 1st measure beat *Four* to cut off, raising the baton only slightly; pause and repeat *Four* to prepare. The 3rd beat in bar 2 and the 4th in bar 3 are treated similarly. Use the pattern of Diagram 57a.

Ex. 287a: Stop on *Three* in the 1st bar, cutting off with the left hand; repeat *Three* after the pause (Diagram 57b). Use the left hand again when you stop on *Three* in the 3rd measure, and resume the tempo on *Four* (preparation).

Ex. 287b: Since the notes before the first hold are pizzicato, just stop on *Four*, which is repeated.

Ex. 288: The 4th beat in both bars is repeated.

Ex. 289a: Use the pattern of Diagram 23a. In the 2nd bar, stop on *Two* by moving the baton to the left with a short turn of the wrist. The clarinet now plays the cadenza without being directed until it comes to the last Bb (⌢). Beat *Two* again, this time as an up-beat leading into bar 3, using a gesture which prepares *f* legato. The stop on *Two* and repeated beat are done in a similar manner in the 4th measure, but the up-beat is now *p* staccato. (Note that the sidewise motion used here on *Two* for the stop is much more convenient than carrying the 2nd beat to the top of the field.

Ex. 289b: Subdivide in bars 1-3 for good rhythmic control. After the pause at the end of bar 2, beat *One* directly in the 3rd bar without preparation.

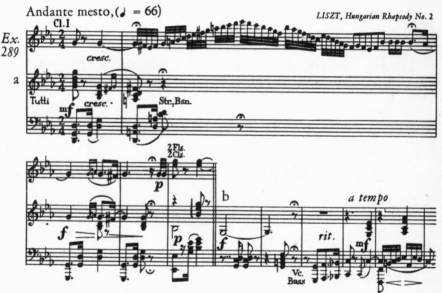

Ex. 290: *One* in the 2nd measure is repeated. Inexperienced conductors sometimes try to prepare the repeated beat with an extra gesture, instead of following the regular procedure, in the erroneous belief that this increases their control. By beating the *pp* chords light-staccato at about shoulder level, you have plenty of space for the second down-beat after the pause. This down-beat is a vigorous full-staccato.

PUCCINI, *La Bohème*

Ex. 291: Stop and wait on the down-beat in the 4th measure, then continue as shown in Diagram 57d. Bring in the strings with a gentle but definite upward movement of the baton. A similar upward movement, but slower (Meno presto!) leads the winds after the second fermata.

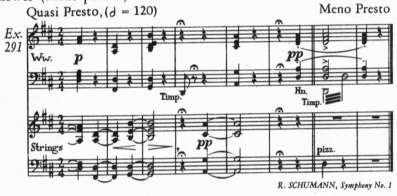

R. SCHUMANN, *Symphony No. 1*

Ex. 292: The same technique is here applied to accompaniment. Cut the chord in bar 2 by beating *Three* and wait for the singer; then repeat *Three* as preparation.

HAYDN, *The Creation*

Ex. 276: The 3rd beat in bar 2 is repeated.

Additional examples for the study of fermatas on rests:

Bizet: *Carmen*, 2nd act, *Toreador Song*—bar 24.
Haydn: Symphony No. 103, 1st movement (development section), and
    4th movement.
Hindemith: *Mathis der Maler*, 3rd movement—1 bar before No. 10.
Kodály: *Háry János* (Suite), 5th movement—upbeat.
Tchaikovsky: Symphony No. 6, 4th movement—11th, 14th, and 16th bars
    after F.
Weber: Overture to *Oberon*, bar 9.

DIFFERENT NOTE VALUES UNDER A FERMATA

When some instruments have a different note value under a fermata
than others, the conductor must be careful not to omit any necessary
beats. *Cf.* Exx. 240-242.

Ex. 293: While the left hand sustains the tutti *ff*, the baton waits on
Two, moves quickly through *Three*, and cuts off the tympani on *Four*.
This *Four* is done with a small gesture; a larger one is used for the repeated 4th beat which cuts off the tutti and prepares the next bar. In bar
2, the first wait is on *One*, and the second wait occurs on the 3rd beat
which also ends the tympani roll.

BEETHOVEN, *Die Weihe des Hauses—Overture*

Ex. 294: The 3rd beat must be given very clearly to start the double-
tonguing in the trumpets, the tremolo in the strings, and the percussion.
Save the left hand for the crescendo.

COPLAND, *A Lincoln Portrait*
Reprinted by permission of the copyright owners,
Boosey & Hawkes, Inc., New York, N. Y.

Ex. 295: While the baton sustains the strings (on the 6th beat), cut off the flute quietly with the left hand.

BRAHMS, *Symphony No. 4*

Ex. 296: In the 3rd bar, indicate the entrance of horns, trumpets, and tympani after the count with an extra down-beat (small!) or with a gesture of the left hand. *One* in the next bar cuts the hold.

Additional examples for the study of different note values under a fermata:

Beethoven: Symphony No. 8, 1st movement—42 bars from the end.
Berlioz: *Marche Hongroise (Rakóczy March)* from *La Damnation de Faust*, last bar.
Enesco: *Roumanian Rhapsody No. 1*, 2nd bar.
Haydn: Symphony No. 102, 1st movement—last bar of the introduction.
Liszt: *Les Préludes*, before the double bar after D.
Schuman, William: Symphony No. 3—Part 2, bar 141 (contrabass!).

INTERRUPTIONS

Most interruptions are executed by stopping the beat, if necessary with cut-off. After the pause, which may be short or long, prepare the next attack. Since the players may overlook an interruption, especially if it is not clearly marked, it is sometimes advisable to use a sudden warning gesture of the left hand.

Exx. 297-299: The regular preparation follows the break. Use no rebound in bar 4 of Ex. 298, since you need the upward gesture for preparation. In Ex. 299, use the left hand for cut-off; after the interruption beat clearly the 4th eighth in preparation for the next phrase.

By permission of Novello & Company, Ltd., London

BEETHOVEN, *Symphony No. 9*

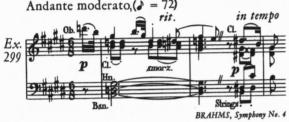

BRAHMS, *Symphony No. 4*

Ex. 300: The traditional interruption is very slight. Do not bounce the baton in bar 3, but keep it down as in a tenuto beat. Immediately after the 3rd quarter-note begin the legato preparation, which is somewhat shorter than the regular whole-beat; otherwise the interruption would be unduly prolonged.

J. STRAUSS, *Vienna Blood*

Ex. 301: The most practical way of indicating the interruption is to use an extra *quarter*-beat at the end of bar 2, which virtually becomes a 5/4 bar (♩ ♩ ♩). The extra beat serves as cut-off and is followed by the down-beat of bar 3.

R. STRAUSS, *Don Juan*

After a very short interruption between two bars, the music can be resumed by moving the baton downward immediately after a stop at the top of the field of beating. This use of the down-stroke is the only exception to the rule that the baton must change direction in order to lead the orchestra into an attack. The forearm always participates in the downward gesture with a motion which is gentle in *p*, forceful in *f*. This procedure for attacking the 1st count in a bar is applied occasionally to directing certain other entries (*cf.* "Free preparatory gestures", p. 252). However, it requires considerable skill and does not lend itself to general use; the student should use this technique only for interruptions of the type discussed in the following three examples.

Ex. 302: An extra quarter-beat (♩ ♩ ♩ ♩) may be used to indicate the pause and to prepare the next measure. For a very short interruption, however, the following procedure is preferable. Subdivide the 3rd count, the last quarter-beat being a somewhat sudden upward gesture which, after a very short stop at the top of the field, is succeeded by a gentle down-beat. The latter starts the next bar without preparation. The motion of the baton may be supported by a smooth gesture of the left hand.

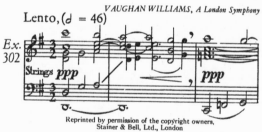

Lento, (♩ = 46)

VAUGHAN WILLIAMS, *A London Symphony*

Ex. 302

Strings *ppp*   *ppp*

Reprinted by permission of the copyright owners,
Stainer & Bell, Ltd., London

Ex. 303: Subdivide the second half of bar 1, using an accented up-beat on the last eighth. Hesitate on this beat and proceed directly into the new tempo. Since this leaves no time for preparation, the first two beats in "molto più mosso" must be sharp and determined. In bar 3, use the accented up-beat again on *Four* and continue with the down-beat after a momentary break.

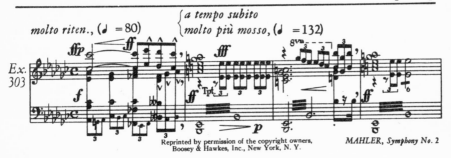

MAHLER, *Symphony No. 2*

Ex. 173: Cut the tutti fermata, wait, and beat *One* (bar 5) as preparation; hesitate briefly after a small but snappy *Two*. (In bar 4, do not forget to indicate the cut-off for the percussion instruments!)

Additional examples for the study of interruptions:

Brahms: *Variations on a Theme by Haydn*, after each variation.

Gershwin: *Rhapsody in Blue*, 7th bar after No. 15, 3 bars before No. 37, 1 bar before No. 39.

Hindemith: *Mathis der Maler*, 1st movement—double bar before No. 12; 3rd movement—double bar after No. 34.

Moussorgsky: *A Night on Bald Mountain*, 4 bars after F.

Sibelius: Symphony No. 2, 1st movement—double bar after N, and at O.

Chapter 20

ACCENTS AND SYNCOPATION

ACCENTS

FOR THE INDICATION of an accent, the beat which precedes the accent is always used for preparation. The preparatory gesture is similar to that at the beginning of a piece, its size and character depending on the degree of the accent to follow. The accented count itself is indicated by the strength of the beat. The emphasis that is put on the accented beat can be varied widely. For a subtle accent in legato, either a larger beat or clicking on the accent may be employed. Tenuto, marcato, or even staccato may be used for stronger accents. In staccato passages emphasis is obtained by the increased sharpness of the beat.

An especially strong accent requires a particularly effective preparation, a gesture that is referred to in this book as "*sf*-motion". An unusual amount of space and energy is needed to co-ordinate the players in a powerful attack. If the accent is on the 1st count of a measure, the accented up-beat of Diagram 21 is used. To accent the last count of a measure, prepare with a backward thrust of the arm as described in Ex. 32. For a strong accent on *Two*, in 4- or 3-beat, the regular patterns do not allow enough space for adequate preparation. Therefore in 4-beat carry the baton to the *right* on the rebound of the 1st beat with a quick curved motion, then sweep to the left for the accented *Two*. In 3-beat this procedure is reversed.

The object of the combined preparation and emphasis is to secure a unified attack on the part of the players. Conductors sometimes try to get this result by hesitating just before the accent, a procedure that often fails in its purpose because the players do not co-ordinate properly. The method given above is an aggressive one in the sense that it actually carries the players into the accented count. In soft music, of course, in order to avoid overemphasis, the aggressiveness should not be made too obvious. This can be accomplished by beating the unaccented counts with a minimum of gesture. In that case a small preparation will still suffice.

The left hand may also be used to indicate an accent, either together with the right hand, or by itself. This is a matter of personal preference. The left-hand gesture includes the preparation on the preceding count and the indication of the accent itself. The preparation is made by an upward motion of the left arm (while the right hand continues its motion undisturbed!). The accent may be indicated in several ways. For example: in *p*, a sharp motion toward the players, the tip of thumb and index finger together; in *f*, a strong downward movement with the hand or the fist, the gesture varying from very small to very large.

Exx. 304a and 305a: The accents are indicated by > and *sf*. Naturally a stronger gesture is needed for an accent in a *f* passage than in a *p* passage. Practise each of these exercises with different degrees of force and with several techniques.

Ex. 306: Lift the baton slightly higher than usual on *Four* in the 1st bar, to prepare the accent in the 2nd bar. The left-hand technique may also be used. In 306b prepare the accent in *ff* with an accented up-beat.

Ex. 196 (bar 3): A staccato gesture cuts off on *Three* and also provides the preparation for the accented 'cello attack; beat *Four* legato and somewhat larger than the following *One*.

Ex. 307: For these accents use very incisive gestures.

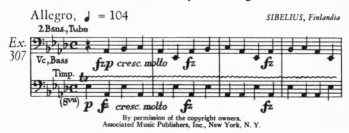

Ex. 308: For the accented 4th counts, use a forceful preparation on *Three*. *Four* is done with a sharp staccato gesture. Observe that in Ex. 308a the accent is followed by a neutral beat. In Ex. 308b, bar 3, beat *One* with a snappy rebound and *Two* in a *down*-left direction and stop, skipping *Three*; prepare the new tempo on *Four*. This means that here the preparatory beat starts from down-left instead of from the right, as is customary.

VERDI, *Aida*

Exx. 142 (bar 3) and 199 (bars 2 and 3): For a sudden tutti staccato chord, use the same technique as for an accent.

Exx. 265, 309, and 310: Various accents in 3-beat. In fast tempo, the gesture indicating accents must be made with very little arm motion; the necessary quick turns of the baton should be made with a flexible wrist.

Copyright, 1941, by G. Schirmer, Inc.

Ex. 311a: Only a very slight beat is needed on *One* in the 4th bar, so as to use a minimum of gesture for the accent.

Ex. 311b: Raise the baton only slightly to prepare the accents on *One*.

Ex. 312: Use large beats on *Two* to prepare the accents; use small gestures elsewhere so that the accents are more prominent.

Used by permission of the copyright owners,
The John Church Co., Philadelphia, Pa.

Ex. 313: Because of the accents, carry the 2nd beat to the left and use a smaller gesture than usual for the 4th beat.

Ex. 314: The beat in the 2nd measure does not follow the regular pattern but is a preliminary beat, just as if the piece started in bar 3. Beat staccato for the *sf*.

Ex. 296: The accents in bars 1 and 5 are made with a slightly emphasized staccato. The rebound in the 2nd measure must be vigorous.

Ex. 127: Because the right hand indicates *f* in the 5th measure with a large gesture, the left hand is needed for the accent in bar 6.

Ex. 156: The accent in *ff* is expressed by marcato, the one in *p* by tenuto.

Additional examples for the study of accents:

Beethoven: Symphony No. 4, 2nd movement.
Beethoven: Piano Concerto No. 5, 1st movement.
Borodin: *Polovetzian Dances* from *Prince Igor*.
Brahms: *Academic Festival Overture*.
Gershwin: *Rhapsody in Blue*.
Haydn: Symphony No. 92, 1st movement (development section).
Haydn: Symphony No. 97, 1st movement (*Vivace*).
Tchaikovsky: *Nutcracker Suite, Ouverture miniature; Danse russe* (*Trepak*).
Wagner: Overture to *Tannhäuser*.

SYNCOPATION

(1) *Syncopated passages without accents* require no special beat. The gestures must be very definite and the rhythm steady. You must beat, so to speak, between the notes, not on them. Discipline yourself to keep strictly in tempo, neither rushing nor dragging. Occasionally it is better to beat tenuto or staccato even in legato phrases, to give the orchestra a solid feeling for the rhythm.

Exx. 315-318, and 133: Syncopations in various rhythms. Ex. 318 requires special concentration and a beat that is very precise without becoming stiff. If two pianos are available, practise this entire section of the concerto; have the solo part played on one piano and the orchestra part on the other. Conducting this accompaniment is a very challenging problem for any young conductor, and quite difficult. A phonograph recording may be used to advantage.

By permission of the copyright owners,
Associated Music Publishers, Inc., New York, N. Y.

Copyright by C. F. Peters
Reprinted by permission of the copyright owner, Mr. Walter Hinrichsen

(2) *Syncopated notes with accents* are indicated on the preceding beat, which is staccato. The sharpness of the beat increases with the degree of the accent. In contrast with an ordinary accent, which is on the count, this staccato beat is not prepared. The beat itself is the preparation for the syncopated note that comes after the count. Again, never beat the syncopation, beat the rhythm! Be especially careful not to beat the count after the syncopated note too soon.

Ex. 267: 4-beat. This demonstrates a staccato accent in a legato passage; in bar 1, beat staccato on *One* and *Three*, legato on *Two* and *Four*.

Exx. 319 and 320: 3-beat. In Ex. 320, bars 2 and 4, do not accent the 2nd beat or you will weaken the strong accent on the 3rd.

Courtesy of J. & W. Chester, Ltd., London
Galaxy Music Corporation, New York

Exx. 152 and 321: 2-beat.

Allegro molto con brio, (♩ =152)

BEETHOVEN, *Prometheus—Overture*

Ex. 322: Though this can be done in free style (p. 304), practise with the syncopation beat, a vigorous staccato.

Allegro energico, (♩. = 72)   SMETANA, *The Bartered Bride*

Additional examples for the study of syncopations:

Without accents:

Beethoven: Symphony No. 4, 1st movement—*Allegro vivace* (also with accents).

Debussy: *Nuages*, 5 bars from the end; also strings pizzicato in the next bar.

Mascagni: *Cavalleria Rusticana*, Arrival of Alfio (*Allegretto* 2/4).

Mozart: *Die Zauberflöte*, 2nd act, No. 17—Aria, 3 bars from the end.

Shostakovitch: *The Golden Age*, 4th movement at No. 62.

With accents:

Brahms: Symphony No. 2, 4th movement at F.

Gershwin: *Rhapsody in Blue.*

Prokofieff: *Classical Symphony*, 1st movement at No. 17.

Puccini: *Tosca*, 1st act, bar 4.

Weber: Overture to *Der Freischütz*, passage starting at bar 53.

ACCENTS ON OFF-BEATS

Accents on off-beats are indicated in the same way as syncopated notes with accents, i.e., by a sharp staccato on the preceding beat.

Exx. 187b and 304b: These exercises, directed in 2-beat, are very instructive for accents both on and off the beat. Remember that the rests not used for preparation are neutral. In Ex. 187b, the short *f* chords on the off-beats are treated as though they were accented. Use a neutral beat for *Two* in bars 1 and 2, and for *One* in bars 4 and 5.

Ex. 305b: In music directed in 1-beat with the accent on an off-count, use a sharper staccato with a larger and very quick rebound.

Exx. 197 and 323: While the indication of the accented off-beats in Ex. 197 offers no problems, the staccato chords in Ex. 323 require much concentration on the part of the conductor. The beat should be primarily concerned with the chords and not the string passage. In the 1st bar, *One* is *f* staccato, *Two*, light-staccato, and *Three* is the preparation for *Four*. In the 2nd bar, *One* is a sharp down-beat for the off-beat chord, *Two* again is light-staccato, and so on. Use rather small gestures.

Ex. 324: The *f* chords that end the phrases are treated like syncopations with accents.

Exx. 325 and 326: For the beats that are followed by accents, use a clear staccato with a quick rebound on *Two*.

Permission granted by Durand & Cie, Paris, and
Elkan-Vogel Co., Inc., Philadelphia, Pa.
Copyright owners

Exx. 122 (bar 3) and 123 (bars 6 and 7): The same for 1-beat.

Ex. 180 (bar 2): Accented off-beat in a subdivided pattern.

Ex. 327: The off-beat accent is combined with sustained notes, but the technique remains the same. This is also true for the syncopated entry on *One* in the 2nd measure.

Ex. 327

Allegro ma non troppo, ♩ = 66   BARBER, *Symphony No. 1*

Copyright, 1943, by G. Schirmer, Inc.

Ex. 328: The serenade from the 2nd act of *Die Meistersinger* is difficult to conduct, because of the continually changing fermatas (with and without repeated beat) and accents (both on and off the beat). Repeat the beat on the fermata in the 1st and 3rd bars, but not in the 2nd bar in which *Three* (preparatory!) follows the hold directly. The accents in the 2nd bar are on the beat, those in the 1st and 3rd bars are after *Three* and *Four* respectively.

Ex. 328

Moderato, ♩ = 76   WAGNER, *Die Meistersinger*

Additional examples for the study of accented off-beats:

Barber: Symphony No. 1, 2nd and 3rd bars after No. 50.
Beethoven: Symphony No. 4, 3rd movement.
Beethoven: Symphony No. 6, 4th movement.
Brahms: *Variations on a Theme by Haydn*, Variation No. 5.
Brahms: Violin Concerto, 3rd movement.
Mozart: Overture to *Die Zauberflöte, Allegro.*
Schuman, William: Symphony for Strings, 3rd movement—passage starting at bar 58.
Tchaikovsky: *Romeo and Juliet* (Overture-Fantasia), 3 bars from the end.
Wagner: Overture to *Tannhäuser, Allegro.*

Fp

Fp is executed in much the same manner as an accent. It requires a staccato beat, and the left hand is used often to secure a unified and sudden drop in the dynamics. This warning gesture (palm facing the players) comes almost together with the *fp* beat.

Exx. 42, 210, 220, and 239: *fp* on sustained chords. In anticipation of the *p*, the bounce of the baton is reduced to a minimum. The left hand should be used in Exx. 42 and 239.

Ex. 329: *fp* in strings, tremolo, requires a very definite and unhesitating preparation. You get the best results with a clear sweep of the *point* of the baton. In the 1st measure, the beats on *One* and *Two* indicate both the tutti chords and the tympani *ffz* on the off-beats; *Three* is non-espressivo, giving the tympani enough time to fade away; *Four* is the precise preparation for the sharp down-beat (not too large) indicating the *fpp*.

Ex. 330: Control of the *fp* is especially important for the operatic conductor, because of the frequent occurrence of a soft accompaniment immediately after a sharply attacked chord.

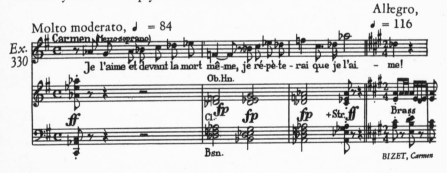

Exx. 331 and 332: The same technique is used for a change from *f* to *p* within one beat. Since the baton cannot indicate both *f* and *p* with one gesture, the left hand is needed.

It sometimes happens that there is a change from *p* to *f* within a single beat. This is not, strictly speaking, an accent, but it is convenient to discuss in this chapter the technique for directing such a change. The gesture used must bring out the element of surprise inherent in the music. Hence, in contrast to an accent, no preparation should be felt on the preceding beat. The effect is achieved by suddenly enlarging the beat on which the *f* enters.

Ex. 333: Start to beat the 4th measure as though the *p* would continue uninterrupted, but extend the down-beat sharply with the baton tipped downward. Use the left hand for the *p* subito in bar 5.

Ex. 334: The 2nd beat in bars 3 and 7 is larger, but the 1st beat must not give away the change prematurely. Left hand in the 5th measure.

Additional examples for the study of *fp*:

Barber: *Essay for Orchestra*, 4th bar after No. 19.
Beethoven: Symphony No. 1, 3rd movement.
Beethoven: Symphony No. 2, 1st movement—Introduction.
Franck: Symphony in D minor, 3rd movement—bar 5; also bar 53.
Prokofieff: *Classical Symphony*, 1st movement—1 bar before No. 9.
Rossini: Overture to *Guillaume Tell*, *Allegro vivace* 2/4.
Smetana: *The Moldau*, bar 126.
Wagner: *Lohengrin*, 1st act—1st scene.

Chapter 21

PHRASING

To indicate phrasing, several different techniques are used. They will be explained in connection with the examples. Although the methods of phrasing differ, they have this in common: there is a decreased intensity at the end of a phrase, and by contrast a fresh motion at the beginning of a new one. A slight break results but with no delay in the rhythm, which remains steady. Thus the players shorten slightly the last note before the break.

Ex. 335: In the 1st bar, beat tenuto (the "dry" tenuto) on *Two*, not leaving it until just before *Three*, so that the 3rd beat is somewhat hurried. In the 2nd measure, go only half-way to the right for *Three*, and immediately start *Four* with an espressivo gesture. In the 3rd bar, beat tenuto on *Three* in the manner described in Ex. 227. Refer to Diagram 58a for details of the gestures.

The following six examples show different phrase endings after the 1st beat; the method of directing them varies. Notice the difference between the techniques used here and those used for interruptions (p. 198). In the latter case the rhythmic structure of certain bars had to be altered; in phrasing, however, the rhythmic continuity is not affected.

[216]

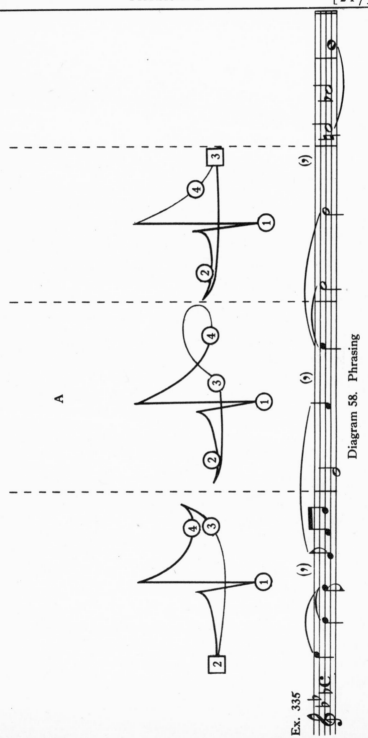

Ex. 335

Diagram 58. Phrasing

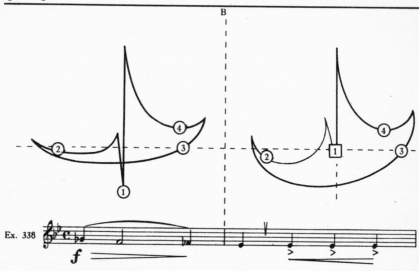

Ex. 338

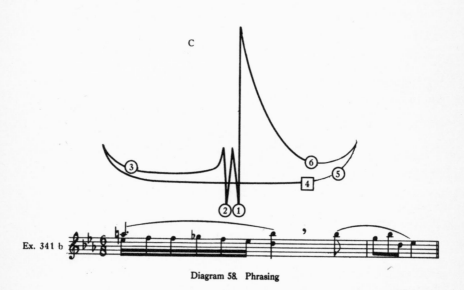

Ex. 341 b

Diagram 58. Phrasing

Ex. 336: Beat *One* in bar 4 with a vigorous staccato and a large rebound, just as if the piece started on *Two*.

Ex. 337: The 1st beat in bar 5 is given with a fairly large legato rebound which provides breathing space and introduces the new phrase on *Two*.

By permission of the copyright owners,
Associated Music Publishers, Inc., New York, N. Y.

Ex. 338: In the 3rd measure, the composer indicates the phrasing. Beat tenuto on *One*, then swiftly prepare the accented *Two* (Diagram 58b).

Ex. 339: The 2nd beat in bar 3 is very small. Continue the 1st beat in the next bar below the left-right line with an espressivo gesture, thus gaining an animated start for the new phrase. Use the same technique for the next phrase, which begins after a rest.

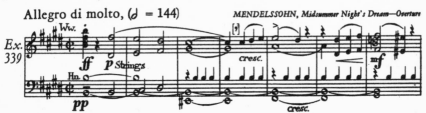

Ex. 97: Stop on *One* in the 4th measure, and prepare a new start on *Two* with a very soft and gentle gesture.

Ex. 266: In bar 5 there is a break because of the rest, and a calm legato beat would be sufficient. If a pronounced break is desired, beat tenuto on *One*.

Ex. 340: The phrasing in the 2nd measure is marked by the composer. Lead the horns by interrupting the legato line with a tenuto beat on *Three* (Diagram 58a, bar 3).

Lento, (♩ =60)   CARPENTER, *Sea Drift*

. Copyright, 1934, by G. Schirmer, Inc.

Ex. 139: Beat tenuto on *Three* in the 2nd measure and resume the staccato on *Four*. A straight gesture is used to reach ③ . After the staccato beats in bars 1 and 2, the holding quality of the tenuto brings out the structure of the musical phrase.

Ex. 341a: For the 2nd measure, apply a technique similar to that used in Ex. 335, bar 2.

Ex. 341b: Beat tenuto on *Four*, prepare with *Five* (Diagram 58c).

Andante con moto, (♪ = 96)   SCHUBERT, *Symphony No. 5*

There are other cases of phrasing in which the object is not to build the melody, but to achieve clear separation between successive chords or to secure a sharp release after a sustained note. These are illustrated in the remaining examples of this section.

Ex. 342: In the 2nd and 3rd bars, beat tenuto on *One* and *Three*, using *Two* and *Four* for preparation (staccato).

By permission of G. Ricordi & Co., Milan

Ex. 236: In this typical symphonic ending, a separation must be made before the last chord is attacked. Stop on *One* in bar 2 and use a delayed *Two* to prepare the final chord.

Ex. 265 (bars 6 and 7): To separate the chords, beat *One* with a gentle staccato beat, followed immediately by a small preparatory gesture which leads into the next chord.

Ex. 343: A rhythmic figure following a sustained note gains clarity if an energetic beat is used to cut the long note. Thus, *Three* in bars 1 and 2 of Ex. 343a is a sharp staccato. The same thing occurs in the 2nd measure of Ex. 343b; both *Two* (accent) and *Three* (cut) are given sharply.

Ex. 344: While *Three* in the 1st bar is neutral, *Three* in the next bar is preparation, as is *Two* in bar 3. Cut the phrase with a sharp down-beat in bar 4.

Ex. 345: A sharp beat on *Four* in the 3rd bar.

WAGNER, *Die Meistersinger—Prelude*

Ex. 310: A sharp staccato beat on *Three* in bar 2 secures a unified ending of the trill in the wood-winds and trumpets, and indicates a slight pause.

Exx. 126 (bar 13) and 215 (bar 6): The same technique in 1-beat.

Additional examples for the study of phrasing:

Brahms: Symphony No. 3, 3rd movement at I.
Gluck: Overture to *Iphigénie en Aulide*, bar 20.
Liszt: *Hungarian Rhapsody No. 2, Andante mesto*.
Prokofieff: *Classical Symphony*, 2nd movement.
Tchaikovsky: Symphony No. 5, 1st movement—Introduction.
Wagner: *Siegfried Idyll*.

SUSTAINED NOTES

After a sustained note has been attacked, the remaining counts are very often treated as though they were rests. To beat during soft held notes with anything more than a small neutral beat is meaningless. In *f*, sustained notes are held most effectively with the left hand.

Exx. 131 (bars 5 and 7) and 233 (bar 3): *Two* and *Three* are neutral, while *Four* is preparation. In each of these the left hand maintains the dynamic intensity.

Ex. 346: This music is a combination of sustained notes and accents, and its adequate direction requires a well-controlled baton technique. The left hand maintains the intensity, while the function of the baton is limited to a sharp indication of the accents on and off the beats; neutral beats are used for the unaccented counts. Use 4 strokes (subdivision) for the accents in bar 14.

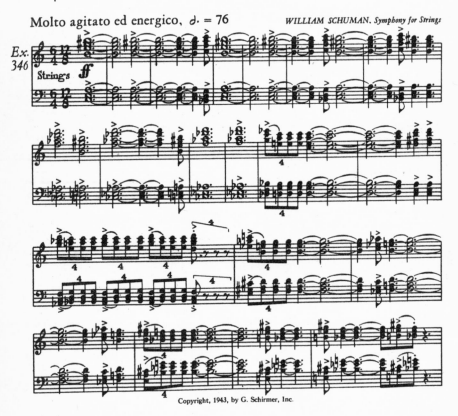

Molto agitato ed energico, ♩. = 76   WILLIAM SCHUMAN. *Symphony for Strings*

Copyright, 1943, by G. Schirmer, Inc.

Crescendo and diminuendo on a sustained note are not usually directed in the same way as in a melodic line. The change is expressed chiefly by the left hand, while the intensity of the beat increases or decreases. In other words, the size of the beat is not as important as the change in tension revealed by the general attitude of the conductor.

Ex. 347: If the forearm has sufficient tension and the facial expression is convincing, you can indicate the crescendo with small baton gestures even without using the left hand.

Ex. 347

Ex. 259: The diminuendos may be expressed with the left hand while the baton, on the 2nd and 3rd counts, simply marks time and stops on the fermata. Subdivide *Four* in each of the first 3 bars and use the last eighth for preparation in order to avoid interfering with the diminuendo.

Ex. 348: Diminuendo with the left hand, fairly small beats with the baton. After the eighth-note preparation (staccato) for bar 1, you need not subdivide on *One* and *Two*. Subdivide *Three* to bring the strings in because, in this slow tempo, a quarter-beat would not indicate the attack clearly. Continue subdividing so as to lead the descending octaves securely.

Ex. 348

Ex. 349: Staccato eighth-note preparation and staccato down-beat (*fp!*). The following 2 eighth-beats are neutral, the next leads into the new chord. This beat, the 4th eighth, also prepares a unified pizzicato attack. Hence, it is somewhat larger than the neutral eighth-beats and is very precise. The left hand, which had been raised in the *fp*, helps to lead the change of harmony and the pizzicato. The 6th eighth is used for an unobtrusive cut-off (winds). It is not necessary to beat on the 7th eighth, but keep in time so that the preparation on the last eighth is strictly in tempo. The 2nd bar is done like the 1st, except that the preparatory last eighth indicates *p* and legato (the tempo is well established and the pizzicato will work without staccato beat). Because of the crescendo in the 3rd measure, the beats are no longer neutral. You may use tenuto on the 5th and 7th eighths to build the crescendo. In bar 4, the left hand sustains the 1st violins, the right cuts off the rest of the orchestra by clicking on the 3rd eighth. On the 4th eighth the baton picks up the legato, while the palm of the left hand turns quickly toward the violins, indicating the sudden *p*.

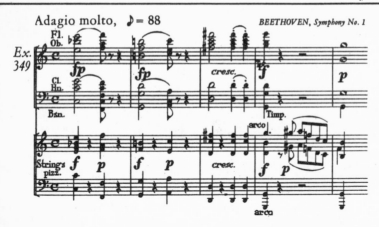

Ex. 350: Cut off the violins, 'cellos, and basses on the 2nd eighth in bar 3, then count to yourself, but do not beat until the last eighth, which prepares the tutti chord. Beating out this measure would weaken the tension among the players. The brilliance and dramatic tension of the sudden *ff* are increased by beating the preparation a trifle late rather than strictly in tempo. Do not forget that the bounce after the down-beat carries the baton into the position of attention for the violin attack (Allegro).

Additional examples for the study of sustained notes:

Beethoven: Symphony No. 3, 2nd movement—bars 158 and 159.
Beethoven: Symphony No. 5, 2nd movement—bar 149.
Brahms: Symphony No. 4, 3rd movement at I.
Gounod: *Faust*, 1st act—Introduction.
Sibelius: *Finlandia, Andante sostenuto.*
Wagner: Prelude to *Lohengrin*, passage starting at the entrance of the trumpets.
Wagner: *Die Götterdämmerung*, 1st act—Prelude.

MELODY BUILDING

The manner of interpreting a melody is one of the most individual characteristics of a musician. Just as a melody played by different soloists may produce varying impressions, so a melody played by an orchestra under different conductors may not affect the listener in the same way. In the case of the orchestra, the gestures by which the conductor conveys his intentions to the players are at least as important as verbal explanations during rehearsal. In fact, a competent conductor, at the first rehearsal with an unfamiliar orchestra, can lead a melody according to his intentions by means of his gestures alone.

In short, the shaping of a melodic line is achieved by means of a purposeful combination of the basic techniques that have been discussed. The use of legato, staccato, and tenuto beat for indicating articulation has been taken up previously. It has been shown that changes in the size of the beat affect not only the dynamics but also the phrasing. In addition, subtle variations in the size of the beat, even from count to count, can express the inflections in the melody that are not indicated by interpretation marks but are "behind the notes". The value of variations in the intensity of the beat, from very intense to completely neutral, has also been treated.

Only by a vital and natural combination of all these elements can the conductor's beat present his conception of the melody to the players. The manner of doing this cannot be put into any formula; the natural feeling for the melody must be developed in each individual. Your feeling for the music will be reflected in the size, intensity, and shape of your beat.

Now that you have all these techniques at your disposal, it will be helpful to review some of the melodic passages among the examples. You will find that you now have more flexibility and freedom in conveying your intentions.

Ex. 27: Beating this music espressivo with the same size and intensity on all counts would not get much personal reaction from the players. Personal reaction means that each player, in this case in the string section, has the same feeling of initiative he would have in a solo performance. To inspire the musicians, the beat needs variety of size and intensity, corresponding to the musical expression. The student should try several ways of expressing the melodic contour, to find which of them best suits his own musical personality. One way is suggested, but it is not the only possible way, nor the "right" one.

Use a large beat with clicking in the 1st measure, decreasing size and intensity in the 2nd, but with a large and expressive preparatory gesture on *Four*. Clicking is not needed in the 3rd bar. A smaller beat on *Four* in this bar and more relaxed beats on *One* and *Two* in bar 4 make for a good contrast before the crescendo, which is rendered more effective by the sudden increase in intensity. The first 2 beats in bar 5 are large, *Three* is very incisive. The 2nd beat in bar 6 is small, the 3rd an expressive preparation. In the 8th bar, the beat becomes smaller and more relaxed.

Ex. 260: It is impossible to express the whimsical charm of the music by academic time-beating. Every aspect of the conductor's appearance is important—the way he stands, his facial expression, and the variety in his beat. Here again, every player must be inspired to feel like a soloist and to put himself completely into the music. One way of using contrasting beats to bring out the life of the whole passage follows.

Remain motionless after the cut-off of the first fermata. With the small staccato preparation (*Three* in bar 1), relax your manner and facial expression. In bars 2-4, use a legato downbeat and a small "dry" tenuto on *Two* for cut-off; then staccato on *Three* and *Four*, the preparation becoming a little more animated each time. The down-beat in the 5th bar is hardly noticeable because of the sudden appearance of the left hand (*p* subito), which remains lifted during the rests and is used for the cut-off on the second fermata. The right hand gives a delicate staccato beat on *Three* (bar 5), changing into legato on *Four*.

In 1-beat, the continued up-and-down motion of the baton may easily become monotonous, which would have a fatal effect on a melodic passage. This may be avoided in two ways—either by using a graceful curved motion of the baton rather than a straight up-and-down motion, or by changing the size of the beat. A good passage on which to try these methods is the second theme of the first movement of Beethoven's Fifth Symphony.

Ex. 351: Direct the first 4 bars with small forceful gestures, indicating the secco character of the 5th and 7th bars with an incisive downward gesture of both arms (bar 6 is preparatory). The gesture in bar 8, to lead the entry of the French horns, should have an up-beat character. The three *sf* notes are marcato. Immediately after the third, the gesture changes to prepare the entry of the *p* legato melody. The rise and fall of the melody is brought out by the size of the beat; in the unstressed measures the beat is very small. An alternative method is to use small gestures throughout and lead the melody with the left hand. If the 'cellos and basses tend to enter late in bars 14 and 18, let the beat in these bars have a slight staccato quality.

Chapter 22

DIFFERENT USES FOR BASIC PATTERNS

THE TREATMENT OF THE SIX basic patterns has so far had for its object the mastery of each of the individual patterns. Consequently, in most of the examples the beat has followed the notation, so that when legato was marked a legato beat was used, and similarly for staccato. There have been a few exceptions. In actual conducting, however, it is often necessary to use a beat which does not conform to the notation. While there can be no specific formula for the application of the patterns, the following discussion will cover the most frequent cases.

NON-ESPRESSIVO

As explained previously, this beat is used for soft and emotionally neutral passages. It is also used to mark time when nothing rhythmical occurs (sustained notes) and to indicate rests. It is very useful in accompaniment to keep the orchestra subdued. While primarily used for legato, the non-espressivo may also be applied to detached passages, as shown in the following example.

Ex. 352: In bar 3ff., a staccato beat would lead the players to overemphasize the detached quality of the notes, and a tenuto would impress them as stiff and academic; non-espressivo lets the music flow in a simple and natural way.

Allegretto, ♩ = 76   BEETHOVEN, Symphony No. 7

Ex. 352

Thus, when the conductor does not want the orchestra to play a very detached staccato, he may use non-espressivo instead of staccato. This principle can be applied to the beginning of Exx. 16 and 166. Here, and in the following discussion of choice of beat, the pattern chosen should often depend upon the way the orchestra responds to your gesture. The beat may assume a corrective function. If the orchestra's playing is too detached, the non-espressivo will tell the players to decrease the sharpness of the staccato; if the music is not played sharply enough, the staccato beat will bring out the desired articulation.

ESPRESSIVO-LEGATO

This beat has such a definite character that it is applied only when the music is both legato and espressivo.

LIGHT- AND FULL-STACCATO

The appearance of single staccato beats in legato passages has already been discussed; they are used for phrasing, for accents, and as preliminary beats to strengthen a start in *f*. To attack a sustained note in *f*, a full-staccato preparation is always used.

Slurs do not necessarily mean legato. Often, as in the following example, they refer only to the execution.

Ex. 353: In bar 3ff., use light-staccato.

There are many legato passages in fast tempo where the rhythmic element is predominant and a legato beat would be artificial and would not carry the rhythm strongly and clearly enough.

Exx. 148, 354, and 355: Full-staccato is used despite the phrase markings. Try to beat legato and you will see how inadequate it is.

A staccato beat may be used in passages where no staccato is marked but where you wish to concentrate the players' attention on the rhythm.

Ex. 356: Light-staccato beats starting on *Two* in the 2nd measure help to emphasize the rhythm and assure unified playing by the strings on *Four*. Be sure not to slow down in your anxiety to stress the rhythm—a typical mistake which upsets the orchestra more than it helps.

The use of a *gentle staccato*, between non-espressivo and staccato, has already been suggested several times. This beat uses a quick motion before the counts, but there is no stop. Apply it where the detached quality is not felt very strongly but where legato would be inappropriate.

Ex. 357: Gentle staccato is applied to this music because of the rather slow tempo. Staccato with full stop on the count would be too jerky and the legato beat would not express the rhythmic vitality.

MARCATO

The aggressive character of this pattern makes it applicable only to strong and forceful music. Sometimes a marcato beat may be used in espressivo-legato on *One*, or on *Four* and *One*, to emphasize the rhythm strongly, but this procedure causes monotony if repeated too often.

TENUTO

The use of the expressive form of the tenuto beat has already been discussed. The "dry" form used on single counts for purposes of phrasing has also been treated. When employed for whole bars, the "dry" form (Diagrams 49 and 51) indicates the rhythm in an academic manner. Use it chiefly as a corrective measure to maintain the ensemble, or when for other reasons the rhythm must be stressed in a completely neutral way. It is helpful in accompaniment, to point out the counts clearly and avoid misunderstanding. In the first few bars of Ex. 131, this beat prevents the brasses from dragging; be sure to keep strictly in time, and do not delay the beat by waiting for the sixteenth-notes.

Strangely enough, the "dry" tenuto beat is sometimes taught as the standard pattern. The lifeless nature of this beat, however, prevents adequate musical expression and results in mere time-beating. This undesirable effect does not occur in rapid tempo, especially in 2-beat; here the "dry" tenuto is convenient as a substitute for legato. In this case, the legato rebound on *One* would make the quick gestures confusing. In the first bars of Ex. 270 the "dry" tenuto beat, done by the wrist alone, is easily seen to be the most convenient gesture.

LEGATO AND STACCATO SIMULTANEOUSLY

When legato and staccato are played simultaneously by the orchestra, the beat usually has the character of the leading melody.

Ex. 358: Beat legato; the moderate staccato needs no special attention.

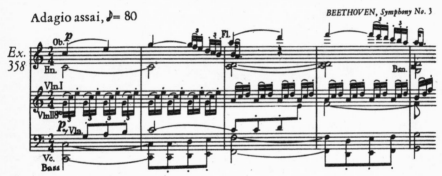

Ex. 359: The staccato beat changes to legato with the entrance of the main theme in viola and bassoon. You may use an occasional gentle staccato beat to express both melody and counterpoint.

Ex. 360: The wood-wind passage in bar 3ff. would be conducted legato if it stood alone. The staccato beat is used, however, for two reasons: the brisk viola figure requires more attention, and the winds would naturally play legato. Furthermore, the staccato beat insures a good attack on the triplet figures in the violins and bass instruments.

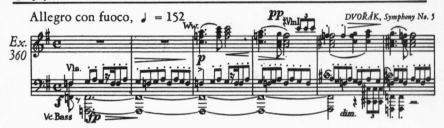

There are passages where several important but different melodies occur and to which the same pattern cannot be applied for any length of time. Sometimes the gentle staccato is useful as a compromise beat. Often it is necessary to change quickly from one pattern to another to get the best results.

Ex. 361: Use a gentle staccato motion.

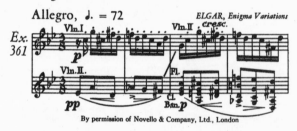

By permission of Novello & Company, Ltd., London

Ex. 362: Beat non-espressivo, changing to poco espressivo in the 2nd measure. Return to neutral beats in bar 3; in the next bar, add some staccato quality to the beat, for the release of the sustained brass chord and to lead the detached notes. Then change back to non-espressivo.

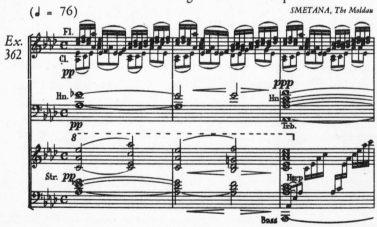

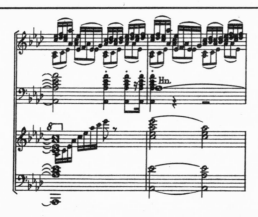

Additional examples for the study of passages in which legato and staccato are played simultaneously:

Berlioz: Overture *Le Carnaval Romain*, passage starting at the 35th bar of the *Andante sostenuto* 3/4.

Haydn: Symphony No. 101, 2nd movement.

Mendelssohn: Symphony No. 4 (*Italian*), 2nd movement.

Tchaikovsky: Symphony No. 5, 4th movement—bar 414.

Verdi: *Otello*, 3rd act, beginning.

Wagner: Prelude to *Die Meistersinger*, 38 bars before *Sehr gewichtig*.

SIMULTANEOUS DIFFERENT DYNAMICS

An orchestral score often has different dynamic markings occurring simultaneously. The tympani or brass may enter softly while the rest of the orchestra is playing a loud passage, or a solo instrument may play *f* while the rest of the orchestra plays *p*. In most cases the baton directs the larger group of instruments and the left hand takes care of the others if needed. Thus, the left hand may give the warning *p* gesture while the right has a large espressivo beat, or a non-espressivo with the baton may be combined with a stimulating gesture of the left hand.

Ex. 363: The right hand beats *fp* in bar 3, as it did in bar 1. The left hand sustains the *f* in the violins in the 3rd measure and indicates their sudden *p*.

When crescendo and diminuendo occur at the same time, both hands are needed. The baton again is concerned with the larger group and the left hand leads the others.

Ex. 364a: The left hand cues in the *p* entrance of 1st violins and 'cellos, while the baton indicates *f*. In the second half of the measure the size of the beats decreases. The left hand takes over the diminuendo of the wood-winds in bar 3, while the right directs the crescendo in the other instruments.

Ex. 364b: The left hand leads the instruments on the top staff and the baton leads the others.

Additional examples for the study of passages with simultaneous different dynamics:

Barber: *Second Essay for Orchestra*, passage starting 2 bars before No. 11.
Berlioz: *Symphonie Fantastique*, 4th movement—39 bars from the end.
Brahms: Symphony No. 2, 4th movement—12 bars after C (109th bar of the movement).
Dvořák: Symphony No. 5 (*From the New World*), 1st movement—passage starting at No. 9.
Mendelssohn: *Fingal's Cave Overture*—several passages.
Sibelius: Symphony No. 2, 2nd movement—several passages.

PROBLEMS OF ORCHESTRATION

Generally speaking, the nature of the instrumental groups is such that the winds need an especially clear and precise beat while the strings call for a warmer gesture. The combination of both requires an intelligent mean, the nature of which is an essential part of the relationship between the conductor and his players. This will be discussed in greater detail in Chapter 24.

Similarly, the extent to which the conductor should indicate articulation and dynamics is closely connected with the response of the different instruments and groups. Certain results are obtained rather easily from the strings but you must work harder to get them from the winds, and vice versa. A crescendo in the wood-winds requires a larger gesture than in the brass. It is an erroneous notion that the massive effects of the brass need a huge gesture. On the contrary, a small and very definite beat controls the brass instruments most effectively and prevents them from dragging.

How to beat pizzicato depends entirely on the musical context. Lack of unity in pizzicato is a very common mistake, but the young conductor must not assume that he is always to blame. Even a correct beat does not secure a unified attack if the players are not attentive. Generally, string players tend to anticipate pizzicato entrances, and the conductor must be especially careful when such an entrance occurs in combination with other instruments. The preparatory gesture must be distinct and incisive.

When pizzicato occurs alone, it is directed like staccato.

Ex. 365: The last chord requires a sharp full-staccato, but not too large.

Exx. 142, 198, and 366: The soft pizzicato needs a small staccato beat and may be assisted by the left hand. The left-hand gesture uses the preceding count for preparation and imitates the action of plucking the string. Some conductors use this so effectively that they rely on it alone for the pizzicato.

When some strings play pizzicato while others play arco, or play pizzicato in combination with wind instruments, there are two possibilities. If the rhythm is established and steady, a special gesture would disturb the players rather than help them. But when the rhythmic pulsation is not continuous, and often after rests, a staccato preparation helps secure a unified attack.

Exx. 62, 163a, and 367: Beat legato, with no special gesture for the pizzicato.

Ex. 190: In bars 17 and 19 the same instrumental combination is used, but the strings play arco the first time, and pizzicato the second. Consequently the preparation for the second chord has staccato quality.

Additional examples for the study of passages in which pizzicato occurs alone or in combination with various instruments:

Beethoven: Symphony No. 4, 1st movement—Introduction.
Beethoven: Overture to *Coriolanus*, last few bars.
Franck: Symphony in D minor, 2nd movement.
Haydn: *The Seasons*, No. 18—Recitative.
Mendelssohn: Symphony No. 3 (*Scotch*), 3rd movement.
Prokofieff: *Peter and the Wolf*, several passages.
Schuman, William: Symphony for Strings—3rd movement.
Strauss, Johann: *Pizzicato Polka*.
Tchaikovsky: Symphony No. 4, 3rd movement.
Tchaikovsky: Piano Concerto No. 1, 2nd movement.

Chapter 23

ACHIEVING COMPLETE PHYSICAL CONTROL

GENERAL APPEARANCE

COMPLETE CONTROL OF PHYSICAL GESTURES and movements, necessary to everyone who appears on a public platform, is especially important for the artist, because his poise and ease of movement not only impress the public, but—and this is far more significant—also affect his own performance. The conductor needs freedom of motion more than any musician, because his work consists of communicating musical expression directly by gestures. It is not necessary, of course, for a conductor to be trained as rigorously as a dancer. Still, he must find the happy medium between tension and relaxation; he will show this in the way he mounts the podium and faces the players—and indeed in every gesture he makes.

Authority over the players, knowing what you want musically, and confidence in your technique enable you to overcome gradually personal idiosyncrasies such as stamping the feet, wandering about the podium, moving the body unnecessarily, and making grimaces. The two extremes to be avoided are shyness and exhibitionism. Every gesture the conductor makes should say something to the players. The genuinely inspired musical leader concentrates upon meeting the demands of the music and of the orchestra; he has no time or energy for superficial gestures having only audience appeal. Nevertheless, there must be a harmonious continuity of gesture, each movement blending with the next, resulting in an appearance of smoothness and security.

The conductor must not be carried away by his emotions. Despite the intensity and passion of his feeling for the music, some part of his mind must act as a control mechanism and prevent him from losing himself in the music to the extent that his ears no longer bring him an objective perception of what the musicians are doing. In this way the conductor is able to think ahead and is alert for any emergency, and the players feel that they can rely on him in any situation.

FIELD OF BEATING

It is important to remember that the field of beating is described by the *point of the baton*, and it is here that the attention of the orchestra must be focused. This object cannot be achieved if the center of motion is the hand, with the baton carried along as a life-less appendage. With the point of the baton as the center of motion, it is easy to co-ordinate the playing of groups seated relatively far apart. Then the conductor does not feel the necessity of "going to the orchestra with his gestures", but rather draws the players toward himself, strengthening his feeling of security and authority.

The center of the field of beating in the standard form (as used for the diagrams) is directly in front of the conductor, about midway between the shoulder and the waist levels. Therefore it is important that the conductor's desk, just high enough for the score to be read easily, should not interfere with the beat. Sometimes it may help to have the desk slightly to the conductor's left, in order to allow for greater freedom of motion of the right arm.

Moving the field of beating slightly up or down may bring variety into the beat, but the student is cautioned against the continual use of an abnormally high or low field. Moving the center of the field sidewise, either by carrying the arm over or by turning the body, should be done only when it accomplishes a definite purpose, such as addressing one particular group very strongly. The players on the opposite side of the orchestra must never be allowed to lose sight of the baton. Too frequent change of the field of beating disrupts the continuity of gesture and confuses the players. This is also true for moving the field toward or away from the body.

Much has been said in previous chapters about the relation of the size of the beat to the dynamics. It has also been pointed out that the intensity of the gesture is at least as important as the size. For this reason, loud music does not always require a large beat, and a conductor can use small but intense motions most effectively. Several prominent conductors, in fact, have achieved magnificent results by keeping their field of beating always quite limited in size. But this technique must only be used by a particular type of personality, otherwise it lacks expression and tension.

There are situations in which, for reasons other than dynamics, the size of the field must not be too large. In fast tempo, large gestures are easily blurred and lose their effectiveness. In leading a small group, the gestures can be smaller than those used in leading a large group. Also, an operatic conductor, directing in a darkened orchestra pit, must be certain that his gestures are within the small lighted area of his desk.

USE OF THE EYES

The eyes are an invaluable means of establishing personal contact between the conductor and the players. Therefore they should be used as much as possible, and a minimum amount of time should be spent in looking at the score. If you cannot entirely memorize the music, you must still be able to keep your attention on the orchestra most of the time, referring to the score only at intervals of several bars. This ability can be built up by training. Learn to see a number of bars at once, so that by glancing down at the score you know what is coming. Of course, you must know the score so well that you will have no fear of losing the place while you are looking away. Without this knowledge you are apt to turn your eyes toward the players too late, with a resulting feeling of discomfort. Not only the preparatory gesture but the way you look at a player should tell him in advance what kind of expression you expect. However, you must exert discretion in using your eyes when there is a tricky solo passage—your staring at the player might make him nervous.

INDEPENDENCE AND USE OF THE LEFT HAND

That the left arm must be independent of the right is generally taken for granted. The conductor must be able to beat steadily with the right arm and feel no muscular tension in the left. The achievement of this independence, however, is a problem for the student, who will often automatically make some kind of rhythmic movement in sympathy with the right arm.

There are many exercises that are useful for training the arms to perform different gestures simultaneously. Some of the best follow.

Describe a circle with one arm while moving the other up and down. Practice first with the forearm, then with the entire arm. Alternate arms suddenly.

Beat time steadily with the right hand while the left independently makes typical conductor's gestures, such as indications for dynamics, accents, warnings, etc. Use various rhythms in the right hand and be sure to include 12 beats in a measure.

Practise beating different rhythms in both hands. Start by tapping the edge of a table, since hearing the rhythm makes it easier to co-ordinate. Tap 3 against 2, and 3 against 4. It helps to think of the fractional values within the bar:

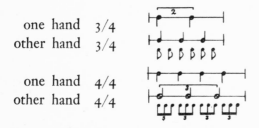

one hand   3/4
other hand   3/4

one hand   4/4
other hand   4/4

It is a good rule to avoid doubling the baton gestures with the left arm, because it is a waste motion. Nevertheless, even the best conductors do it occasionally, but only at moments of great climax. To double continually is a sign of lack of control.

In general the function of the left hand is to indicate details of interpretation, while the baton focuses attention on the rhythm. The ability of the left hand to express the most subtle nuances as well as the most dramatic accents is one of the characteristics of fine conducting. When and how to use the left hand are matters of individual taste, but it should always tell the orchestra something essential. If the conductor uses the left hand continually, the players will ignore it.

In earlier chapters the use of the left hand has been discussed in connection with dynamics, articulation, cuing, accents, etc. These gestures may reinforce the indications of the baton, or express details that the baton cannot bring out adequately, or even, in some cases, express the opposite of the baton gestures. The rest of this chapter will deal with some of the typical functions of the left hand.

The left hand is used often to bring out a particular group of instruments (*cf.* the instruments on the top staff in Ex. 364b). When you want to cue in a group without disturbing the general line of the baton, use the left hand. In Ex. 355 it can indicate the entry of the strings in bar 3, or the trumpets and tympani in bar 4. In Ex. 324 use the left hand for emphasizing the off-beat chords in bars 2 and 9. Apply a sharp downward gesture with the fist. This must not interfere with the smooth progress of the baton to the following neutral beat. (Note that in bar 9 the left hand is lifted simultaneously with the down-beat of the baton!)

The left-hand gesture may differ from that of the right in regard to phrasing, dynamics, and articulation. In Ex. 364, for instance, each hand indicates a different degree of dynamics.

Ex. 368: In bars 3 and 4, the baton indicates non-espressivo while the left hand builds the expressive ——————.

Ex. 369: The right hand beats staccato throughout and the left indicates tenuto for the 1st violins in bar 3, and the 'cellos and basses in bar 4.

Another helpful gesture of the left hand is the raised finger for attention, e.g. when an instrument is about to enter after a long rest. Also, a number of fingers may be raised to warn the orchestra that you will change the number of beats in a measure. For instance, if you are beating all the counts in 4-time and at a più mosso want to beat alla breve, raise 2 fingers one bar before the change. This is an emergency gesture, not necessary when the change is marked in the parts or has been sufficiently rehearsed.

When not in use, the left hand should be in a neutral position. It is best to hold it on or near the lapel, whence it can move easily for the various gestures. Occasionally you may keep the hand at the side, though this sometimes looks stiff or gives the conductor an appearance of indifference if used too often. Resting the hand on the desk, on the hip, or in the pocket is not recommended.

Turning a page must not interrupt a left-hand gesture; it is better not to begin a motion than to stop it in the middle. Better still, know the score so well that turning a page can wait a few bars.

Chapter 24

ON PREPARATION IN GENERAL

TECHNIQUES OF STARTING

THE FIRST THING TO DO after reaching the conductor's stand is to make sure that all the players are present. There have been occasions when the conductor was compelled to stop the music after the first few bars because of the absence of one of the musicians. The manner in which you pick up the baton must be authoritative, and fussy gestures should be avoided. A well-disciplined orchestra does not require a noisy tap on the stand to call it to attention. With one motion take the position of attention, which can in itself set the mood, and face the group of instruments that plays first. Do not look at the score before the playing begins! The left hand need not be used for every start. The baton is usually raised to about shoulder level; if it is held too high, the preliminary beat may be awkward.

To secure a good opening attack is a very difficult problem, which is not always solved successfully—even with the best orchestras. While part of this problem has to be worked out in rehearsal, and consequently is not discussed here, a good beat is still necessary for clean execution. The first requirement is that all the players be ready and alert; do not give the preliminary beat until all eyes are on you. It is also indispensable that conductor and players be in agreement on the number of beats in a measure.

In a large majority of cases the regular preliminary beat will secure a unified attack. However, certain instrumental combinations present difficulties that require special consideration. The inexperienced conductor may find it difficult, especially in soft entrances, to bring in wind instruments simultaneously, or winds combined with harp, or high strings. The problem is caused by the purely physical difference in the way each instrument "speaks". For instance, the oboe player

[246]

reacts differently at the attack than the trumpet player, and various other instruments respond differently in very high or very low registers. Despite these differences, a good ensemble must be achieved, or the entrance will be "arpeggiated". This difficulty occurs not only at the beginning but also in the course of a piece, especially after rests.

The solution, of the problem depends to a certain extent upon the understanding between the conductor and his players. As far as the beat is concerned, two extremes are possible—a dry beat or a flexible one. Some German conductors use an anticipatory beat. The played attack does not coincide with the baton movement but follows it by as much as half a second or longer. The conductor uses a rather dry beat (tenuto, or, for *f* attacks, marcato), stops on the opening count and *waits* for the orchestra, then proceeds as usual. Thus the first beat (but not the count!) takes a little longer than the following ones. Some orchestras are accustomed to the use of this technique, either for the entire group or only for certain soft entrances in the winds; the conductor visiting these orchestras will do well to adapt his beat to this well-established habit, for it would take a great deal of training to replace it.

The reason that such an anticipatory beat works is that the players are accustomed to adjusting their attacks so that they follow immediately after the beat. Many conductors, however, adhere to the principle of always beating *with* the orchestra. A flexible and more rounded beat is needed to secure a good ensemble at these difficult attacks. With this beat, you "breathe" with the players and almost "put the notes in their mouths". After the preparation the beat curves down and up with a very plastic gesture, while the attitude and facial expression say to the players: Now—start! Every conductor must find the method that is most effective for him.

Ex. 370: The difficulty here is caused by the oboe, 2nd bassoon, trumpets in the low register, and trombones, all of whom start *ppp* and must be synchronized with the rest of the orchestra. The anticipatory beat may be used here; a small, clear down-beat anticipates the played attack. If the flexible gesture is used, the left hand can help express the inviting quality with a smooth, gentle motion toward the orchestra.

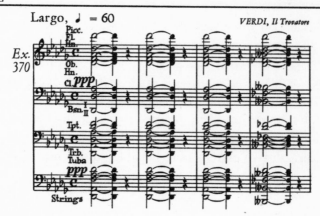

Ex. 8: In a well-trained orchestra, the strings will listen to the solo English horn and adjust their playing in case of a slight delay in the attack. No special beat is needed.

Ex. 164: The difficult wood-wind entrance in the 2nd measure is best handled by the flexible beat.

Ex. 170: Because the rhythm is so strongly felt here, the regular preparation is sufficient to secure a unified attack from the winds in bar 2.

Ex. 352: This is a particularly difficult start. No amount of rehearsal will do the trick, unless the beat is clear and helps the players to concentrate on a unified attack.

ENTRIES

It is not compulsory to indicate every cue; in fact, there are cases where cuing can even be harmful. When the players know the music very well and you give an unnecessary cue with an emphasized gesture, it may be interpreted as an indication to play loudly. In fast tempo, it is often impossible to give many cues within a few bars; do not let your gestures become too involved or confusion will result. Still, the conductor should not spare himself in giving cues, as they constitute one of the chief means by which he maintains contact between himself and his players, giving the latter a feeling of security, and identifying himself with them.

Cues are given for three purposes:

(1) You may simply remind the players to enter after a number of rests. This depends partly on the reliability of the individual players, but certain entrances are so difficult for the musicians that cues must be given in any case. Besides, there are cues which are expected as a matter of habit, and their omission may cause uncertainty.

Ex. 371: There is nothing particularly difficult about the oboe entrance since it occurs after a rest of only 5 bars. The player, however, may be surprised if the cue is not given and may not enter in time.

(2) A cue may be given to insure precision of attack.

Ex. 372: The eye is sufficient for the wood-wind entrance in the 5th bar, and a gesture would be superfluous. However, the strings in the next bar do need some gesture, not because they would get lost after only the 1-bar rest, but to insure a clean and precise attack. A staccato motion on *Two* strengthens the rhythmic feeling of the players; it should be small and delicate. At the same time the left hand takes care of the *p* in the winds.

Ex. 373: A gentle staccato gesture on the 2nd quarter in bar 3 helps the violins to enter precisely—an assistance especially needed here, because the fast passage starts after the count. Most conductors subdivide this count. It should be done unobtrusively, resuming the legato line by the 3rd quarter.

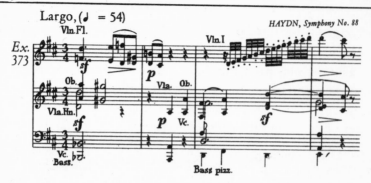

There are certain cases where there is danger of a delayed entrance: for instance, heavy brass entrances in fast tempo. This can be avoided by beating the preceding count slightly ahead of time. Thus, in Ex. 117, *Two* in the next to the last bar is somewhat hurried, and *One* in the last bar is actually an anticipatory beat. While this is a matter of individual preference, a conductor with good control may execute such an entry without using an anticipatory beat, especially with the help of the left hand. There are certain passages in accompaniment, however, which can hardly be done without this type of beat.

Ex. 374: Beat the preparation for the tutti entrance a little ahead of time, to avoid a delayed attack. Just how much in advance to beat depends partly upon the soloist, who sometimes hurries this passage, and partly upon the conductor's experience with the orchestra.

(3) Often the conductor wants to lead an entry in a particular way: loud or soft, expressive or emphatic, lyric or dramatic. His purpose is not just to give a cue, but to convey to the orchestra his detailed intentions concerning the interpretation of the music. This use of the preparatory gesture to lead an attack in which the cuing *per se*

is unimportant is so fundamental that it is treated under a separate heading.

PREPARATION IN ITS BROADER ASPECTS

It is entirely erroneous to think that preparatory gestures are used only to start a piece. On the contrary, they are used continually and constitute one of the most effective tools by means of which the conductor brings life and variety into the performance. In a sense, all conducting is preparation—indicating in advance what is to happen. With the preparatory gestures the conductor not only brings in the instruments with a particular shading and expression, but also emphasizes the salient points of the melody and underlines the phrase groups.

Mere time-beating would never be enough to accomplish musically significant results. If you did not use preliminary gestures in Ex. 179, the players would still play the notes correctly. But to bring out the tenderness of the string entry on *Three* in the 1st measure and the strong, noble staccato chord in the 2nd, preparatory gestures are needed; in fact, they are more important than the beats themselves. The more the conductor can express in these gestures, the more response he will get from the players in the way of shading, articulation, and expression.

Ex. 375: The purpose of a stimulating 2nd beat in bar 2 is not so much cuing as expression; a strong gesture secures a brilliant entry in the violins. Use the same kind of preparation on the 4th beat for the 'cellos and basses. Lead the energetic 'cello passage in the 1st measure with small gestures, so as not to confuse the violas, who are playing *p*.

Often it is necessary to use one or more smaller and less intense beats before the preparation, so that the larger and stronger preparatory gesture may be more effective. If you were to use large beats for the crescendo in Ex. 173, it would be difficult to find a more powerful motion for the preparatory down-beat in the 2nd bar which is needed for a rhythmic *ff* attack of the motive ♪♪♪ . Therefore, indicate the crescendo with the left hand and save the larger baton gestures for this preparation.

Ex. 376: Use forceful beats for the chords and the preparations on *Three*, and very small beats for the violin passages. This treatment is not only helpful technically but also conforms to the structure of the music.

Ex. 377: The beats in the 2nd and 4th bars should be sharp but without too much intensity, so that the down-beat preparation and accented *Two* in the 3rd and 5th bars will be more effective. In the 6th measure, however, *Two* is used to prepare the important entrance in the bass instruments.

FREE PREPARATORY GESTURES

There are exceptions to the rule that the preliminary beat must be strictly in time. Some of these exceptions have been discussed in the chapter on holds and interruptions. There are also other cases in which the rule may be neglected. Often it is not possible to give a strict preparation in an emergency, especially when following a soloist. It may be necessary to cut the preparation short, so that the orchestra will not enter late. A typical example is the beginning of Beethoven's Piano Concerto No. 5. In the first movement, bars 3 and

5, it is quite difficult to achieve perfect co-ordination of the tutti attacks with the end of the piano cadenzas. Only skilfully timed, free preparations will bring about the desired effect. Even in the absence of an emergency it may be more convenient to dispense with a strict preparation, namely, when a correctly timed gesture may be either too long or too short.

Ex. 378: The tempo marking is disregarded in the preparations for the fermatas. The preliminary beats are free and take into consideration the quiet feeling of the opening. The first beat, which is strictly in time, is the preparation for the violin entrance in the 6th measure.

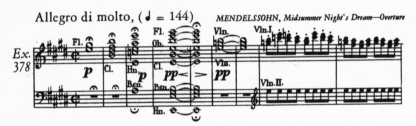

Apart from these exceptions, some conductors prefer to use a freely timed preparatory gesture. This is justified only if the results are satisfactory. The student should first master the strict technique; he will then find it an interesting experiment to try other methods. It is quite possible that very dramatic or very delicate attacks may be executed in an extremely effective way by ignoring the tempo in the preparation.

PREPARATION WITH SUBDIVISION

In slow tempo a full-beat preparation may be too long and it will be necessary to subdivide the count preceding the entry. This will result in a clearer gesture and establish closer contact with the musicians.

Ex. 347: Subdivision on *Four* allows one beat for the cut-off and an eighth-note preparation for the violin entrance in the 3rd bar.

Ex. 379: While quarter-beats are adequate in the 1st bar, a good attack on the *f* in the 2nd requires a vigorous eighth-note preparation, both in the interest of clarity and to express the sudden change in the music. Therefore subdivide on the 3rd count.

Larghetto, (♩ = 50)

Ex. 379

BEETHOVEN, *Violin Concerto*

Ex. 380: The 4th counts in bars 1 and 2 are subdivided by some conductors to obtain a precise sixteenth-note. The same subdivision is indispensable in the 3rd bar, because without the clear indication of *Four-and*, the violins would not feel secure in their triplet.

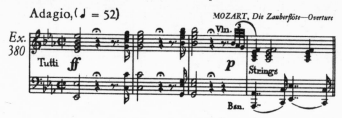

Adagio, (♩ = 52)

Ex. 380

MOZART, *Die Zauberflöte—Overture*

Exx. 141 and 170: Even at the very start of a piece, subdivision may be useful to facilitate the playing of a short anacrusis. Beating *Four-and* at the beginning leaves no doubt about the tempo. For the first eighth-beat use a small sidewise motion; the up-beat on the second eighth is the actual preparation and requires a larger gesture. This type of subdivision is a special case of the use of an extra beat for a start after the count. (*cf.* p. 104).

Study and practise scores Nos. 5 and 6 discussed in the Appendix.

Chapter 25

NUMBER OF BEATS IN A MEASURE (I)

GENERAL CONSIDERATIONS

THE CONDUCTOR CANNOT rely upon the time-signature to tell him how many beats he should use in a measure, because the composer does not always think of this problem when he sets the rhythm. Nowadays, composers are more apt to consider conducting problems when marking their scores, but the indications on many older compositions may be confusing to the conductor who is not familiar with the various traditions. The metronome markings are a more reliable indication, but even these can be misleading. No one would use 1-beat for the Allegro molto (4th movement) of Beethoven's First Symphony, although the metronome reads ♩ = 88 (*cf.* Ex. 260).

In general, you may use

for	12 units in a measure:		12 or 4 beats
"	9	" " " " :	9 or 3 "
"	8	" " " " :	8 or 4 "
"	6	" " " " :	6, 2, or 1 "
"	4	" " " " :	12, 8, 4, 2, or 1 "
"	3	" " " " :	9, 6, 3, or 1 "
"	2	" " " " :	6, 4, 2, or 1 "

There are three factors to be taken into consideration: the tempo of the music, the players' need for rhythmic security, and the degree of intensity you desire on the weak counts or in the smaller rhythmic values. The last is more a question of style and interpretation than of technique.

The speed of the music sets a limit to the number of possible beats in a measure. Thus, in Presto or Allegro molto in 4/4, a 4-beat would often be uncomfortable for the conductor and confusing to the players. The musical pulsation, moreover, is far more likely to demand an alla breve beat than a stroke on every written count. Mendelssohn's *Wedding March* (*cf.* Ex. 134) is marked **C** , but conductors generally lead it in 2. The same is true of the Allegro vivo in Rossini's Overture to *Il Barbiere di Siviglia* (*cf.* Ex. 258). On the same principle Exx. 155 and 156 need 1-beat, although marked 2/4.

On the other hand, many slow movements written in 2/4 or **₵** have to be directed in 4, for otherwise so much time would elapse between beats that the rhythm would no longer be clear. *Cf.* Exx. 16, 25, 37, and 306. In these slow movements there is room for genuine disagreement as to whether the fundamental musical pulse is in 2 or in 4. For the conductor, however, the beat is influenced by practical considerations. The musicians must have a definite sense of the rhythm; if 2-beat were used in the above examples, they would miss the security that they have a right to expect from the beat.

When the conductor feels strongly that the rhythm consists essentially of 2 pulses in a measure, but still has to indicate 4 beats for technical reasons, a subdivided 2-beat (Diagram 42) is the most practical. This is also the best procedure for music to which neither 4-beat nor 2-beat can be applied continuously, but which requires changes in the beat, as in the slow movement of Schubert's Symphony No. 9 (*cf.* Ex. 229) and the Andante of Haydn's Symphony No. 103 (*Drum-roll*). In these movements, the alternating use of the regular and subdivided 2-beat allows the conductor to adjust his gesture to the pulsation of the music. If the transition from one pattern to the other is performed with ease and flexibility, the change, sometimes even from bar to bar, will not upset the clarity of the beat.

Even for the conductor who is unfamiliar with the traditions, some experimentation should show the number of beats which is most effective. The slow movement of Mozart's Violin Concerto, K.216 (Ex. 381) is not very well known and is therefore a good illustration. It is marked **C** in Adagio. If you try to beat 4, you will find that the first half of bar 1 may turn out satisfactorily, but both the continuation of the melody and the triplets in the accompaniment demand 8 beats in a measure.

The problems which arise in triple time are treated similarly. 1-beat in its straight or subdivided form is often used for fast movements in 3-time (*cf.* pp. 83 and 131). In slow 3-time, use subdivision with 6 beats or, when triplets occur on each count, 9 beats in a measure. 2 beats in a bar may be used for fast 6-time, 3 beats for 9-time, and 4 beats for 12-time.

Ex. 382: The metronome marking suggests 2 beats in a measure, but it would be difficult for the flutists to co-ordinate their playing unless the conductor indicates the eighth-notes. Use a subtle subdivision (Diagram 46).

*In all cases the choice of beats must not affect the choice of
tempo. Do not drag when using more beats than indicated
in the time-signature; do not hurry when using fewer beats.*

In addition to the tempo of the music, there are considerations other than technique that determine the number of beats in a measure. It may happen that there is a choice between two ways of beating, both technically correct, but having different effects on the musical interpretation. The rule, sometimes taught, that no more beats should be used than are absolutely necessary to mark the time, may be good for time-beaters but is never followed in artistic conducting. It is obvious that if one beats the smaller rhythmic values even though this may not be "absolutely necessary", the weak beats are played with more intensity. On the other hand, the indication of fewer strokes can result in a broader flow of the music. Thus, the mode of beating may have a marked influence on the meter of the music, which in turn can affect the interpretation of a whole piece. It is self-evident that Exx. 95 and 167 require a different number of beats, though both are marked 6/8 and are played in about the same tempo. 2-beat is adequate for the lilting melody of the Barcarolle, while 6-beat is needed to bring out the polyphonic interweaving in the example from Bach.

Ex. 383: This music is usually directed in 2-beat. It has been conducted in 4-beat without altering the traditional tempo significantly. The shape of the theme is quite different in the two cases, because of the sub-accent on the third quarter in 4-beat.

Allegro con brio, ($\downarrow$ = 88)

BEETHOVEN, Coriolanus Overture

There are other cases in which stylistic considerations determine the number of beats in a measure. A particular feeling for rhythm may be an essential characteristic of a composer's style, and failure to do justice to this feeling may result in a performance which either lacks intensity or is overemphatic.

Ex. 384: This music has been conducted with 4 beats in a bar and with 12. The difference is that in the latter case the eighth-note values receive more stress, even though the tempo for both interpretations is the same. The choice of pattern therefore depends on whether or not the conductor wants to emphasize these small values, although such emphasis may not conform to the best traditions of performing Bach.

Largo ma non tanto, ($\downarrow.$ = 50)

BACH, Concerto for Two Violins

Ex. 385: This melody (and in fact the entire first movement of this symphony) is done with 2-beat. 4-beat would be possible from a purely technical point of view, but would not convey the typically Mozartean flow of melody.

That the baton technique can be closely related to the musical language of different composers may be seen by comparing certain passages from the works of Verdi and Wagner. Verdi's music often demands a beat which gives to the smaller time values that intensity which is so characteristic of Italian rhythmic feeling. For Wagner, on the other hand, an alla breve beat is often used to bring out the broad line of the music, although the time-signature is 4/4.

Ex. 386: Outside of Italy this may be heard conducted alla breve. Such treatment loses the dramatic effect of the music and makes the melody sound rather banal.

Ex. 387: In these two passages, typical of Verdi's style, the composer's metronome markings indicate half-beats; but most Italian conductors use 4 strokes, generally with the subdivided pattern. This results in a more exciting performance, and at the same time secures better rhythmic control. Thus the violins will play the descending figure in Ex. 387a clearly, whereas the passage is apt to be muddy when directed alla breve. In Ex. 387b, the syncopated rhythm will hardly come out distinctly unless the conductor indicates 4 beats in a bar.

Allegro agitato, (♩ = 88)

Ex. 388: The section marked **C** requires an alla breve beat, although the string passages look as though they need 4-beat. The latter, however, would not bring out the grandeur of the melody.

SIMULTANEOUS DIFFERENT RHYTHMS

Another case in which the conductor must determine how many beats he will use in a measure occurs when different rhythms are played simultaneously by various groups of the orchestra. The principle to be followed is this: avoid gestures that would disturb the rhythm of any group. This is best done by weakening or omitting such disruptive beats.

Ex. 389: The melody is in triplet quarter-notes against the 4/4 rhythm of the accompaniment. A change to alla breve is not recommended; it is not difficult to play the triplets against the regular 4-beat, provided *Two* and *Four* are somewhat weakened. This will help the triplet figure without confusing the accompanying instruments.

Ex. 390: In the 1st measure, 6 beats are needed for clear direction of the various groups. In the next bar only slight subdivision is recommended, so as not to interfere with the smooth execution of the triplet. Do not subdivide at all for the triplet in bar 3; then you may return to subdivision.

Ex. 391: Since the rhythmic figures in the wood-winds and trumpets are predominant, continue beating 2 in the 3rd bar. Violins and horns thus play their 3/4 rhythm as a syncopation.

HARRIS, When Johnny Comes Marching Home

Ex. 177: Because of the very slow tempo, 4-beat in bar 2 would make the players feel insecure. Use 12 beats in a measure, so that the violas and 'cellos play their couplets against the rhythm in the tympani. You can help the string players by emphasizing the 2nd, 5th, 8th, and 11th eighth-beats.

Ex. 392: For the quintuplet in bar 3 use 1-beat, in bars 6 and 7 use 2-beat with weakened *Two*. For the entrance of the first violins (bar 6) it is advisable to indicate a sharp *Two* with the left hand, a gesture which does not interfere with the brass figure. Be sure that the 1-beat is strictly in time, ♩ = 63.

STRAVINSKY, Le Sacre du Printemps

Ex. 393: Mentioned in the composer's *Traité d'Instrumentation*, this passage has become a classic example of simultaneous different rhythms. As

Berlioz points out, the Allegro movement in the violas is maintained in the Allegretto by subdividing bar 3. The 4th bar, however, is not subdivided, for this would disturb the rhythmic feeling of the solo melody.

Ex. 394: The 8/8 and 7/8 against 3/4 cannot both be included in the beat. Use 3-beat, but with weakened 2nd and 3rd beats, which facilitates the synchronizing of the odd rhythms with the beat. Apply a similar technique to bars 3 and 4.

Ex. 395: The flute and clarinet players calculate for themselves where their notes coincide with the 4-beat. Their triplets will be sufficiently well established and will allow a smooth execution in the 2nd measure, even though the rhythmic figures do not always coincide with the beat. However, the conductor may find it necessary to help the flutes and clarinets by indicating 6 beats in a measure with the left hand while beating 4 with the baton. (This procedure is recommended as an interesting exercise to achieve independence of the two hands!)

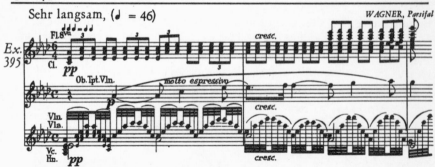

Additional examples for the study of passages in which different rhythms occur simultaneously:

Barber: *Second Essay for Orchestra*, passage starting at No. 19.
Brahms: *Variations on a Theme by Haydn*, Finale.
Debussy: *Nuages*, passage starting at the 7th bar after No. 2.
Hindemith: *Mathis der Maler*, 3rd movement—passage starting 5 bars before No. 25.
Tchaikovsky: *Overture 1812*, passage starting at bar 188.

IRREGULAR MEASURES

There are occasions when the composer includes more counts in a measure than are allowed by the time-signature. The treatment of such measures depends on the musical context.

Ex. 396: Beat the first three counts distinctly, stopping at *Three* while the strings continue playing. Listen to the solo clarinet, and synchronize the preparatory gesture so that the attack on the 2nd bar will not interfere with the steady pizzicato. Whether to use a free or an eighth-beat preparation depends on individual experience.

Ex. 397: Use *Two* for the cut-off and preparation, with the strings playing the G on the off-beat. Direct the remaining notes of the figure with two or three small extra strokes on the left side of the field of beating. (The third can be omitted, if this results in a smoother flow of the *rubato*.)

Beat the regular *Three* on the B

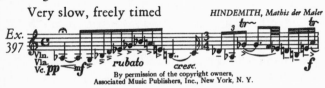

Additional examples of irregular measures:

Copland: *A Lincoln Portrait*, bar 183.
Respighi: *The Pines of Rome*, Part II (*Lento* 4/4)—5th and 9th bars.
Verdi: *La Traviata*, 2nd act—Germont's aria (*Di Provenza il mar*), 4th bar.
Verdi: *Otello*, 3rd act—1 bar before Q.

Chapter 26

NUMBER OF BEATS IN A MEASURE (II)

CHANGING THE NUMBER OF BEATS
FOR ONE OR MORE BARS

IT SOMETIMES BECOMES NECESSARY in the middle of a piece to change the number of beats in a measure. This situation can be caused by a change in the rhythmic structure of the music, as, for instance, by the appearance of triplets in duple or quadruple time. Another cause is the occurrence of intricate rhythms or rapid passages that may be played indistinctly unless the conductor has the added control over the players gained by beating the smaller values. This technique may be compared to the routine of counting "one-and, two-and", familiar to all instrumentalists as an aid in the precise performance of rhythmically difficult passages. Whether to beat the smaller values or not may also depend upon the ability of the particular orchestral group; experienced and technically superior musicians may not need such help. Furthermore, a change of beats may be desirable, not for technical reasons, but for the sake of expression. In slow or moderate tempo, the regular strokes often will not allow sufficient indication of intensity. The conductor then feels that his gestures are becoming purely mechanical instead of "being with the orchestra", and that only by adding more beats to the bar can he regain close contact with the players. Or else, in lively tempo, he may sense that there is too much excitement in his gestures, and that only by reducing the number of beats can he make the music flow more calmly.

As far as baton technique is concerned, such changes require an especially clear beat that leaves no doubt about the conductor's intention. This is particularly true when the change is not marked in the players' parts. A change from 4 to 2 beats or vice-versa can be the cause of trouble if it is not executed properly. It is dangerous to use

[266]

curved espressivo gestures during such a change because the orchestra may be unable to see "where the conductor is". The main counts should be easy to recognize, while smaller gestures should be used for the weak beats. The subdivided patterns lend themselves readily to temporary changes. They are also used to achieve a gradual transition, applying the technique discussed on pp. 152 ff., except that now the tempo is not changed.

Ex. 398: The triplets in the 5th bar may require a change from 4-beat to 2-beat. The change should be marked in the parts.

PUCCINI, *Madama Butterfly*

Ex. 399: Change to 1-beat in the 3rd bar and return to 2-beat at rallen-tando.

Ex. 400: Because of the slow tempo, the triplet in the 6th measure ("breit") is directed with 3 strokes, applying a regular 3-beat.

BRUCKNER, *Symphony No. 4*

Ex. 401: The structure of the music calls for a change of beat. The 3rd and 4th bars are directed with 4 strokes; subdivide in the second half of bar 2 to get an effective preparation for the *ff*. Return to 2-beat in the 5th measure, at the same time giving a clear indication of the sudden *p*.

Ex. 402: The 4th bar requires 3-beat because of the traditional ritenuto.

Ex. 403: Beat 3 in the fermata bar, to indicate clearly where the hold occurs.

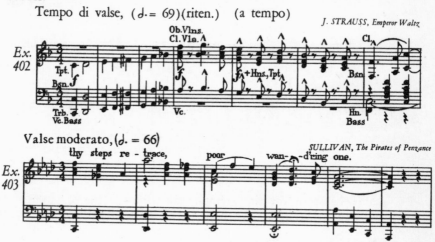

Ex. 404: Because of the slow pace (ritardando) the syncopated passage in bar 3 must be directed with 8 beats in a measure, or the violins will lose the feeling of security.

Ex. 405: According to tradition the first 3 sixteenth-notes of the "precipitando" are held back slightly; the others are played quickly and violently. Hence, subdivide the first half of the 3rd measure with sharp gestures, but use only one stroke for the second half. The following bar is legato.

Ex. 406: Here the conductor must know to what extent the orchestra needs his help for a flawless rhythmic execution. Subdivision may not be necessary when the players are thoroughly familiar with the music and have strong rhythmic feeling of their own. In many cases the conductor, instead of taking a chance, will prefer to subdivide for the triplet figure in Ex. 406a, bar 3 ff., either by using 6 small beats (Diagram 46), or by beating *One-Three-Four-Six* with downward gestures for *One* and *Three*, upward gestures for *Four* and *Six*. Beat legato in the first two bars and then change to staccato. In Ex. 406b, bar 2, use 6-beat with neutral gestures but with staccato on *Six;* return to 2-beat in the 3rd measure. Bars 4 and 5 need no subdivision.

Allegro con brio, (♩. = 66)   *BRAHMS, Symphony No. 3*

Ex. 406

Ex. 407: Direct the opening with a very calm 3-beat. In bar 2, however, change to subdivision to lead the flute passage and the harp chords. In the next bar return smoothly to the calm 3-beat.

Largamente e molto rubato, ♩ = 48   *GRIFFES, The White Peacock*

Ex. 407

Ex. 408: Although this music is marked 2/2, 4-beat is advisable, even for the best orchestras, to secure precision in the violin and viola passages. Change to 2-beat in the 5th measure.

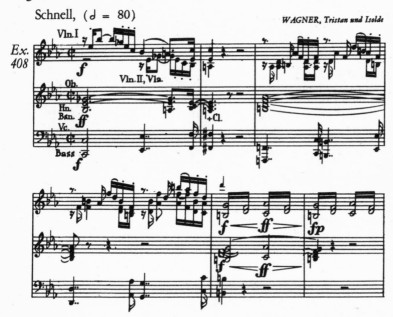

Ex. 409: Though conductors differ in the way they lead the 12/8 section of this movement (4 or 12 beats in a measure), there is no doubt that, starting from the last quarter of the 1st bar, the beat must be subdivided.

Ex. 410: In most orchestras the violin run in bar 3 will be muddy unless directed with 6 beats (Diagram 46), light-staccato. Return to 2-beat legato in the next measure.

Ex. 411: The rhythmic figure requires 8 beats in a measure. In the 4th bar, change to a calm 4-beat, but return to subdivision on the 4th count in bar 5.

Ex. 412: As the metronome marking indicates, this music is directed with 1-beat. However, the first violin section may need your help to co-ordinate the 32nd-notes; subdivide the 1st bar (Diagram 30b).

Ex. 413: Although the metronome marking suggests 8 beats in a measure, most conductors find that continual subdivision would upset the calmness of the line. You may subdivide slightly just for the syncopations and for the staccato chords (winds), but you must subdivide to prepare the horn entry.

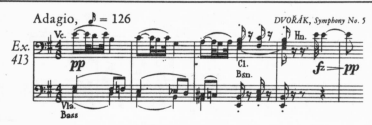

Ex. 346: In case the off-beat accents (bars 3, 6, etc.) lack precision, skilful subdivision on the preceding counts may give a satisfactory result.

Ex. 414: It is not necessary to use 4 strokes in bars 3 and 4, but many conductors do so, in order to have the rhythmic figure played with more élan. Resume the alla breve in bar 5 for the natural flow of the music.

Ex. 415: Here again, subdivision is not compulsory, but the use of 6 beats in bars 2 and 4 underlines the expression of the melody.

Ex. 416: The entire movement from which this passage is taken requires frequent change from regular to subdivided 3-beat, partly for technical reasons, partly for the sake of expressiveness. In the 4th measure, the eighth-note values must be indicated to secure a smooth execution of the dotted rhythm. Start to subdivide unobtrusively on the 1st count in that measure. In bar 6, the subdivision is hardly noticeable since the rhythm is now established. In the next bar, however, subdivision helps greatly to give ntensity to the lyric passage.

Ex. 417: The last part of this theme (bars 1-4), the second theme of the movement, is done with 3-beat. Some conductors continue to beat 3 at "a tempo". However, this *pp* section achieves its quality of lightness and suspense when directed with a small 1-beat. This entire movement demands flexibility on the part of the conductor; he brings life into his interpretation with a skilful mixture of 3-beat, 1-beat, and the subdivided pattern *One-(two-)Three.*

Additional examples for the study of passages in which the conductor usually changes the number of beats for one or more bars:

Berlioz: Overture *Le Carnaval Romain, Andante sostenuto* 3/4; whether to direct the 3rd bar with 3 beats or with subdivision depends on the individual conductor. Most conductors subdivide at the change to E major, also at the change to A major.

Brahms: Symphony No. 1, 4th movement; for the Introduction, *cf.* Ex. 211. Subdivision is necessary for the passages with 32nd-notes, but return to 4-beat 3 bars before *Più Andante*. In the *Allegro non troppo*, conductors change frequently to 2-beat, for instance at *animato* (118th bar of the movement), but resume the 4-beat whenever necessary.

Dvořák: Symphony No. 5 (*From the New World*), 4th movement. Use 4-beat at the start but change to 2-beat in bar 10; resume the 4-beat at No. 2. Similar changes are applied to the rest of this movement.

Leoncavallo: *Pagliacci*, Intermezzo. Subdivision is used in bars 1 and 3.

Puccini: *La Bohème*, 1st act, Rodolfo's aria. In the *Andante lento*, subdivision is applied to the measure before the 2/4 bar.

Tchaikovsky: Symphony No. 6. In the 3rd movement, change to 2-beat for the concluding section. In the 4th movement, the beat changes frequently from regular to subdivided 3-beat.

Verdi: *Aïda*, 1st act, 1st scene. In Aïda's aria (*Ritorna vincitor*) 2-beat is used at *Cantabile*, with subdivision for the triplet at *tremendo*. Return to 4-beat after the fermata.

Wagner: Overture to *Der Fliegende Holländer*. In the *Andante*, change from 6-beat to 2-beat at *Animando un poco*.

SUBDIVIDING A SINGLE COUNT

Subdivision of single counts has been discussed as a means of directing ritardando. It may be used occasionally, even though the tempo does not change, either for secure playing or for the sake of intensity. The skilful application of this technique adds vitality and expression to the interpretation. Indeed, to use it without interrupting the flow of the musical line or upsetting the clarity of the beat is the mark of a master. However, young conductors are warned against too frequent subdivision of this kind, especially in espressivo; many curved gestures in a bar are hard to follow if they are not used in a completely convincing way. Perfect control of the baton is required for the application of such intermediate strokes.

On the other hand, subdividing single counts can be very useful in slow passages with dotted rhythm when a small note-value follows a larger one, as in Ex. 379. Beginning on *Four* in the 2nd bar, use subdivision to secure correct playing of the 32nd-notes; subdivide only on the counts on which the dotted rhythm occurs.

Ex. 418: Subdivide on *Four* in bars 2 and 3; subdivision can also be applied to the first two counts in bar 4, to control the triplets.

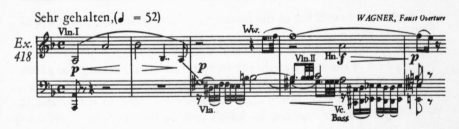

Sehr gehalten, (♩ = 52)   WAGNER, *Faust Overture*

Ex. 418

Ex. 419: Should there be any difficulty with the after-beat of the trill in flutes and violins, a skilful subdivision of the 3rd count in bar 2 will keep the instruments together. The gesture must be small and precise, without any delay.

Andante tranquillo, (♩ = 66)

Ex. 419

MENDELSSOHN, *Midsummer Night's Dream—Nocturne*

Ex. 420: Subdivision on *Two* in bar 5 leads the violins (C and D♭ played with two up-bows!) to indicate the tender expression of the phrase.

Andantino affettuoso,   PUCCINI, *La Bohème*
(♩ = 69)   *poco affrettando*
                                    a tempo   Vln.I   *rall.*

Ex. 420

Ex. 421: The accented notes in bars 3 and 4 require subdivision so that each of these notes may be directed with great intensity. To achieve a clear release of the dotted quarter-note, use an incisive beat on *Two* in each of these bars.

Chapter 27

5-TIME AND 7-TIME

THERE ARE TWO WAYS of beating these odd counts. If the tempo is not too fast, each count receives one beat. When the tempo is so rapid that this cannot be done distinctly, several counts are included in one gesture. Such rapid successions of uneven bars first appeared in the music of Stravinsky and has since become characteristic of modern scores.

5 BEATS IN A MEASURE

Several patterns may be used, depending on the way the groups of notes fall within the bar. A 5/4 signature may stand for continual alternation of 2/4 and 3/4, in which case Diagram 59a is applicable (this diagram indicates staccato, and the other types of gesture may easily be deduced from it). Some conductors actually alternate 2-beat and 3-beat in the same size, but the 5-beat pattern shown on the diagram has this advantage: since the second group (*Three-Four-Five*) is kept smaller and toward the top of the field of beating, the downbeat on *One* stands out and the orchestra has a definite point of orientation.

Ex. 422: Apply Diagram 59a. The entire third movement of the symphony follows this beat.

Allegro con grazia, ♩ = 144   TCHAIKOVSKY, Symphony No. 6

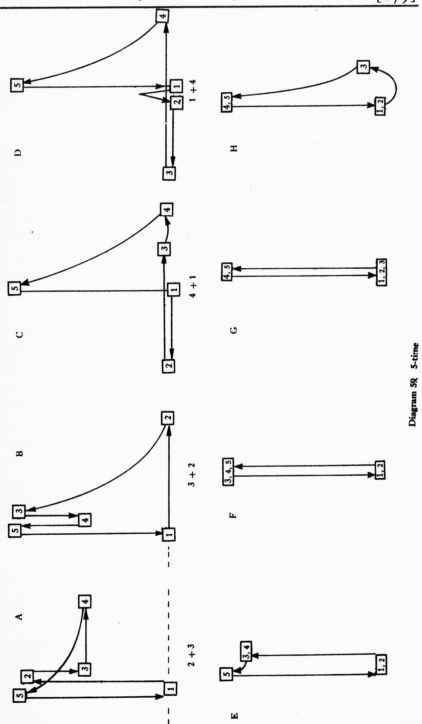

Diagram 59. 5-time

Ex. 423: The notation indicates the rhythmic groups (3/4 + 2/4).
Apply Diagram 59b.

Ex. 424: No division of the 5-group is apparent. The pattern of Diagram 59c is the best (4/4 + 1/4), because it is close to the 4-beat of the preceding and following bars.

Ex. 425: The 1st measure follows the pattern of Diagram 59c, and the next three bars use that of Diagram 59d, which is simply 4-beat with a repeated downbeat (1/4 + 4/4).

Additional examples for the study of the 5-beat patterns:

2+3 beats:

Barber: *Second Essay for Orchestra*, 3rd bar after No. 25.
Carpenter: *Sea Drift*, passage starting 3 bars before No. 15.

3+2 beats:

Respighi: *The Pines of Rome*, Part II—13th bar; also at *Ancora più mosso*
 (the pattern 4 + 1 can also be applied).
Strauss, Richard: *Salome*, 1st scene, passage starting at No. 15.
Wagner: *Tristan und Isolde*, 3rd act, 2nd scene—31st bar.

4+1 beats:

Griffes: *The White Peacock*, passage starting at bar 7.
Shostakovitch: Symphony No. 1, 2nd movement—bar 2.
Strauss, Richard: *Salome, Salome's Dance*, bar 30.

5-TIME WITH 1, 2, OR 3 BEATS IN A MEASURE

When the tempo is too fast to beat clearly and easily on each count, fewer beats are used in a measure. In Diagram 59e there are 3 beats: the 1st includes *One* and *Two*, the 2nd *Three* and *Four*, and the 3rd, with a small turn of the wrist, indicates *Five*, which has a preparatory quality. There are only 2 beats in Diagrams 59f and g, giving rise to an asymmetric pattern. Which pattern to use depends on the rhythmic stress of the music and, to a certain extent, upon what is most convenient for the individual conductor. If you have a flexible wrist, you may prefer 59h for bars in which *Four* is accented.

Ex. 426: Execute the 4th measure according to Diagram 59e, since the feeling is 2/4+1/8.

Reprinted by permission of the Oxford University Press, London
(U. S. A. Agents: Carl Fischer, Inc.)

Ex. 427: The 5/8 rhythm in bars 4-7 seems to conform to Diagrams 59e or f. But the entrance of the wood-wind passage in the 6th measure calls for an especially clear indication of the small rhythmic values. Since changing the pattern would disturb the players, direct these four bars according to Diagram 59a, using small gestures.

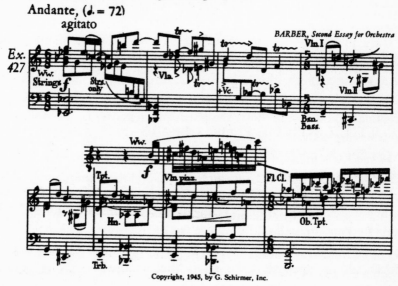

Copyright, 1945, by G. Schirmer, Inc.

Ex. 428 (bars 2, 3, and 5): Diagrams 59f or g could be used; if pattern f is used, the *ff* figure ♪♪♪ is felt as a syncopation, while with pattern g the up-beat coincides with the attack of that figure.

Courtesy of Edition Russe de Musique, Paris
Galaxy Music Corporation, New York

If the music moves very quickly, it becomes necessary to use 1-beat. This requires a definite feeling on the part of the conductor for the 5 small note-values within each beat. Control over this intricate rhythm is by no means as difficult as it seems, and a few hours of concentrated practice should enable the average student to master it. The following exercises are recommended.

(1) Set the metronome at 50. Count aloud, starting with *One* for each tick, and repeat several times. Then double the count, with *One*, *Two* on every tick. Continue to increase the count, one at a time, up to five counts for each tick. The sequence of counts within each tick must be kept smooth and continuous. In this way you learn to alter the rhythmical unit while keeping the measure fixed. The entire exercise should be repeated, replacing the metronome by walking steadily, each step representing one tick.

(2) The next exercise trains the rhythmic control by changing the measure and keeping the unit. Set the metronome at 208 and beat 1-beat. Start with 2 ticks per beat, then use 3, 4, and 5. You will find that with 5 ticks per beat the metronome is not fast enough for a con-

venient 1-beat. Hence, use one of the Diagrams 59e-h. Next, dispense with the metronome and increase the tempo until 1-beat becomes convenient in 5-time.

(3) Apply both procedures to Exx. 429a and b.

Ex. 430: The 5/8 bars are conducted with 1-beat.

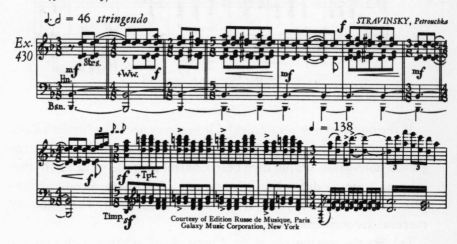

Courtesy of Edition Russe de Musique, Paris
Galaxy Music Corporation, New York

7 BEATS IN A MEASURE

Diagrams 60a-d show different methods of execution depending on the groups within the measure.

Ex. 431: The composer has indicated the grouping. Accordingly, Diagrams 60c and d are used alternately.

Courtesy of J. & W. Chester, Ltd., London
Galaxy Music Corporation, New York

Ex. 432: Apply Diagram 60a.
Ex. 433: Apply Diagram 60b.

By permission of the copyright owners,
Associated Music Publishers, Inc., New York, N. Y.

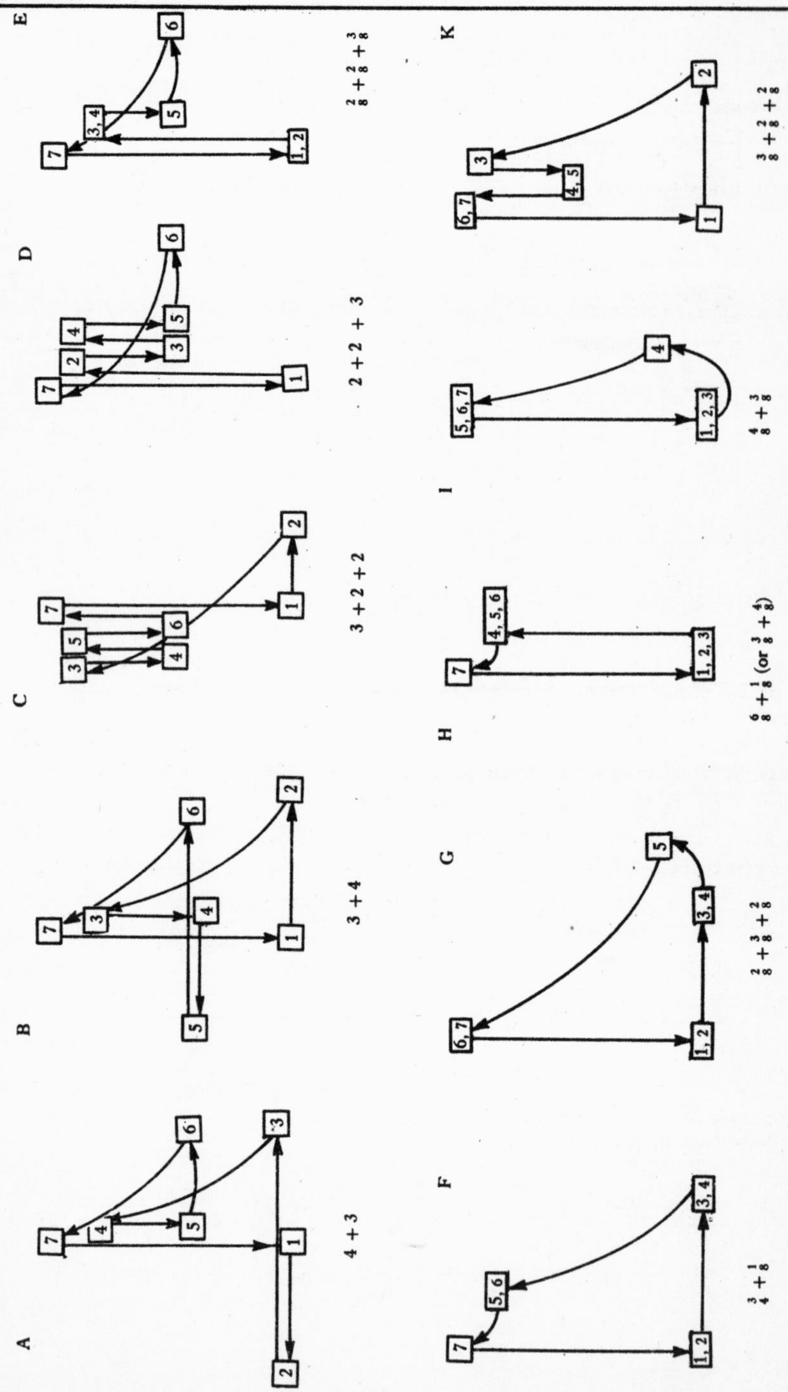

Diagram 60. 7-time

7-TIME WITH 3, 4, OR 5 BEATS IN A MEASURE

Diagrams 60e-k. The 4th bar in Ex. 428 is best executed with 60g.

Ex. 434: For bars 2 and 5, use Diagram 60e or f. The 6th measure can be done with pattern g. For the 5/8 (bar 4) use Diagram 59e.

By permission of the copyright owners,
J. & W. Chester, Ltd., London

Ex. 457: Use Diagram 60e for bars 1-3, Diagram 60k for the 4th bar.

Additional examples for the study of 7-time:

3+4:

Stravinsky: *Le Sacre du Printemps*, 2nd part—2nd bar after No. 106.

4+3:

Barber: *Second Essay for Orchestra*, 11th bar after No. 21.
Griffes: *The White Peacock*, 2 bars before A.
Stravinsky: *Le Sacre du Printemps*, 1st part—*Rondes Printanières*, 2nd bar after No. 48.

Chapter 28

CHANGES OF RHYTHM AND TEMPO

CHANGES OF TIME-SIGNATURE and of tempo are not found frequently in the music of the classic composers, but occur quite often in scores by Wagner and later composers. When they are found in the older music it is usually between sections of the composition, while in modern scores they occur from phrase to phrase and even from one bar to another. In all cases these changes require clear gestures and, for change of time-signature, the new rhythmic pattern must be unmistakable.

CHANGE OF TIME-SIGNATURE WITHOUT CHANGE OF TEMPO

While change of time-signature in itself involves no new technical problems, a rapid succession of changes requires a clear mind and a flexible hand. Exx. 435-438 contain, in the form of exercises, typical rhythmic changes such as occur in modern music. As in all music of this sort, the conductor must study carefully the rhythmic arrangement of the measures before he even lifts his baton.

There are two types of changes. (1) Most often the *rhythmic unit remains constant* although the time-signature changes. In this case the conductor must be certain that, for instance, ♩ equals ♩ exactly. Exceptions to this rule are usually specifically indicated by the composer. (2) Sometimes, although the rhythm (time-signature) changes, the tempo (pulse) is maintained by keeping the *bar length constant*. This is usually indicated in the score.

Ex. 435: 1-beat in bar 5, 3-beat in bar 10.

Ex. 436: Resist the temptation to slow down in the 7th and 15th measures! 1-beat in bars 9, 10, and 16; 2-beat in bar 17.

Ex. 437: Keep the rhythmic value of the beat constant in bar 4. The change in the 7th measure makes one old bar equal to half of a new bar. *In bar 10, the 2-beat remains constant.* According to tradition the special indication (𝅗𝅥=𝅗𝅥·) is omitted; in fast tempo when 2-beat is used throughout, it is customary that at the change to 6-time, bar equals bar. On the other hand, it is taken for granted that at the change from ¢ to 3/2 (bar 14), ♩ equals ♩. As a result of these traditions, which contradict strict logic, bars 10 and 14 are of different length.

Ex. 438: 1-beat in bars 3-7. Use Diagram 59e for bar 15. Be sure that the sixteenth-note values remain constant in bars 3, and 10-13, and beat accordingly with unmistakable down-strokes.

Review the following examples in which the rhythmic value of the beat remains the same, although the pattern of the beat changes with the time-signature: Exx. 213, 230, 279, 368, 392, 394, 424, 426 (bar 2), and 433.

Ex. 439: This shows clearly the difference in applying 6-beat for the time-signature 6/4 (Ex. 439a), and subdivided 3-beat for the time-signature 3/2 (Ex. 439b). (Unfortunately, composers do not always indicate this correctly; they may mark double time, 6/4, in passages which actually are in triple time, 3/2; in such cases the conductor must use his own judgment.) Note that in the following two passages the value of the quarter-note remains constant.

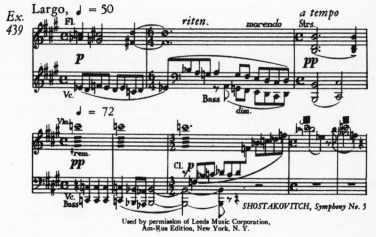

SHOSTAKOVITCH, Symphony No. 5

Used by permission of Leeds Music Corporation,
Am-Rus Edition, New York, N. Y.

Ex. 440: The 3/4 bar offers no particular problem, because the quarter-beat was present in the subdivision of the previous measures.

COPLAND, A Lincoln Portrait

Reprinted by permission of the copyright owners,
Boosey & Hawkes, Inc., New York, N. Y.

Ex. 441: At the Alla breve the composer indicates that the bar length is unchanged.

BEETHOVEN, *Symphony No. 3*

Additional examples for the study of passages in which the time-signature changes while the beat remains constant:

Barber: Symphony No. 1, from the beginning until No. 4 (study score pages 1-10).

Berlioz: *Roméo et Juliette*, 4th part (Scherzo)—transition to *Allegretto* 3/4.

Brahms: *Tragic Overture*, double bar at K, *Molto più moderato* 4/4.

Puccini: *La Bohème*, 1st act, passage between Nos. 9 and 10.

Rimsky-Korsakov: *Scheherazade*, 2nd movement, transitions at H and N.

Sibelius: Symphony No. 2, 2nd movement.

Tchaikovsky: Symphony No. 4, 4th movement—*Andante* 3/4.

Wagner: *Siegfried*, 1st act—1st scene.

In the above examples, the beat was constant regardless of the change of time-signature. In the examples that follow, the rhythmic value of the beat changes with the time-signature. Hence the conductor must "think" the important rhythmic unit. The slightest uncertainty in the beat may jeopardize the ensemble.

Ex. 442: The ♪ remains constant throughout; therefore the 1-beat starting in the 4th bar must be very precise and sure, securing a steady sixteenth-note movement. Be especially careful of the return to 2/4 and do not delay *Two!* (An ambitious student will do well to beat the entire 3rd scene of the 3rd act of *Die Meistersinger*.)

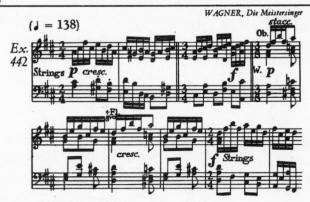

Ex. 443: 3/4 is done with 1-beat; 4/4 is beaten alla breve while the quarter-unit remains constant. The 2nd scene of the 3rd act of *Tristan*, from which this is taken, has other examples of this type of rhythmic change.

Ex. 427: Be sure to keep the tempo steady when returning to 2-beat in the last measure; do not rush!

Ex. 428: In conducting this passage as a whole, the main problem is to keep the ♪ steady. Set the metronome at 144, which gives the quarter-beat. Thereby the eighth is easily established. Beat bar 6 strictly in tempo, each half-beat representing 4 eighth-units.

Ex. 430: A passage of this type need not be as confusing as it looks. In effect, the metronome marking means ♩ = 160. The tempo increases up to about ♩ = 178 in the 8th measure. Start with a definite feeling for the eighth-unit, which is best maintained by counting to yourself and using sharp down-beats in bars 1-12. Counting the small units to yourself in this fashion is indispensable for certain passages in modern scores.

Ex. 434: Apply the techniques described above.

Additional examples for the study of passages in which the rhythmic unit remains constant while the beat changes:

Dvořák: *Scherzo Capriccioso*, passage in 2/4 (bar 561).
Strauss, Richard: *Don Juan*, bar 30.
Strauss, Richard: *Don Quixote*, transition to Variation No. 8.
Stravinsky, *Le Sacre du Printemps*, 1st part—*Jeu du Rapt*, passage between
    Nos. 43 and 48. ..
Wagner: *Die Götterdämmerung*, Interlude between the Prelude and the
    1st act (*Siegfried's Rhine Journey*), transition from *Schnell* 6/8
    to *Rasch* 3/4.

CHANGE OF TEMPO WITH RHYTHMIC RELATION MAINTAINED

Sometimes the rhythm of the new tempo has a relationship with the previous rhythm, which may be indicated by the composer by means of such markings as *doppio movimento, mezzo tempo,* or ♩ = ♩ , etc. Concerning this last indication, composers are not in agreement as to which note value represents the old tempo and which the new. In classic music the musical context gives the clue, while modern composers generally use the relation: ♩ (old) = ♩ (new).

Ex. 444: This exercise illustrates a number of typical changes of tempo and rhythm. Use 2-beat in the 6th measure, 1-beat in the 13th. Observe that the relation between bars 16 and 17 is based on the equality of the two bars.

Ex. 445: The marking "Tempo stretto come avanti" indicates that ♩♩♩ equals ♩♩♩ ; therefore the quarter-beat equals the previous half-beat.

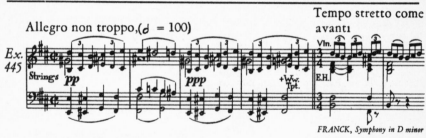

FRANCK, *Symphony in D minor*

Ex. 446: In the Presto (1-beat) the whole measure equals the quarter-beat of the previous tempo.

BRAHMS, *Symphony No. 2*

Ex. 447: For an unmistakable indication of the tempo change ($\flat = \downarrow$) it may be helpful to subdivide the last quarter-beat in bar 2. In any case, "think" the eighth-note values in the old tempo just before starting the "Doppio mosso".

Copyright, 1943, by G. Schirmer, Inc.   BARBER, *Symphony No. 1*

Ex. 448: The quarter-beat of the Allegro is twice as fast as the quarter-value in the Lento.

Reprinted by permission of the copyright owners,
Boosey & Hawkes, Inc., New York, N. Y.   COPLAND, *A Lincoln Portrait*

Ex. 449: For bar 2 apply Diagram 59b; the eighth-beats are twice as fast as the quarter-beats in the preceding measure. The 2nd beat in each bar should be sufficiently sharp to bring out the syncopations.

Ex. 450: Subdivide the 3rd quarter-beat in bar 2; the second eighth of the subdivided beat serves as preparation for *Four* in the new tempo, which is twice as fast as the old tempo.

Ex. 451: If the metronome markings are strictly observed, each of the slow beats in bar 5 equals *four* fast beats of the preceding tempo. Good control is needed to indicate the sudden change with calm, small gestures.

Ex. 353: The tempo change is in effect ♪=♩ .

Ex. 388: Change from slow to fast (♩ = ♩).

Additional examples for the study of tempo changes with rhythmic relation maintained:

Brahms: *Academic Festival Overture, Maestoso* 3/4.
Kodály: *Psalmus Hungaricus,* transition to 4/4 at No. 9.
Rimsky-Korsakov: *Scheherazade,* 2nd movement, *Moderato assai* 4/4 at F.
Sibelius: Symphony No. 3, 2nd movement, 13th bar after No. 6, *Tranquillo.*
Strauss, Richard: *Till Eulenspiegel, Gemächlich* 2/4, 19th bar, *doppelt so schnell,* 25th bar, *wieder noch einmal so langsam.*
Stravinsky: *L'Oiseau de Feu* (Suite), Finale—*Doppio Valore Maestoso* at No. 19.

CHANGE OF TEMPO WITHOUT RHYTHMIC RELATION

Sometimes when the tempo changes, there is no relationship between the last beat in the old tempo and the first beat in the new. If there is an opportunity in the music for a preparatory beat, the new tempo is established just as at the beginning of a piece. This is the case in Exx. 141, 275, and 295 (after a fermata), Ex. 298 (after an interruption), Exx. 308b and 330 (after a rest), Ex. 329 (after a sustained note), Ex. 293 (after the last beat in the bar, but feasible only because of the slow tempo which allows subdivision on the last count!), and Ex. 216 (at the end of a ritardando).

However, a sudden transition may leave no opportunity for a preparatory beat. This requires a clear and determined gesture, especially for the first few beats in the new tempo. The conductor must be absolutely sure of the tempo and the players must be convinced of his certainty. Still, some sudden changes are so difficult that they can be played satisfactorily only as a result of careful practice at rehearsal.

Ex. 452: The first three beats in the 2nd measure must be given without any hesitation or faltering, yet without rushing, and not too heavily. (The same is true for the 3rd bar of Ex. 267.)

Andantino moderato, (♩ = 76)   Un poco più animato, (♩ = 100)

NICOLAI, *The Merry Wives of Windsor—Overture*.

Ex. 453: No interruption is intended in the 3rd bar; simply start the new tempo on *Three*.

ENESCO, *Roumanian Rhapsody No. 1*

Ex. 454: Use a simple and very clear wrist motion at the start of the Presto, addressing the first violins.

BEETHOVEN, *Leonore Overture No. 3*

Ex. 455: Some conductors subdivide for the sudden poco meno, but it is better just to slow down the 1-beat. Allow the instruments time for the 2nd and 3rd quarter-notes in your calm and graceful up-beat.

J. STRAUSS, *Voices of Spring*

Ex. 456: The transition to a quicker tempo in bar 5 must be indicated with particular certainty because of the syncopation; use a precise staccato.

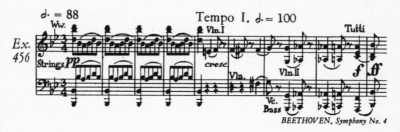

BEETHOVEN, Symphony No. 4

The following five examples show change of tempo in combination with change of the rhythmic pattern.

Ex. 457: The gesture on *Two* in bar 5 uses the accented up-beat and is timed as a preliminary beat in the slower tempo.

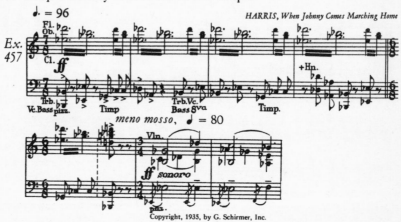

Ex. 458: In the 4th measure, an incisive *Two* is needed to establish the new tempo firmly.

WILLIAM SCHUMAN, Symphony No. 3

Ex. 459: An energetic full-staccato beat is needed for the Vivo.

RIMSKY-KORSAKOV, *Capriccio Espagnol*

Ex. 460: In bar 3, the composer indicates not only a change of pattern (1-beat) but also a suddenly faster tempo. Therefore lead the first 2 bars of the Più mosso with especially clear down-beats. The gradual increase of the tempo is interrupted by a sudden slowing down at Meno. Direct this with a subdivided 1-beat (Diagram 30b); 2 bars later, at molto ritenuto, change to regular 3-beat. For A tempo primo use staccato beats, not too large but very determined.

Copyright, 1941, by G. Schirmer, Inc. BARBER, *Overture to The School for Scandal*

Ex. 430 (bar 13): This illustrates a change to slower tempo and to the 3-beat pattern.

Additional examples for the study of sudden tempo changes without rhythmic relation:

Beethoven: Symphony No. 5, 2nd movement—bars 205 (*Più mosso*) and 218 (Tempo I).

Beethoven: Symphony No. 6, 3rd movement—bar 234 (*Presto*).

Berlioz: *Menuet des Feux-Follets* from *La Damnation de Faust*, several changes from *Moderato* to *Presto*.

Dvořák: Symphony No. 5 (*From the New World*), 3rd movement, *a tempo* at No. 2.

Enesco: *Roumanian Rhapsody No. 1*, several sudden changes.

Schuman, William: Symphony No. 3, Part I, start of the Fugue (bar 146).

Shostakovitch: *The Golden Age*, 1st movement at Nos. 13 and 17; 3rd movement (Polka), 4 bars from the end.

Tchaikovsky: Symphony No. 5, 2nd movement—*Moderato con anima* (bar 66).

Verdi: *Aïda*, 2nd act, 2nd scene (Gran Finale)—start of the ballet music (*Più mosso*) at E.

Study and practise scores Nos. 7 and 8 discussed in the Appendix.

Chapter 29

FREE STYLE

FREE STYLE OF CONDUCTING

It often happens that a student attends a concert that is led by an eminent conductor and finds that the leader's gestures do not correspond with the patterns and methods studied so arduously. He wonders if he has been wasting his time, and whether conducting can be taught at all. It seems to him, indeed, that what he has learned has little application to actual conducting.

What this book has called good usage in conducting conforms to the traditional patterns, but it is not always easy to recognize the patterns, since there is room for considerable variation. Furthermore, the rapidity with which the gestures follow each other makes it difficult to discern them. The student's plight may be compared to that of a person with a good theoretical knowledge of a foreign language who, entering the country where the language is spoken, has difficulty with the swiftness of everyday speech. In both cases increasing experience and familiarity will clear up the confusion.

Nevertheless, the student is correct in concluding that the conductor uses some gestures that do not conform to any of the patterns. This is due to the fact that there are gestures that can be described as "free style". Some of these gestures are discussed below.

The direction of any beat may be changed to secure a particular result. For intense lyricism in 4-beat, it is effective to carry ②higher than usual and to reach ③ with a diagonal movement, especially when the 3rd beat is emphasized. In very strong passages, down-beats may be used on each count to stress the attack. (This should not tempt the young conductor to adopt an all-down-beat technique!)

Ex. 461: The chords in bars 5-7 are done by many conductors with successive down-beats. Use four strokes in the 4th measure (subdivision).

Ex. 462: These bars conclude the entire movement. Since it would be awkward to end with an upward gesture, use a down-beat for *Two* in bar 4. This down-beat is a sharp motion to direct the accented off-beat.

Reprinted by permission of the Oxford University Press, London
(U. S. A. Agents: Carl Fischer, Inc.)

In fast 2-beat, the gesture easily becomes monotonous and does not lend itself to the directing of expressive passages. Therefore conductors sometimes use curved motions, carrying the baton to the right on *One* and to the left on *Two*. This method avoids the continual stress on the 1st beat, which in certain lyric passages (*cf*. Ex. 463) can become quite disturbing.

Copyright, 1943, by G. Schirmer, Inc.

Also in 2-beat, it is possible to emphasize *Two* by using a not too large but energetic sidewise stroke, preferably to the left, when an upward *Two* would be inconvenient; this means that the 1st beat is very small.

Ex. 464: The beginning of this movement (bars 1 and 3) can be done by beating *Two* to the left with a strong but short gesture.

It has already been pointed out that certain beats may be weakened in order to emphasize others by contrast. In free style the weakening may be carried to the point where such beats disappear altogether. In all cases, however, the 1st beat should be omitted only when there is no likelihood of a misunderstanding. Many players follow the music by counting bars, and need the down-beat. The same applies to skipping rests, which is done fairly often because the conductor does not want to make gestures that are not essential. For instance, in Ex. 189, bars 1 and 2, the 5th eighth-beat may well be omitted, though the rhythm must be maintained strictly. Generally, a conductor with limited experience will do well to indicate all the rests if there is the slightest possibility of a misunderstanding—which is one of the most frequent causes of mishaps.

In orchestral accompaniments, a careful handling of rests is required when the orchestra pauses for several successive measures. In each of these measures (*general pauses*) the first count should be indicated by a clear down-stroke, omitting the other counts. In many cases this *free style* procedure is more secure than the indication of all the counts. Not to beat at all during passages of this kind is advisable only if the players have been informed at which bar the conductor will resume the regular beat. This should generally be done in the measure which precedes the one in which the orchestra enters after the pause. (*Cf.* the end of the violin cadenza in the first movement of Mendelssohn's Violin Concerto; from the beginning of the cadenza do not beat for 35 bars, but resume the regular 2-beat one measure before the entrance of first violins, first flute, and first oboe.)

Whether to beat or omit rests is a particularly important problem in accompanying recitatives. Most Italian opera conductors traditionally use a down-beat for all chords regardless of the count on which they fall. This is practicable only when the orchestra parts include the words of the recitative; otherwise the beats must be very clear and the first counts must be unmistakable, even while the orchestra is waiting during several rests.

Not beating at all for a number of bars while the orchestra is playing must also be classified as a free style characteristic. When not indulged in for the sake of showmanship, this can have a genuine musical purpose. Soft passages, similar in style to chamber music, may need little or no indication from the conductor. The fact that no beat is given may challenge the players' initiative and result in an especially well-balanced and delicate performance. Incidentally, it may be very helpful for the young conductor to realize on such occasions that the musicians can to a certain extent play without him, and that he need not control every single count. This realization may cure him of holding the reins too tightly, and increase his poise and relaxation. But if the beat is stopped, it must be resumed smoothly at the proper moment, or the performance will become shaky.

It may sometimes be effective to beat with the left hand instead of the right. In Ex. 193 you may direct the tympani solo (bar 5) with the left hand, saving the right for the tutti in the next measure.

In certain syncopated passages in which the syncopation is in effect a change of time-signature, you may beat the accents instead of the rhythm. Do this only when all the instruments have the same rhythmic pattern and no misunderstanding is possible. The conductor must be sure that his clear-cut control allows him to return to the regular rhythm with absolute certainty.

Ex. 322: You may use 3 beats for the first two bars, beating on each *sf* and returning to 1-beat in bar 3, as though the music were written:

The use of free style for preparatory gestures has already been discussed on p. 252. While free style adds variety to the beat and sometimes brings out effects which the regular pattern cannot achieve, it loses its meaning if used too frequently. It can be dangerous if it weakens the players' feeling of security, especially in unfamiliar music. Also, it may confuse an orchestra that is not highly experienced.

A useful if merely mechanical and limited way of handling the baton is "finger conducting". It displays the conductor's complete control over his stick, because well-trained fingers are required to execute the various rhythmic patterns without any motion of arm and wrist. Its application is confined to cases in which the conductor wants a very small beat with a minimum of effort. Finger conducting is not an indispensable part of the conductor's equipment, and teaching it to beginners would be a doubtful procedure. It is difficult to do and demands strong and disciplined fingers; otherwise the hand tires and becomes tense. Premature attempts to master this free style technique may do more harm than good.

THE ART OF ACCOMPANIMENT

In conducting an orchestral accompaniment you face essentially the same problems as in accompanying a soloist at the piano, but the particular kind of alertness and flexibility that a good piano accompanist has are required to an even greater degree by the conductor: his gesture must both follow the soloist and lead the orchestra. For even though the players adjust to the soloist to a certain extent, they must rely upon the leader for most of the co-ordination.

The main problem is to obtain perfect ensemble between the soloist and the orchestra. In those rare cases when the conductor and the soloist have worked out their interpretation beforehand, the task is easier, though even then the conductor must be ready for unexpected changes of tempo. However, considerable skill and attention are demanded of the leader in order to maintain a good ensemble when there have been relatively few rehearsals.

A few technical hints follow. In slow tempo, resist the temptation to subdivide the beat unless subdivision is absolutely necessary. It is much better to use slightly larger and very calm gestures which, so to speak, contain the smaller values, and make the musicians listen to the soloist. If they listen carefully, they will follow even rubato passages without the conductor's help. The desire to stay together with the soloist must not result in stiff gestures with overemphasized beats, or the accompaniment will drag. Do not hesitate unnecessarily on the counts, but keep the gesture moving with a light forearm. Be prepared to delay or hasten toward the next count. A special warning is given against waiting on the last count in the bar with uplifted arm; if a delay is necessary, move slowly upward, then come down quickly. Generally, such adjustments must not cause the rhythm to become uneven. Despite rhythmic nuances the conductor cannot afford to lose sight of the basic rhythm. Both the soloist and the orchestra expect a certain firmness from the conductor.

This brings up the question of when the conductor should lead and when he should follow. To decide this, he must understand the nature of the instrument or voice that he is accompanying. There are cases in which it is evident that the conductor leads the soloist, as in the opening of Ex. 465, where the pianist must follow the beat.

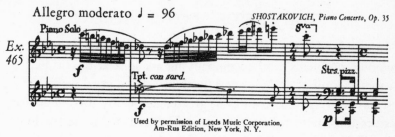

Used by permission of Leeds Music Corporation, Am-Rus Edition, New York, N. Y.

On the other hand, the conductor should know where to wait for a singer to breathe, or for a difficult shift of position in the violin, or where to speed up with a quick run on the piano—to mention only a few such adjustments. It goes without saying that the conductor should listen carefully to the solo part. Above all, he must know it thoroughly. In rapid passages with many notes on each count, he must know the groupings of the notes within the bar so as to synchronize his beat with the soloist. It is sometimes easier to follow the left hand of a piano part when this is rhythmically simpler than the right. Also, it may help to watch the soloist when the ear alone is not adequate. For good dynamic balance, however, the conductor must rely on the ear alone. The dynamic marks, as printed in the parts, are more or less relative and must be corrected by the conductor's indi-

cations whenever necessary. If you cannot hear the soloist with rea-
sonable ease, you may be sure that the audience cannot either.

The student should get some practical experience in accompanying
instrumentalists and singers as soon as possible, even though he may
only have at his disposal a piano or a small ensemble. Nos. 9-11 in the
Appendix include typical examples of orchestral accompaniment. In
this practice the soloist should occasionally avoid watching the conductor, and may even make it hard for him by taking various liberties.

Chapter 30

APPLICATION OF BATON TECHNIQUE

APPLYING BATON TECHNIQUE TO THE SCORE

THE DISCUSSIONS in the Appendix show how to apply baton technique to a complete score. Some of these detailed suggestions may be considered too personal, in fact, certain passages can be directed in several different ways. The further the student advances, the more he will develop his own technique and will use the gestures that suit his artistic personality. Some musicians maintain that a detailed planning of gestures has little value, and that if the conductor knows the score thoroughly, his gestures will follow automatically. Since the gestures of even experienced conductors are not always adequate at first rehearsals, the inexperienced leader should certainly prepare himself as well as he can. It is only after many years that a conductor can react automatically to a difficult score without having organized his gestures in advance. As the foregoing study has shown, it is not always easy to co-ordinate the various motions. Especially in difficult passages, the student may have to conduct his imaginary orchestra again and again, before the sequence of motions is smooth and fits the music.

In preparing to conduct a score the student should keep in mind two basic requirements. (1) A strong feeling for the rhythm of each individual part as well as for the whole, which combines different rhythms, is needed to direct the players with authority. (2) Only if all the dynamic gradations are firmly fixed in the leader's mind, can his gestures be combined in a simple and natural way. Even highly talented young musicians, especially if their experience has been limited to the piano, often need great self-discipline to achieve certainty with regard to rhythm and dynamics.

Ex. 466: In order to direct this theme with conviction the conductor must study its rhythmic structure, especially the frequent change from 6/4 to 12/8.

Molto agitato ed energico, ♩. = 76   WILLIAM SCHUMAN, *Symphony for Strings*

Ex. 466

Copyright, 1943, by G. Schirmer, Inc.

Ex. 467: A polyrhythmic passage of this type needs careful study. You must know the various rhythmic figures and the way they are combined, or your gestures will lack firmness. The student will do well to direct each of the three groups separately before he conducts the whole.

Con spirito, (♩ = 80)   WALTON, *Viola Concerto*

Ex. 467

Reprinted by permission of the Oxford University Press, London
(U. S. A. Agents: Carl Fischer, Inc.)

Furthermore, the importance of knowing the orchestration thoroughly cannot be overestimated, not only for cuing but for the conductor's planning as well. As the baton moves, the mind follows a succession of instrumental parts. *The conductor thinks in a line that contains all the important musical elements and interpretation marks in terms of the instruments.*

Which musical elements are important? The conductor must decide when he will direct the melody, how much attention he will give to the inner parts, and which details need special attention. The choice of "what to conduct" lends individuality to the interpretation. For example: when two groups play the melody, the larger one is usually led more directly, but if a particular orchestral color is desired (as strings with solo wood-winds, the wood-wind color predominating), the smaller group is addressed. The effect of a passage may be greatly enhanced by directing counter-voices more strongly than the main melodic line. Generally speaking, however, it is unwise to pay too much attention to inner parts and to use elaborate gestures for a great number of small details, for this disturbs the logic of the over-all musical picture and may easily become a mannerism.

It must be pointed out that not every interpretation mark requires a gesture. The fact that all of the individual techniques have been discussed does not mean that they must *always* be applied. It is not necessary to indicate every accent or to lead every detail of the phrasing. This would result in an overloading of the gestures and would detract from the spontaneity of the performance. The mastery of baton technique is not an end in itself, and the student must develop a feeling for the proper use of this tool. He will then know how to use his gestures economically and will not miss the forest for the trees.

Another danger which the conductor must avoid is the tendency of his planned gestures to become so firmly fixed in his mind that during the performance he will not consider the players sufficiently. He must always remember that he is leading human beings and not the idealized orchestra of his private practising. He must not let his imagination and temperament carry him away, causing him to lose sight of reality and to neglect the needs of the musicians. The solution is to have a clear conception of how the score should sound, and yet be able to adapt the gestures to the actual response of the players. The leader must be mentally and physically alert in order to sense the players' reactions and to control them even when things occur that he did not anticipate.

Factors such as the quality of the players are important, because with less-experienced musicians the conductor's concern is with elementary needs, while with well-trained players his indications are directed more toward interpretative ends. In experienced orchestras the players themselves supply a good deal of precision and expression upon which the conductor can rely. Still, details of tempo, dynamics, and articulation that are *not* marked in the orchestral parts need stronger gestures than those that are. The results of rehearsal must also be considered: well-rehearsed details require less indication during the performance than those that have not been prepared.

ADJUSTMENTS WHILE IN ACTION

No one can foresee at all times how the players will respond; hence, the conductor's ear must be keen enough to realize what the orchestra is doing and, if the results are not as desired, the gestures must be adjusted accordingly.

The importance of the ability to maintain a definite tempo has already been stressed. If the players hurry or drag the music, a firm beat must counteract this. It may even become necessary to use staccato or tenuto (especially the "dry" tenuto) although the music is legato. If the tempo threatens to become uneven in staccato, the sharpness of the beat should increase. Such corrective measures, however, must not take the form of jerky gestures. Caution must be exercised particularly in accelerating the tempo when the players are dragging, because the acceleration may become too great. On the other hand, the common error of using an enlarged, spasmodic beat sometimes causes the tempo to drag still more. The best way of maintaining control is with relatively small but firm beats. This is also important for cases when the conductor may have to correct his own tempo. In general, it is easier to speed up after having started somewhat slowly than to do the contrary. In slow tempo, a subdivided beat may effectively prevent hurrying.

But the beat is secondary; it is most important that the conductor's feeling for the tempo be so strong that it cannot be affected by any irregularities on the part of the orchestra. Even though the beat may have to yield to the players for one or two counts for the sake of ensemble, the conductor must be able to bring the orchestra back to the correct tempo with flexible but firm gestures. As an invaluable exercise, the student should practise with a pianist who can follow the beat as an orchestra would, but who deliberately slows down or hurries, forcing the student to find the proper gestures with which to lead him back to the original tempo. This exercise should be practised with different rhythms, legato and staccato, and at different speeds.

Such flexibility is particularly useful in accompaniment because of unexpected delays, stops, and other emergencies. It is usually easier to wait than to catch up. If the latter is necessary, small beats are much more effective than large ones. Nervousness may lead to frantic motions that aggravate rather than help the situation. The conductor must train himself to remain calm in an emergency and should learn to anticipate difficulties before they arise. The same is true for adjusting entrances that are either missed or played prematurely. A useful technique to smooth out an early entrance is to hold the offender with a left-hand gesture while leading the rest of the group with the baton, being sure to bring the former into unity with the others. An angry wave of the hand only confuses the issue. The conductor's job is to help the performance and not to discipline the players. If the entrance is late, encourage the player to catch up while holding back the rest of the orchestra if necessary.

The conductor's consideration for what the musicians need should include even such mechanical problems as putting on and taking off mutes, or turning pages at a crucial moment during which he may have to wait slightly.

However well-rehearsed the ensemble and however well-marked the parts, only the actual sound of the music tells the conductor which gestures to use for dynamics. If the orchestra plays too loud in a f passage, the conductor may decrease the size of his gesture and even use the left hand to subdue the group. On the other hand, a p passage may not stand out sufficiently unless the conductor gives a large beat.

The degree of intensity in the gesture clearly depends upon the musicianship of the players. Occasionally the conductor will allow an individual player considerable freedom in the performance of a solo passage and will simply accompany him with the rest of the orchestra. For a well-balanced performance the leader must sense how much emotional intensity the players have, so that his gestures will strengthen weak sections but not give unnecessary stimulation to groups that do not need it. However, it does not follow that the conductor should ever be lacking in intensity. He must never allow himself to adopt a passive attitude, for the orchestra expects that he will do his share of the work, and if he does not, it is inclined to lose interest.

All this discussion may provoke the questions: to what extent do the players watch the baton, and how much can their playing be influenced after the rehearsals have been completed? Of course this depends partly on the individual player's technical ability and alertness. But except for the rare occasions when his attention is completely absorbed by a very difficult passage, the average player gives a considerable part of his effort to watching the baton. If this were not so, it would be hard to explain the remarkable influence exercised by an able conductor at a first reading of unfamiliar music. Still, the conductor should co-operate with the players by assisting them with very clear and, if necessary, larger gestures, either in passages of great technical difficulty or when something goes wrong and decisive leadership is demanded.

Another question that is often asked is: how much does the conductor accomplish during a performance, as compared with the work done in rehearsal? One opinion is that practically all of the conductor's effectiveness is due to the drilling that the orchestra undergoes during rehearsal. On the other hand it has been argued that baton technique may be developed to the point where the orchestra can perform in all details according to the conductor's desires, even without rehearsal. Neither of these extreme answers is satisfactory. A carefully prepared reading can be spoiled in public performance if, for any reason, the conductor's baton technique does not match the standard set in rehearsal. Nervousness may give rise to a vague beat or to the indication of an incorrect tempo. Nevertheless, there are many details that must be clarified orally in rehearsal. If these oral explanations are accompanied by a sound baton technique, the conductor can achieve, in a short time, results that would require much longer practice on the part of an orchestra unassisted by visible guidance. This has been proved in the case of conductorless orchestras, where it was actually necessary to schedule four times as many rehearsals as would have been needed with a competent conductor.

But the conductor's function goes far beyond the mere exercise of control. His technique must be a means through which to vitalize the orchestra. The music must always sing within him; then his gestures will not become mechanical. When technical mastery is combined with musical inspiration, the conductor makes his players feel that he is working *with* them. In the absence of these qualities the players feel restricted and are affected *negatively*. A good conductor works as an artistic leader and not as a disciplinarian; he is stimulating and affects his players *positively*. Perhaps only experience can reveal how crucial a distinction this is. For only a direct and positive approach inspires the players; this is the secret of vital and dramatic orchestral performances.

APPENDIX

Discussion of Complete Works or Movements

1.

Edvard Grieg

THE DEATH OF ÅSE

from *Peer Gynt Suite No. 1, Op. 46*

Miniature Scores: Kalmus No. 20; Baron No. 98
Recordings: Sir Thomas Beecham conducting the London Philharmonic
Orchestra—in Columbia Album X-MX-180
Eugene Goossens conducting the Cincinnati Symphony
Orchestra—in Victor Album M-DM-1100
Walter Goehr conducting the London Symphony Or-
chestra—Decca Record No. K1319

You may pause for a moment before starting, to prepare the calm
atmosphere. Then give the preliminary beat and direct the first 4 bars
poco espressivo. In bars 1 and 2, keep *Three* small so that *Four*, which
is a sort of preparation for the next phrase, is expressive without being
too large. You may give some indication of vibrato with the left hand
in bars 3 and 4. On *Four* in the 4th measure, turn the palm of the left
hand toward the orchestra. Beat non-espressivo in bars 5-8. The emphasis which is put on *Four* in the 8th measure cuts off the players together and prepares the *mf* (espressivo). It is better to do the crescendo with the baton, saving the left hand for later. *One* in bar 10
is a small gesture to start the repetition of the phrase softly again. Use
the left hand for the *p* in bar 13. At the beginning of the 15th bar, keep
the gestures especially small, then increase their size for the crescendo.
In the 16th measure, *Two* is suddenly small, the left hand indicating
p. *Three* is larger for the crescendo and *Four* is full-staccato for the *fz*.

From bar 17, beat molto espressivo. For the accents, click on the counts. In bar 24 sustain the volume of the half-note with the left hand. Cut off on *Four* with both baton (staccato) and left hand (*cf.* p. 135). This staccato beat changes quickly into a legato preparation for the *p* attack. The gestures in bars 25 and 26 should not be too small, so that they may be decreased for the *pp*. Express the slight ⎯⎯⎯ ⎯⎯ with the baton. Be economical with the left-hand gestures and they will be more effective at the end of the piece. A strong warning gesture for *pp* is to put the index finger of the left hand to the lips. The fading away in the last bar is discussed on page 168.

The orchestration presents no particular problems. Lead the entire group, giving slightly more attention to the 1st violins. In bars 15-21, bring out the 'cellos either by looking at them or by directing an expressive left-hand gesture toward them. In the 27th measure the violas should be emphasized; it is sufficient to look at them. Bring in the basses in bar 33 in the same way.

2.

Wolfgang Amadeus Mozart

SYMPHONY NO. 39, K.543—MINUET

Miniature Scores: Boosey & Hawkes No. 165; Kalmus No. 33; Baron
                        No. 16; Harcourt, Brace "Arrow" Scores; Pro Art
                        No. 30; Eulenburg No. 415; Broude
Recordings: Sir Thomas Beecham conducting the London Philharmonic
                        Orchestra—in Columbia Album M-MM-456
                        Bruno Walter conducting the BBC Symphony Orchestra
                        —in Victor Album M-DM-258
                        Walter Goehr conducting the National Symphony Orchestra—Decca Record No. K1238

3-beat, ♩ = 132. In contrast to the preceding piece, the music is gay and joyous. This must be felt as soon as you lift the baton for attention. Do not wait long; too much hesitation may spoil the players' enthusiasm for the opening. Beat the 1st bar with a snappy and stimulating beat (full-staccato), but not too large! In playing Mozart *f* should never be exaggerated. The rhythmic element in this music is very strong, and once the tempo is established, it is not necessary to emphasize it any longer. Thus, small beats may be used in bars 2 and 3, but they must express the energy of the violin passage. When the melody ends in bar 4, the wind chords must not be dull. Therefore, give the players a stimulating glance, or use a left-hand gesture to bring out the staccato brilliantly. Save the contrast of a larger baton gesture for the up-beat on *Three* which prepares the start of the second phrase.

In the 8th measure the winds take care of themselves, playing *f* to the end. Lead the violins into the *p*. Use a slightly larger down-beat in bars 9 and 10 for the *mfp*. For this, lift the baton higher on the preceding up-beat than you would for a regular *p*. Beat light-staccato in the 11th, legato in the 12th measure. Cue the winds in; since they are playing legato while the strings have some staccato notes, use a gentle light-staccato with the detached quality not felt very strongly. The last 2 beats in bar 15 are legato. In the 16th measure *Two* is very small, but *Three* is a large preparation. Do not forget to look at the trumpets and tympani for their cue.

The slurs in bars 21 and 22 are for bowing and not for expression; beat staccato. An espressivo beat in the next 2 bars would distort the character of the music, because the rhythmic element is still predominant. The beat is essentially staccato but not sharp. *Three* in bar 24 is done with a lifted forearm for a good attack on the repetition. On *Three* in bar 38, lift the baton again for the closing tutti; by doing it gently you will not disturb the *p*.

3.

Johann Sebastian Bach

AIR FROM SUITE NO. 3 IN D MAJOR

Miniature Scores: Baron No. 149; Boosey & Hawkes No. 263; Broude; Associated; Longmans Green "Arrow" Scores; Eulenburg No. 818

Recordings: Arturo Toscanini conducting the NBC Symphony Orchestra—in Victor Album M-DM-1080 (Record No. 11-9344)

Serge Koussevitzky conducting the Boston Symphony Orchestra—in Victor Album M-DM-1123

Adolf Busch conducting the Busch Chamber Players—in Victor Album M-DM-339
Felix Weingartner conducting the Paris Conservatory Orchestra—in Columbia Album M-MM-428

Subdivided 4-beat, ♪ = 72. The entire piece is done with a legato beat. The main function of the baton is to keep the rhythm moving steadily but unobtrusively, and to bring out the various melodic impulses. The continuous flow of the melody must be maintained without undue emphasis of the 1st beat in each bar.

Use a clear eighth-note preparation for the start, and beat the 1st measure non-espressivo with a slight click on each beat to establish the rhythm. The espressivo starts on the 2nd eighth in bar 2. Address the 'cellos and basses in the 1st measure by looking in their direction. Turn your head toward the 1st violins in bar 2, always beating in the center for all to see. It is advisable to turn the palm of the left hand toward the 1st violins just before the 3rd bar, to insure a soft attack. At the same time turn your head to the 2nd violins and lead their melody. Turn back to the 1st violins on the 5th eighth.

In a similar manner bring out the various melodic ideas in the inner parts throughout the piece. To do this well, you must know the polyphonic structure and think with the 4 different parts as they move along. In places like the first half of bar 5 and the last half of bar 10, there is no melodic movement and consequently no espressivo is needed. When bar 6 is played the first time, lead the bass instruments in their sixteenth-note movement. The second time, beat non-espressivo in the second half of that bar. The fermata in the last bar applies only to the repetition; stop on the 5th eighth-note and keep the baton up as long as you want to sustain the chord, then cut.

Since no dynamics are marked in the original score, each conductor must decide for himself how he wants to shade the music. In any event, the rise and fall of the melody requires changes in the size of the beat, depending on the individual interpretation. The subdivided beat, however, must be clear enough so that the players are never in doubt as to where you are.

4.

Ludwig van Beethoven

SYMPHONY NO. 7–THIRD MOVEMENT

Miniature Scores: Baron No. 7; Boosey & Hawkes No. 114; Kalmus
                    No. 7; Eulenburg No. 412; Pro Art No. 15
Recordings: Arturo Toscanini conducting the Philharmonic-Symphony
              Orchestra of New York—in Victor Album M-DM-317
              Eugene Ormandy conducting the Philadelphia Orchestra—
              in Columbia Album M-MM-557
              Felix Weingartner conducting the Vienna Philharmonic
              Orchestra—in Columbia Album M-MM-260

SCHERZO. It is indispensable for conducting this music to know
how the phrase groups are built. Thus, the 1st section up to the double
bar is divided into phrases of 2, 4, 4, 6, 4, and 4 bars. The 2nd section
starts with a 4-bar phrase in the strings followed by an 8-bar phrase in
the flutes and clarinets, and a 4-bar phrase in the violins and violas. The
next phrase ends with a sudden *ff*. The succeeding 16 bars are metri-
cally similar. The following 5 bars (starting with the 61st measure)
have the oboe and bassoon entrance 1 bar before the end of the 4-bar
phrase in the strings; this overlapping entrance starts a 2-bar phrase all
within bars 61-65. Now there are 4 phrases of 4 bars each, then 4+3,
leading back to the repetition. Bars 89-98 are similar to the beginning
but with different orchestration; the 8-bar inversion following this is
new, as is the next 4-bar phrase divided between the strings and winds.
After the 6-bar phrase (starting with the 111th measure) the section
ends with 8 regular 4-bar phrases.

Familiarize yourself thoroughly with the orchestration, especially
in connection with the phrase groups, and the dynamics.

Use 1-beat, staccato throughout. Start with an energetic full-staccato; the preliminary beat has up-beat character (*cf.* Ex. 153). Be sure
that the sudden *p* in the 3rd bar is well expressed by the baton and
left hand, which requires mental preparation on the part of the conductor. While the orchestra is playing the entire 2nd measure *f*, you
must think of the *p* subito that is coming. In terms of gesture, this
means that the right hand changes suddenly from a fairly large and

vigorous beat to a small and light one. Increase the size for the crescendo and use sharper beats for *sf*.

Do not think it necessary to wave dramatically at each group of
strings starting with bar 25. Beat straight ahead and look at the various
groups, scarcely turning the head. Save the left hand for the *pp* in bar
33. The trick of executing the sudden *ff* is to avoid any emphasis on
the down-beat in bar 43, but immediately snap the baton up to prepare
the tutti chords. Return at once to the light *p* beat. Cue in the oboe and
bassoon in the 63rd bar. To get an effective climax, lead in the string
entrances just before the repetition.

In this fast 1-beat the *ff* must be expressed by the intensity of the
beat, not the size; too large a beat would be very awkward. Be careful
of the sudden *p* in bars 99 and 117. The groups of wind chords starting in bar 118 must be light and delicate; how to direct this, using
either hand, is up to the individual.

The left hand sustains the *ff* of the last 4 bars (1st ending) before
the double bar; the right hand beats *ff* only the 1st of these measures,
then marks time with non-espressivo beats for 2 bars and uses the 4th
for preparation. At the 2nd ending use the left hand for the diminuendo. Some conductors make a ritardando in these 4 bars, or beat the
last one in the tempo of the Trio to prepare the change to the slower
tempo. This is not indicated by the composer, and the change of
tempo can be executed just by starting off in the new tempo at
"Assai meno presto"; the beat in the 2 first bars of the Trio must be
very definite to establish the tempo.

TRIO. Many conductors take this at a considerably slower tempo
than that indicated by the composer, but the tempo must not be too
slow because of the length of the movement (double repetition!). The
phrases in the Trio are quite regular and easy to analyze, while the
orchestration presents no particular problem.

Most of the Trio requires the legato beat. There should be some espressivo quality in it because of the ⎯⎯⎯ ⎯⎯⎯, and to lead the
melodic line, as in bar 154. This is more effective if you use non-
espressivo in bars 150 and 152 as well as in 155 and 156.

Starting with the 199th measure there is an 8-bar syncopated passage with gradual crescendo. The beat must be very precise and may

develop some staccato quality. As the beat becomes larger (crescendo) it approaches marcato. The down-beat in bar 205 should be especially emphasized to stimulate the entering instruments. It is more important here to watch the strings than the flutes and 1st horn. A very energetic marcato is used for the *ff*.

In the traditional slower tempo it is advisable to subdivide, beating *One-Three*, particularly in bars 213 and 214, to keep a firm hold on the rhythmic figure in the trumpets and tympani. For the *fp* in the horns use a staccato beat changing immediately to non-espressivo.

To change back to Presto, beat as if the passage were written:

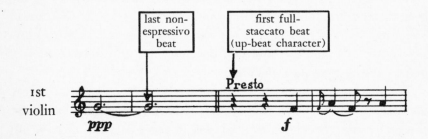

Starting with bar 260 the 1st section of the Scherzo is repeated, but *p*. The gestures are small and precise, to insure a clear and delicate staccato from the orchestra. The left hand is especially needed in bar 285 where the 2nd section begins, also *p*. The tutti chords (bar 303) are now *pp*; the snappy preparation is extremely small.

CODA. While the change to "Assai meno presto" is done the same way as before, the attack of the last Presto requires a preparation strictly in tempo. For this, insert an extra (preliminary) presto beat, which also cuts off the strings, giving them a chance to lift the bow for the *ff*.

In conducting this movement from memory, it is necessary to have a clear picture of how the repetitions differ from one another:

SCHERZO. 1st section repeated
             2nd   "   "

TRIO.   1st   "   "   (repeat written out,
                                  orchestration changed)

             2nd   "   "

Transition

SCHERZO. 1st section repeated (repeat written out,
                                              dynamics changed)
              2nd   "   not repeated (dynamics changed)

TRIO.   1st   "   same as 1st time
              2nd   "   repetition often omitted

Transition

SCHERZO. 1st   "   not repeated
              2nd   "   "   "

CODA.

5.

Michail Glinka

OVERTURE TO "RUSSLAN AND LUDMILLA"

Miniature Scores: Baron No. 52; Russian-American Music Publishers;
                          Eulenburg No. 639
Recordings: Eugene Ormandy conducting the Philadelphia Orchestra—
                   Columbia Record No. 19010D
                   Fabien Sevitzky conducting the Indianapolis Symphony Or-
                   chestra—Victor Record No. 17731
                   Arthur Fiedler conducting the Boston "Pops" Orchestra—
                   Victor Record No. 4427

This piece is sometimes performed faster than the original metronome marking of $\quartnote = 135$, but if it is played too quickly, the rhythmic
precision suffers. A full-staccato preliminary beat sets the very determined rhythm of the beginning, and any hesitation would weaken the
rhythmic thrust of the first few bars.

BAR   1 F.   *One* is very sharp (>), *Two* relatively light.
BAR   12 FF. The desire to keep the passage co-ordinated must not
                  lead to a heavy beat, which hampers rather than
                  stimulates the players.
BAR   19   Because of the speed, the winds must be alerted suffi-
                  ciently in advance so that they will not come in late.
BAR   21   "Brillante" requires a highly stimulating preparatory
                  gesture for the attack.

Bar 25   Syncopation gesture.

Bar 45   Because of the high position on the E-string, the violins must be subdued or they will play *f* instead of *mf*.

Bar 48 ff. Throughout this section the motions should be kept fairly small, even in *ff*, to secure the necessary precision.

Bar 53   The brass section expects a clear-cut *One*.

Bar 58   A small, concise beat controls the off-beat entrances and the pizzicato.

Bar 59 ff. Gentle staccato is best for this passage. Know the cues well!

Bar 62   *Two* is preparatory.

Bar 68 f.   Address the brass instruments and immediately turn to the trumpets and horns (*fp!*).

Bar 77   Sudden change to light-staccato with very delicate motions.

Bar 79   Lead the violas.

Bar 81 ff. Beat espressivo-legato; you may use a free style gesture (page 310).

Bar 85 ff. Bring out the accents and the phrasing.

Bar 97   The third horn has had a long rest, and a reminder at this entrance is helpful.

Bar 101   The gesture indicates only *mf* with the crescendo still to come.

Bar 119   Change to light-staccato.

Bar 120   A clear *One* is needed for the violins.

Bar 133 ff. Use the left hand for diminuendo. Cue in the successive entrances. Use small beats except for the *sf*.

Bar 139   A very energetic gesture is needed to bring out the crescendo in the strings within the short space of 2 measures.

Bar 141   The trumpets enter after a long rest.

Bar 143 ff. Keep the tempo clear even during the rests.

Bar 154   The 2nd violins must be watched for a unified pizzicato.

Bar 156   Tympani cue.

Bar 161 ff. The music is moving rapidly and the cuing gestures must be very clear.

BAR 162   A sharp *Two* brings in the accented clarinet entrance.

BAR 165   Cue in trumpets and double-basses, 2 bars later the trombones.

BAR 190 FF.   Notice the change of orchestration.

BAR 209   Indicate the change to *p*.

BAR 215   Cue in the 1st pair of horns, 2 bars later the trombones.

BAR 229   Although the trombones have not had many measures of rest, they should be addressed clearly.

BAR 293 FF.   Different orchestration, *sfp* instead of >.

BAR 321   This time trumpets and tympani are added.

BAR 346 FF.   Cue in the strings successively (no crescendo!).

BAR 351   Indicate *f* for the tympani.

BAR 357 FF.   Address the brass, violins, and wood-winds in succession.

BAR 373   Sudden increase in tempo ($\boldsymbol{\downarrow}$=160 — 176). The change in tempo is sometimes made with a gradual increase, starting either in bar 349 or 357.

BAR 397   Sharp down-beat so that all the players stop precisely.

6.

Ludwig van Beethoven

OVERTURE TO "EGMONT"

Miniature Scores: Baron No. 43; Boosey & Hawkes No. 121; Kalmus No. 67; Eulenburg No. 604; Hampton Vol. 3

Recordings: Arturo Toscanini conducting the NBC Symphony Orchestra—HMV Record No. G-DB5705

Felix Weingartner conducting the Vienna Philharmonic Orchestra—Columbia Record No. 69195-D

Willem Mengelberg conducting the Philharmonic-Symphony Orchestra of New York—Victor Record No. 7291

In the introduction the 3/2-time is subdivided, and the tempo is generally taken $\boldsymbol{\downarrow}$ = 76 — 92.

BAR   1   Use a quarter-note preparation (staccato) for the opening fermata. The extent to which you indicate the diminuendo depends on the orchestra's response. Use a quarter-beat for cut-off and preparation for bar 2.

BAR 2   Giving equal emphasis to each quarter-beat would result in the rhythmic figure ♩ 𝄾 ♩ 𝄾 , but the notation leads us to assume that Beethoven wanted ♩. 𝄾
♩. 𝄾 . Therefore use the tenuto technique, with strong
emphasis on the 1st and 3rd quarters; the 2nd quarter
is used for a connecting gesture. The 4th is in the
manner of a cut-off, and the 5th relatively weak. The
6th is a strong preliminary beat.

BAR 4   The 6th beat is done with a gentle staccato, now indicating *p*.

BAR 5   Beat non-espressivo with clear subdivision; elaborate
gestures would be out of place here.

BAR 6   The 6th quarter may have a slight staccato quality, to
bring out the separation from the following note.
Clear separations of this kind are typical of classic
style and should always be carefully observed.

BAR 8   Indicate the crescendo with the left hand; do not slow
down the tempo, and use the accented up-beat on *Six*.

BAR 9   Using *Six* for preparation would cut the players off and
result in a quarter rest. To hold the *ff* unison as long
as possible, you may use a shortened preparation for
the next bar.

BAR 14   Do not use too small a gesture for the *p* string entrance,
since it is played with some vibrato. The *pp* gesture
must be still smaller.

BAR 15 FF.   An unobtrusive staccato beat on *Six* secures the rhythmic emphasis for the motive in the 'cellos and basses.

BAR 22   After the previous non-espressivo bars, a small espressivo gesture will be sufficient. The horn entrances
should be controlled if necessary.

BAR 25   The new tempo (♩. = 60 — 76) starts without time
for preparation, and therefore this bar requires an unmistakably clear beat. Whether to use straight 1-beat
or a slight subdivision (in the first 4 bars only!) is a
matter of individual taste. Indicate the crescendo by
increasing the intensity, but not the size, of the beat.

BAR 28	The *sfp* is indicated by subdivision or by a sharp up-beat; legato beat follows.
BAR 42	Change to staccato beat; no crescendo until marked in the score!
BAR 47 FF.	*Gradual* crescendo.
BARS 58, 62	High rebound for strong preparation.
BAR 74 FF.	Beat marcato. By this time the tempo may have increased slightly, but the contrast to the second theme (bar 82) must not be too obvious.
BAR 82	The tempo is slightly slower; the forceful chords on *One* and *Two* must be directed by using 3-beat, though not with the regular pattern, which would be too academic. Beat *Two* with a strong but quite small motion, carrying only slightly to the right. Also, *Three* should be comparatively small but sharp.
BAR 84	1-beat legato.
BAR 93 FF.	Indicate the crescendo by intensity of gesture, saving the first large motion for preparation of the *ff* in bar 99.
BAR 100 FF.	The *sf* may be indicated by a sharp upward motion on *Three*, or by the left hand.
BAR 116	Sudden change to legato gesture, leading into the lyric movement.
BAR 123	The *p* must not be disturbed by the way you lead the *f* chords. Use a sudden staccato gesture.
BAR 146 FF.	A legato gesture with clicking brings out both the melody in the low strings and the rhythmic motive in the violins.
BAR 153 FF.	The beat must remain very steady.
BAR 163 FF.	Because of the changed orchestration (winds) it may be necessary to add some staccato to the beat.
BAR 206	The wind chords are important for the modulation. A strong gesture should obtain the greatest possible volume from the winds.
BAR 215	A strong *One* must be addressed to the 1st violins.
BAR 259 FF.	Use a small but extremely intense gesture.

BAR 263 FF.   By contrast the gesture must express the timid feeling of these 4 bars.

Bar 266   Subdivide *One-(two-)Three; Three* prepares the *ff*.

BAR 278   Beat *One-Three* (*Three* with a sidewise motion) and stop abruptly.

BAR 279   After the pause use a whole-beat preparation.

BAR 281 FF.   Indicate the entrances very quietly.

BAR 286   The cut-off is usually the preliminary beat (♩ = 168 — 184) which must express the subdued excitement of the beginning of the Allegro con brio.

BAR 287 FF.   Do not make the crescendo too early.

BAR 294   Lead the trumpet (*p* ◁ *ff*) and beat a subdivided 2-beat as transition to

BAR 295   Alla breve, but do not rush (not faster than ♩ = 96).

BAR 309 FF.   Subdivision may be useful to keep the violins from hurrying.

BAR 313   At this point the gesture should not be too emphatic, because of the crescendo which follows.

BAR 317 FF.   Use marcato beats.

BAR 319   Bring out the trumpets.

BAR 329   The down-beat is also the preparation for the *sf* (*cf.* Ex. 99).

7.

Johann Strauss

OVERTURE TO "DIE FLEDERMAUS" ("THE BAT")

Miniature Score: Eulenburg No. 1103
Recordings: Bruno Walter conducting the Paris Conservatory Orchestra —in Victor Album M-DM-805 (Record No. 13688)
      Bruno Walter conducting the Berlin State Opera Orchestra—Columbia Record No. 9080-M
      Arthur Fiedler conducting the Boston "Pops" Orchestra—Victor Record No. 12-0189
      Eugene Ormandy conducting the Minneapolis Symphony Orchestra—Victor Record No. 8651

The entrance cues will no longer be mentioned, since a thorough study of the score is presupposed and the techniques of cuing have been amply demonstrated. As a test for himself the student should be able to listen to a recording of the entire piece without being surprised at any entrance.

Conductors differ widely in their interpretation of this work, there being no unanimity even among the Viennese. The following discussion is concerned mainly with baton technique and is based on the general tradition.

BAR	1 FF.	♩ = 132-138, full staccato. Only the preparatory beat is large, as is *Two* in bar 2. In this way you direct the motive |♩ ♩ ♩ 𝄾 | strongly and indicate the rhythm for the run with a minimum of gesture.
BAR	4	Here *Two* is not preparatory; the next preparation is on *One* in the next measure.
BAR	8	Use the left hand for the *p*.
BAR	12	The cut-off gesture should leave the baton at a medium height, to allow a convenient preparation for the next tempo.
BAR	13	♩ = 84 (alla breve), non-espressivo.
BAR	15	The conductor may or may not lead the oboe solo; if he does, any exaggeration should be avoided.
BAR	19	Address the 1st violins with an espressivo-legato beat.
BAR	21	*Two* is staccato to stimulate the piquant violin figure.
BAR	22	Address the 2nd violins; their staccato notes must be audible and played scherzando.
BAR	27	Sudden change to light staccato.
BAR	31 F.	Some conductors make a transition back to the original tempo by means of a stringendo, although this is not necessary. In any event, an intensive gesture is needed for the *p* ⟤ *ff*.
BAR	37 F.	Syncopation beat.
BAR	41 FF.	♩ = 58. Beat marcato on the *fp*, then use tenuto. The tenuto pattern, with its connecting gestures, produces a unified attack by flutes, oboe, and bell, which would not respond very well to a legato motion.
BAR	47	♩ = 100. Light staccato. The first 2 beats in the Alle-

gretto must be given so convincingly that the tempo
is clear to the 'cellos and bassoon and that the violas
have no doubt about their sixteenth-notes. It is possible to use the last eighth in the Lento to prepare the
new tempo; in this case, the eighth-beat must be
lengthened so as to correspond to the following quarter-beat.

BAR 50   Change to poco espressivo.

BAR 55   Light-staccato.

BAR 58   Espressivo-legato, stringendo to about ♩ = 112.

BAR 69   Indicate a sharp *fz* (trumpets!) on *One* and do not fail
to establish the slower tempo (♩ = 100) decisively.

BAR 73   Make a slight ritardando so that *Two* prepares Meno
mosso (♩ = 92).

BAR 74 FF. This passage should be directed with freedom of gesture,
and the alternation of staccato and legato should be
brought out.

BARS 82, 90 Most conductors hold back slightly on *Two*.

BAR 97   Lead the 'cellos with an espressivo gesture.

BAR 99 FF. The poco rit. is usually distributed over the next 5 bars
and should not be exaggerated.

BAR 104   Più mosso (♩ = 116) is traditional here. Beat light-
staccato.

BAR 106   Prepare the pizzicato clearly.

BAR 107   Change to an espressivo gesture suggesting vibrato for
the accompanying strings. These instruments have a
tendency to drag at this point unless led convincingly.

BAR 108   The poco rit. is done one bar early.

BAR 109   Give the flute and violins time for the eighth-note A.

BAR 110   ♩ = 116. Observe that the first ♪ is still *p*, but beat
it staccato.

BAR 114   Use the left hand for the *p*.

BAR 121   This bar is traditionally held back somewhat. Various
editions disagree as to whether the last note is C♯ or D.

BAR 122   ♩. = 69, 1-beat. Some conductors feel that they get a
better *pp* ⟨⟩ *f* by using 3-beat for the first 4 bars,
starting at slightly slower tempo and speeding up until

bar 126. For this you need a very agile beat, or the orchestra will fall behind; use subdivision for the transition from 3-beat to 1-beat (*cf.* Ex. 218).

BAR 126   Address the double-basses strongly.

BAR 128   Beat *One-Three* for the accent on the 3rd quarter.

BAR 131   The ♪♪♩ ♩ requires a dynamic preparation. The same is true for the trombone attack in bar 141 ff.

BAR 165   The end of the musical thought is indicated by a strong marcato beat. Let a fraction of a second elapse before the next attack.

BAR 166   Three different executions of this measure can be heard.
　　　　　(1) 3-beat with ritardando,
　　　　　(2) 3-beat with ⌢ on *One*, the 2 eighth-notes still played with ritardando,
　　　　　(3) 1-beat with ⌢ on the half-note and repeated beat without ritardando; the 2 eighth-notes are thus strictly in tempo.

BAR 168   Beat *One-Three* in free style.

BAR 181   ♩. = ♩ , which means ♩ = 138. Use small gestures.

BAR 200   Use a dry tenuto beat on *One*, indicating a slight pause which gives the 1st bassoonist time to breathe. Then stop on *Two* for the fermata.

BAR 201 FF.   ♩ = 76. Start beating non-espressivo and develop gradually to espressivo.

BAR 209   Change to staccato at "a tempo".

BAR 210   Resume the legato beat, emphasizing *One* for the off-beat accents.

BAR 215   A large gesture on *Three* brings the melody into sharper relief.

BAR 218   According to tradition the oboe plays poco rubato. The conductor may lead the accompaniment unobtrusively or direct the melody, depending on his personality and that of the oboist.

BAR 224   An effect of comic exaggeration, intended by the composer, can be secured with an expressive tenuto beat on each count.

BAR 225   A tempo.

BAR 228   Usually a pause is made before the start of the new theme. For this, cut off the violins with the left hand so that the baton is spared for the preparatory *Two*. Most conductors lead the up-beat staccato and hesitate before attacking the next bar. Usually this section starts at ♩ = 96-108, and the actual Allegro (♩ = 138) is not reached until bar 236. The accents in the melody always require an emphasized beat.

BAR 248 FF.   Use a light gesture to keep the playing from becoming too heavy. As a contrast, direct the motive ♪♩♩ ♪ (bars 252 and 254) with a vigorous beat.

BAR 260   Indicate the *fp* and bring out the horn.

BAR 269   Precise up-beat so that the trumpet will not drag.

BAR 278 FF.   Except for the change in orchestration, this section is the same as when it occurred the first time (*cf.* bar 74).

BAR 315   A smooth transition can be made by beating *Two* so that ♩ = ♩. of the following waltz tempo.

BAR 351 FF.   A slower tempo (♩ = 132) is suggested because of the tricky string passages. If these bars are taken too rapidly, the double-basses may produce disagreeable sounds!

BAR 357   Resume the faster tempo.

BAR 371 FF.   Often conductors play a ritardando, with the theme slightly held back (not as much as the first time) and speeding up until bar 380. However, it is at least as effective when played in tempo, accenting the octave jumps sharply and playing the theme with a sudden *pp*.

BAR 388   ♩ = 160, with small gestures.

BAR 395   Beat *One* sharply in case the brass instruments tend to fall behind.

BAR 404   A definite indication is needed for this contrasting *p* subito.

BAR 412 FF.   Bring out the syncopated motive in the horns and trombones.

BAR 419   Lift the baton for a strong preparation so as to direct the concluding measure with one energetic stroke.

8.

Claude Debussy

"FÊTES" ("FESTIVALS")

(No. 2 from Nocturnes for Orchestra)

Miniature Scores: Kalmus No. 101; Boosey & Hawkes No. 577; Jobert; Harcourt, Brace "Arrow" Scores; Hampton Vol. 7
Recordings: Eugene Ormandy conducting the Philadelphia Orchestra —in Columbia Album No. MX-247 (Record No. 12110D)
Leopold Stokowski conducting the Philadelphia Orchestra —Victor Record No. 2034 (also in Album M-DM-630)
Désiré Inghelbrecht conducting the Grand Orchestre des Festivals Debussy—in Columbia Album M-MM-344

Because of the intricacy of this score it is recommended that the student listen to the phonograph record several times before practising the baton technique.

BAR   1   This is usually taken at ♩ = 176. A subdivided 2-beat is suggested because of the speed and the accents on the 1st and 3rd quarters; prepare either with a half-note or a quarter-beat. Use the marcato gesture for the beginning.

BARS   3, 7   There is a marked difference in intensity of beat between *ff* and *f*, especially in the 3rd measure where three wood-winds must be heard against the entire violin section.

BAR   9   Light-staccato, wrist motion only!

BAR   10   Use a larger beat on *Three*, but a smaller one on *Four*. This brings out the crescendo and secures an immediate *pp* in the next bar.

BAR   13 F.   Indicate the accents.

BAR   23   The tempo is twice as slow. Beat this bar with a strong marcato, using the regular 4-beat. Include in *Three* the preparation for the tympani.

BAR 24   Sustain the *ff*.

BAR 25   Cut off the wind chord sharply and keep strictly in tempo during the *p*══ of the tympani. Subdivide *Four* and use the last eighth-beat to prepare the harp entrance (original tempo, ♪ = ♪ !).

BAR 27   The tempo is slightly faster (♩. = 184). The pattern is 5-beat, grouped into 3 + 2 by the composer. The *sfz* in strings and cymbal requires a sharp gesture on *One*, followed immediately by light staccato.

BAR 29   3-beat (♩. = ♩). After the accented *One* use small beats for a subdued accompaniment; the flutes and oboes play *f* on their own initiative.

BAR 39 FF.   Keep the tempo well in hand.

BAR 41   A slight ═══ ══ of this sort can be indicated effectively by adding a gentle motion of the forearm to the wrist movement.

Bar 44   Keep the beat small and precise. The difficult passages of the English horn and oboes will be impossible to play if the tempo has been hurried previously.

Bar 46   Do not become so preoccupied with the main instruments that you forget the double-bass entrance!

BAR 49   The larger gesture on *Three*, which prepares the next bar, will not disturb the flute passage.

BAR 52   Strong indication of the rapid diminuendo.

BAR 55   A slightly emphasized *Two* helps the oboe.

BAR 63   A definite *One* brings the trumpets in precisely.

BAR 64   Weaken *Two* and *Three* so as not to conflict with the quadruplet.

BAR 70 FF.   Bring out the crescendo in the wood-winds by addressing only this group.

BAR 82   Indicate the *pp* subito in the 1st violins with a sudden left-hand gesture.

BAR 86 FF.   For this passage the beat must express both legato and staccato. Beat a slight marcato on *One*, but legato on

Two-Three, the pattern being the subdivided 1-beat rather than an actual 3-beat.

BAR 97   The left hand may be used for the *sfz* on *Three*.

BAR 102 FF.   The crescendo in the winds needs no indication; save your gesture until bar 106.

BAR 116 $\quad$ = 88 (twice as slow as the quarter-beat in the opening). Light-staccato.

BAR 124 FF.   The precision of the gesture must not be felt as a restraint on the Gallic "esprit".

BAR 138 FF.   Do not speed up the tempo.

BAR 151 FF.   A well-balanced climax requires economy of gesture.

BAR 170 FF.   Use a heavy marcato gesture but without slowing down. (A steady tempo is necessary for the coming transition to I° Tempo.)

BAR 174   If the tempo has been maintained strictly, the last bar in 2/4 is exactly as long as 2 bars in the new 6/8 ($\quad$ = $\quad$ = 176).

BAR 190 FF.   The violins play 3 notes against 2 beats; therefore, weaken *Two*.

BAR 202   Here, as a rule, the faster tempo ($\quad$ = 184) is established.

BAR 209   The cymbal entrance may be indicated with the left hand.

BAR 221   Indicate the crescendo strongly.

BAR 233   Use a sharp wrist motion on *Three* for the pizzicato in the violas.

BAR 236 FF.   Small gestures with the utmost precision.

BAR 252   Slower tempo immediately. Since no preparation is possible, the 1st and 2nd beats must be decisive enough to establish the new tempo.

BAR 260   A well-prepared *Three* leads the pizzicato and the *sf* in the horns, and brings in the English horn, clarinet, and 1st horn.

BAR 264 F.   The 3rd beat must be flexible enough to allow the flutes and oboes time to play their triplet figure without rushing.

BAR 266   Sudden "a tempo".

BAR 269 FF. Delicate handling of the baton and a clear mind are needed for directing the fleeting notes of the close.

9.

Felix Mendelssohn

VIOLIN CONCERTO—THIRD MOVEMENT

Miniature Scores: Baron No. 209; Boosey & Hawkes No. 239; Eulenburg No. 702; Kalmus No. 145; Longmans Green "Arrow" Scores

Recordings: Nathan Milstein, with Philharmonic-Symphony Orchestra of New York, Bruno Walter conductor—in Columbia Album M-MM-577

Joseph Szigeti, with London Philharmonic Orchestra, Sir Thomas Beecham conductor—in Columbia Album M-MM-190

Fritz Kreisler, with London Philharmonic Orchestra, Sir Landon Ronald conductor—in Victor Album M-DM-277

Yehudi Menuhin, with L'Orchestre des Concerts Colonne, Georges Enesco conductor—in Victor Album M-DM-531

Start practising at the Allegretto non troppo. This short transition follows a fermata. Whether there is a pause, caused by applause or tuning, or whether the violinist proceeds directly, be ready for the solo entry. If you do not lift your arm until he starts playing, you will not arrive at the 1st beat in time. Keep the baton in the position of attention, and just as the violinist attacks the up-beat, make the preparatory gesture without hesitation. Follow the traditional rubato in bars 9 and 10, synchronizing *Three* in bar 10 exactly with the A. In the 13th measure the soloist is likely to slow down before the *pp*. Hence, delay the 3rd beat and follow delicately. In the next bar, watch the violin bow so as to end the fermata with the soloist.

Allegro molto vivace. Most of this movement is conducted with 2-beat, although in certain places a subdivided beat is used.

BAR   1   This is often done with 2-beat, using a half-note preparation. The rhythm may be more incisive with a subdivided beat, in which case the preliminary beat would be a quarter-note.

BAR   2   Most violinists like to hurry this figure, but the conductor keeps his tempo.

BAR   4   Use 2-beat from here.

BAR   9 FF.   Precision of gesture must be combined with lightness and elegance; too tense a beat would hamper the fluent movement.

BARS   18, 20 and 21   The entries after *One* must not be late; keep the beat moving to prevent any hesitation.

BAR   23   Neutral beats on the rest.

BAR   24   Be on the alert to catch the pizzicato exactly with the D♯ in the solo. The effectiveness of this depends on a skilful preparation on *One*.

BAR   25 F.   *Two* in this bar prepares the next attack and may be slightly hastened, using a gesture which is not too sharp but rather flexible. This may seem to contradict previous suggestions, but when such transparent passages occur in accompaniment, the conductor must rely to some extent upon his musicians having an attentive ear. An academic beat would not arouse the "chamber music" participation of the individual players which is essential here.

BAR   30   The best way to secure a perfect ensemble is to think with the solo violin. The clarinets will follow.

BAR   35   Use a slight syncopation beat without delaying.

BAR   41 FF.   The soloist's freedom of playing should not be restrained by the accompaniment; pick up the beat when necessary.

BAR   55   *Cf.* Ex. 374. In catching up with the violin the preparation for the Tutti may become so fast that the tempo would be unduly hastened. You can use a clear-cut subdivided beat to prevent this, but return to 2-beat for bars 57 and 58 so as not to lose the grazioso quality of the music.

BARS 63, 65   *fp* beat on *One*.

BAR   71 FF.   A lively gesture must maintain the swift pace of the movement and prevent the wind entrances from being late.

BAR 75 FF. The beat must build the crescendo and prepare the bass entrance, leading to a strong *One* in bar 76. Change to legato in bar 77.

BAR 80 A slight ritardando is traditional; follow the soloist.

BAR 81 FF. The violin resumes the fast tempo; concentrate upon the runs to be with the soloist all the time.

BAR 98 FF. Watch the runs again and do not let the wind entrances drag. The violins also need some indication in bar 100 so as not to be late after the sustained note.

BAR 129 Slightly slower for the tranquillo. Beat *Two* exactly with the A in the violin to get the following pizzicato precisely in time.

BAR 184 Beat the rests, following the soloist strictly.

BAR 193 Follow the slight rubato which is customary and synchronize *Two* with the A, but catch up immediately in the next measure.

BAR 198 The soloist usually speeds up at this point; be sure to follow.

BAR 204 FF. Subdue the accompaniment by using a small gesture (the crescendo in bar 206 applies only to the solo).

BAR 218 Follow the soloist closely, since he needs time to attack the high E.

BAR 222 Indicate *fp* strongly, then go along with the rapid movement of the solo instrument. The violinist will be grateful for not being hurried in bars 226-229.

10.

Wolfgang Amadeus Mozart

RECITATIVE: "E SUSANNA NON VIEN"
From Le Nozze di Figaro, Act III

Vocal Scores: G. Schirmer; Boosey and Hawkes; Novello
Recordings: Maria Cebotari, with Philharmonia Orchestra conducted by Josef Krips—HMV Record No. G-DA1875
Aulikki Rautawaara, with Glyndebourne Festival Orchestra conducted by Fritz Busch—in Victor Album M-DM-315

The remarks made on page 141 are pertinent to this discussion. The words as well as the music of the vocal part should be studied so that the conductor knows on which counts the syllables fall.

No matter what liberties the singer takes with the rhythm, the conductor must always give a clear *One* in each bar. Whether or not to beat the other counts during sustained notes or rests depends upon the speed of the music. Beating on all counts is practicable in moderate tempo, using small and smooth gestures. In faster tempo or when the singer hurries, too many beats may become confusing, in which case it is advisable to skip all beats which are not necessary.

When the beat follows the singer's liberties it is bound to become irregular and to affect the various preparatory beats. Therefore, since the conductor must be on time with the entrances, he will have to use free preparations.

For students who use a piano score: only the strings play in this recitative.

BAR   1   Synchronize *Three* with the singer. Beat in tempo
           (♩ = 60) on *Three-Four*, no matter how fast the
           first 2 quarters were. A gentle syncopation beat on
           Three brings in the orchestra.

BAR   2   Indicate the counts clearly with a slight gesture, unless
           the soprano rushes unduly so that you must hurry
           to the next down-beat.

BAR   3   Use a clear down-beat and cut off quietly on *Four*,
           preferably with the left hand.

BARS 4, 6 Same procedure as in bar 1.

BAR   7   If the singer hurries, it is better to skip *Three* and *Four*
           so as to be ready for the sharp down-beat in bar 8.

BAR   8   Do not beat *Three* before the singer reaches it. The
           tempo changes without preparation, so use a sharp
           Three, beating clearly in the new tempo (♩
           = 100).

BAR   9   Wait on *Four*.

BAR   11   Down-beat only.

BAR   12   Use 4 beats, synchronizing *Three*.

BAR   14   If the singer's tempo is steady, the preparation for the *fp* is easy; but if she hesitates, you must wait on *Two* and then give a quick free preparation. Beat *Three* and *Four* in rapid succession, to be ready for the next down-beat.

BAR 15 F. Here again, be sure not to fall behind the singer. The 2nd beat in bar 16 must coincide with the soprano's C♯ (the violas change to A!).

BAR 18 Beat the 1st and 4th counts only, following the vocal part.

BAR 19 If necessary, wait on *Two* and *Four*.

BAR 21 F. The preparatory beats on *One* in each bar introduce contrasting accompaniment figures; the first is wistful, the second very dramatic.

BAR 23 The conductor takes the lead in this bar, the tempo being identical with the previous Andante.

BAR 24 F. Indicate *fp* strongly and follow the singer closely. A smooth and convincing gesture brings in the closing E-major chord, helped perhaps by the left hand.

11.

Ruggiero Leoncavallo

PROLOGUE TO "PAGLIACCI"

Vocal Scores: G. Schirmer; Sonzogno
Recordings: Leonard Warren, with RCA-Victor Orchestra conducted by Frieder Weissmann—Victor Record No. 11-9790
Lawrence Tibbett, with orchestra—Victor Record No. 6587
Robert Weede, with orchestra conducted by Frieder Weissmann—Columbia Record No. 71261-D

When the Prologue is performed on the concert stage, the orchestra begins 44 bars before the first vocal entry. The numbering of the bars in this discussion starts at that point. The orchestration is also mentioned because it is not included in the vocal scores, and the student would do well to mark it in his copy.

BAR 1 *Str.Cl.Bn.Hn.*
1-beat (♩. = 88), marcato gesture.

Bar 3   *Fl.Cl.*
           Beat staccato.

Bar 9   *Tutti*

Bar 25   Beat this bar with a larger rebound so as to prepare the
           following "pesante" a trifle slower.

Bars 29-36 Gradual increase in tempo. Use a strong gesture for the
           secco effect in bar 36.

Bar 37   A tempo.

Bar 39   *Fl.Ob.*

Bar 43   *Cl.*

Bar 46   Synchronize a neutral down-beat with the vocal part.

Bar 47   *Str.*
           Give a clear staccato beat for the off-beat entrance.

Bar 50   *Pizzicato*
           Wait for the up-beat until the singer, after a short
           pause, attacks the next phrase. In a case like this, the
           simplest thing to do is to watch the singer take his
           breath, thus timing your preparation so as to arrive
           together with him on *One* (bar 51).

Bar 51   *Str.*

Bar 53   *Ob.Bn. enter after the 3rd count*
           Use a flexible gesture which allows for a possible
           rubato.

Bar 54   *Cl.Hn. added*
           A marcato 3rd beat straight toward the right brings
           out the second half of the measure emphatically.

Bar 55   Cut the fermata, and pause in readiness for the up-beat.
           A singer who is a good musician will follow your up-
           beat, but be prepared to catch up if he starts by him-
           self.

Bar 56   *Vc., melody with singer; Fl. Harp, upper staff; Vln.2
           Vla. D.B., lower staff*

Bar 59   The singer starts the sixteenth-note passage after the
           orchestra has stopped on *Three*. Beat *Three* with a
           short gesture to the left, wait, and repeat the 3rd beat
           on the singer's F♯ to prepare the next bar.

BAR 60   *Vln.1, melody*

BAR 64   Tenuto is best for this type of chordal accompaniment; the quick connecting gestures enable you to follow the singer from one chord to the next.

BAR 65   Either separate cut-off and preparation, or do both with the same gesture.

BAR 66   *Vc.Bn.*

BAR 67   Cue in the singer.

BAR 74   *Vln.1,2, con sord.*
       "A tempo" here means maintain a steady tempo.

BAR 88   The sudden change to slower tempo is accomplished by retarding the rebound.

BAR 90   *Vc.D.B.*

BAR 91   *Vla. added*
       There is a pause on the eighth-rest in the vocal part; beat tenuto, the upward motion leading into the next bar.

BAR 92   *Cl.Bn. added*

BAR 96 FF.   If the singer is very slow, the 1-beat may be subdivided or changed to 3-beat.

BAR 99   Cut the chord; for the execution of the pause see bar 50.

BAR 100   *Str.*
       The tempo is faster (1-beat). Follow the singer with sharp and distinct beats until bar 105, then stop as though there were a ⌢ over the rest, and wait. Watch the singer again.

BAR 111   *Ob.Cl.Bn. added*

BAR 114   *Fl.Hn.Harp enter on the 3rd eighth-note*
       3-beat; prepare the entrance on *Three* carefully.

BAR 117   *Vc., melody; Vln.1,2, accomp.*
       Use a calm, flexible espressivo 3-beat.

BAR 121   *Ob.Cl.Bn.Vla. added*

BAR 122   Change to a non-espressivo 2-beat.

BAR 124   *Harp added*

BAR 125   Cut the chord with tenuto on *Two* and use a separate gesture to prepare the next bar.

BAR 126   *Str.Harp*
BAR 128   *Bn. added*
           A tempo.
BAR 129 FF. *Vln.1,2,Cl., melody;Vla.Vc.D.B.Bn.Hn., lower part*
           In these bars the tempo increases gradually as more instruments enter, and the espressivo is intensified, changing gradually to marcato by bar 137.
BAR 139   Give the singer time for a good breath on the eighth-rest.
BAR 140   *Tutti*
           Use an energetic marcato gesture, but not so large that the orchestra will play too loudly and cover the voice.
BAR 142 FF. Execute the heavy ritardando with clear subdivided beats and do not be confused by the syncopations. Beat the cut-off (bar 143) with a sidewise gesture, saving the upward motion for the following preparatory beat.
BAR 144   *Vln.1,2,Fl.,melody;Vla.Vc.D.B.Cl.Bn.Hn.Harp,accomp.*
           Here again the beat is very expressive, but should keep the orchestra subordinated to the singer.
BAR 148   *E.H. Hn., melody*
BAR 151   Hesitate slightly before *One* to give the singer a chance to breathe, and attack the beat with him.
BAR 152   The sudden *p* needs a definite indication.
BAR 156   Beat tenuto on *One* and subdivide the other counts. A fermata is customarily made on the first eighth-note of *Three;* keep the baton perfectly still and (watching the singer!) use a swift connecting gesture leading to the next eighth-beat. These last 3 eighth-beats should not be too slow.
BAR 157   Only *Two* is subdivided; wait for the singer and use the subdivision to prepare *Three.*
BAR 158   *Bn. enter on the 3rd count*
           Cut the hold and use *Two* to prepare the chord on *Three.*

Bar 161 *Tutti*
   Energetic full-staccato; beat the rests with small and
   relaxed gestures.

Bar 162 After the chord on *Three* do not beat *Four* until the
   singer is about to slur down to his concluding note,
   then use it to prepare I° Tempo (1-beat).

LIST OF DIAGRAMS

INDEX OF MUSIC

(Figures in roman indicate musical passages referred to in the text;
figures in italics indicate musical illustrations.)

[347]